W9-AER-689

Gramley Library
Salem College
Winston-Salem, NC 27108

Black Pioneers in Communication Research

In Dedication and
Loving Memory of Dr. Lucia Sheila Hawthorne

Black Pioneers in Communication Research

Ronald L. Jackson II
The Pennsylvania State University

Sonja M. Brown Givens
University of Alabama at Huntsville

Gramley Library
Salem College
Winston-Salem, NC 27108

SAGE Publications
Thousand Oaks ▪ London ▪ New Delhi

Copyright © 2006 by Sage Publications, Inc.

All rights reserved. No part of this book may be reproduced or utilized in any form or by any means, electronic or mechanical, including photocopying, recording, or by any information storage and retrieval system, without permission in writing from the publisher.

For information:

Sage Publications, Inc.
2455 Teller Road
Thousand Oaks, California 91320
E-mail: order@sagepub.com

Sage Publications Ltd.
1 Oliver's Yard
55 City Road
London EC1Y 1SP
United Kingdom

Sage Publications India Pvt. Ltd.
B-42, Panchsheel Enclave
Post Box 4109
New Delhi 110 017 India

Printed in the United States of America.

Library of Congress Cataloging-in-Publication Data

Jackson, Ronald L., 1970-
Black pioneers in communication research / Ronald L. Jackson II,
Sonja M. Brown Givens.
    p. cm.
Includes bibliographical references and index.
ISBN 0-7619-2992-4 (cloth) — ISBN 0-7619-2993-2 (pbk.)
    1. Communication—Research—United States—History. 2. African American college teachers—Biography. I. Givens, Sonja M. Brown. II. Title.
P91.5.U5J33 2006
302.2'092396073—dc22

                            2005022222

This book is printed on acid-free paper.

06   07   08   09   10   9   8   7   6   5   4   3   2   1

Acquiring Editor:	Todd R. Armstrong
Editorial Assistant:	Deya Saoud
Production Editor:	Jenn Reese
Typesetter:	C&M Digitals (P) Ltd.
Indexer:	Nara Wood
Cover Designer:	Janet Foulger

Contents

Dedication   ii

List of Timelines   viii

Acknowledgments   ix

Introduction   1

Black Pioneers (presented in alphabetical order)

1. **Molefi Kete Asante**   11
    Introduction   12
    Biographical Information   14
    Academic Background and Experience   15
    Contributions to Communication Research   23
    Conclusion   31
    References   32

2. **Donald E. Bogle**   39
    Introduction   41
    Biographical Information   43
    Academic Background and Experience   45
    Contributions to Communication Research   49
    Conclusion   58
    References   60

3. **Hallie Quinn Brown**   64
    Introduction   65
    Biographical Information   65
    Academic Background and Experience   66
    Contributions to Communication Research   73
    Conclusion   80
    References   80

4. **Melbourne S. Cummings**   84
    Introduction   85
    Biographical Information   87
    Academic Background and Experience   91
    Contributions to Communication Research   94
    Conclusion   100
    References   101

5. **Jack L. Daniel**   104
    Introduction   105
    Biographical Information   106
    Academic Background and Experience   108
    Contributions to Communication Research   114
    Conclusion   123
    References   124

6. **Oscar H. Gandy, Jr.**   128
    Introduction   129
    Biographical Information   130
    Academic Background and Experience   131
    Contributions to Communication Research   138
    Conclusion   146
    References   147

7. **Stuart Hall**   152
    Introduction   153
    Biographical Information   154
    Academic Background and Experience   158
    Contributions to Communication Research   163
    Conclusion   168
    References   168

8. **Marsha Houston**   172
    Introduction   173
    Biographical Information   174
    Academic Background and Experience   176
    Contributions to Communication Research   179
    Conclusion   183
    References   184

9. **Joni L. Jones / Iya Omi Osun Olomo**   **189**
   Introduction   190
   Biographical Information   190
   Academic Background and Experience   192
   Contributions to Communication Research   196
   Conclusion   200
   References   201

10. **Dorthy L. Pennington**   **205**
    Introduction   206
    Biographical Information   207
    Academic Background and Experience   208
    Contributions to Communication Research   212
    Conclusion   219
    References   219

11. **Orlando L. Taylor**   **223**
    Introduction   224
    Biographical Information   226
    Academic Background and Experience   228
    Contributions to Communication Research   231
    Conclusion   236
    References   237

Index   **243**

About the Authors   **267**

List of Timelines

Molefi Kete Asante   36

Donald E. Bogle   62

Hallie Quinn Brown   82

Melbourne S. Cummings   102

Jack L. Daniel   126

Oscar H. Gandy, Jr.   150

Stuart Hall   170

Marsha Houston   186

Joni L. Jones / Iya Omi Osun Olomo   203

Dorthy L. Pennington   221

Orlando L. Taylor   239

Acknowledgments

First, all honor for making this book possible goes to God, who has continually expanded my life. Moreover, I am thankful for my family, and especially for the strong women in my life: my wife, Ricci Jackson, my mother, Sharon Prather, and others who have given me inspiration—Thelma Gross, Phyllis Gross, Georgie Jackson, Baola Gould, Mary Haiman, Vanessa Carter, Mary Gould-Reed, Tita Jackson, Melbourne Cummings, Trina J. Wright, Brenda J. Allen, Veronica Duncan-Walters, and Robin Means-Coleman. I am also grateful for the influential men in my life: my father, Ronald L. Jackson, Sr.; my brothers, Bruce and Tishaun; as well as friends and intellectual sparring partners Brad Hogue, Keith Wilson, Shaun Gabbidon, Ramone Ford, Carlos Morrison, Maurice Hall, Eric Watts, Tim Brown, Henry Giroux, Michael Hecht, and the men of Omega Psi Phi Fraternity, Inc. Also, I appreciate the support of the Africana Research Collaborative, a dynamic interdisciplinary group of communication scholars, as well as the Penn State University Research and Graduate Studies Office for two grants supporting the writing of this book. Finally, I am also appreciative of the hard work and friendship of my coauthor, Sonja Brown Givens.

—RLJ

I am grateful for the love and support of my family in all that I do. To my husband, Lamont Givens, my father, Louis Brown Jr., and my son, Lyn Scott Jr., who have encouraged me along the way to make a difference. Many thanks to my dear friends and sisters of Sigma Gamma Rho Sorority, Inc. Additional thanks are due to my mentors, who have guided me with unwavering love: Jennifer Monahan, Tina Harris, and Veronica Duncan-Walters. My journey through this project would never have happened without the friendship of my coauthor, Ronald Jackson. Additionally, I am thankful for the support of the Africana

Research Collaborative. Finally, I acknowledge the support of the University of Alabama in Huntsville—Humanities Center for its grant support during the completion of this project.

—SBG

Introduction

*B*lack Pioneers in Communication Research unabashedly celebrates both Africana scholarship and Black scholars. Of necessity, it calls to question a perennial matter it does not explicitly discuss—the politics of mainstream intellectualism. One of the book's primary functions is to interrogate the *center* of mainstream academic scholarship while also providing a nuanced pedagogical tool by discussing the lives and careers of pioneering scholars in communication research. The idea of a *center* suggests a place of focus, a foundational point of significance, or a pivotal location. Since the late 1960s, Black scholars and their scholarship have been an influential part of the *center* of communication inquiry, but have seldom been fully acknowledged and integrated in basic communication theory textbooks and refereed, scholarly writings in communication. The pioneering works of Hallie Quinn Brown, Stuart Hall, Molefi Asante, Donald Bogle, Orlando Taylor, Marsha Houston, and others featured here are indisputably central to the field of communication. However, these pioneers have been recognized primarily within international and interdisciplinary arenas such as Black Diasporic studies, cultural studies, ethnic studies, history, women's studies, and communication sciences and disorders at the expense of overstating the *center* in mainstream communication research during the past 30 or more years. Two primary objectives of this book are to honor 11 pioneering Black scholars and their scholarship by showcasing their lives and careers *and* to demonstrate that a significant portion of what we know about culture and communication has been influenced by these individuals.

Although it is clear that Africana scholars (and their scholarship) have historically been largely ignored as major figures central to the field of communication, their works are becoming increasingly well received among a growing contingent of up-and-coming communication researchers interested in the study of culture. These pioneers continue to be heralded among generations of Black communication scholars.

With this recovery of Black intellectualism in communication research, there is also recognition of a long-standing transcendent quality to Black communication thought. A very large segment of it has historically developed a holistic, self-reflective cultural standpoint that has grappled with the Europeanized binaries of mind/body, self/object, individualism/collectivism, and Black/White, as well as the trialectics of mind/body/soul, symbol/referent/reference, and message/sender/receiver. As you will witness while reading *Black Pioneers in Communication Research*, there is always an active, political, and intellectual act of inverting paradigms. For example, Stuart Hall not only subscribes to the postmodern notion of agency but also invokes a critical communication theory of articulation, which requires that we interrogate the language we use to constrain discursive realities. Similarly, it was Hallie Quinn Brown who spoke of the potential for emancipation via rhetoric and elocution at a time when rhetoric's function was primarily conceived within a tripartite paradigm of deliberative, forensic, and epideictic speech. Brown extended the meaning of deliberative speech to illumine class and labor struggles, social uplift, and basic public political participation. Rather than simply maintaining the broad interest in rhetorical education as a discipline of performance, Brown fought for cultural and linguistic inclusiveness. Another example can be found in the works of Molefi Kete Asante, Jack Daniel, and Melbourne Cummings: Each proposed that call-and-response was a constitutive feature of discursive experiences and the Black oral tradition. As Asante explained, it is odd to think of the speech act as being solely comprised of a speaker, text, and inoculated audience when there is so much more interactivity in the Black oral traditions in churches and elsewhere within Black discursive experiences. These prescient paradigm shifts have been overlooked far too often as critical junctures in our scholarship. It is incumbent upon us as scholars to insist upon intellectual inclusiveness and to insist that multiple voices be heard lest we re-energize the circuitry of uncritical thinking and moral degeneracy that is so often criticized in our own principled writings.

Beyond the act of recovering pioneering works by Black communication scholars, *Black Pioneers in Communication Research* also provides a pedagogical tool. The act of introducing scholars via a biographical method is in and of itself a bold and not very popular but imporant critical-interpretive move. As teachers and intellectuals, we are too often unequipped to convey the origins and significance of foundational conceptual models to our students. One practical function of *Black Pioneers in Communication Research* is to facilitate understanding of key concepts—Afrocentricity (Molefi Asante), the pantheon of Black filmic images such as the mammy and mulatto (Donald Bogle), the TrEE model (Oscar Gandy), articulation theory (Stuart Hall), and guilt provocation

(Dorthy Pennington)—by not only identifying the progenitor but also by offering a glance into his or her personal and academic backgrounds that undoubtedly gave rise to the mind-set that produced the paradigm. Any time you see an excerpt without a citation, it is a direct quote taken from an interview with that pioneer.

Black Pioneers in Communication Research shows how the sociohistorical context in which these writers lived aided in the development of the concepts. This pedagogical and organizing approach to the material thus adds another dimension to how this book can be used to teach communication theory and research. It goes beyond advising students that everything is a potential study waiting to be written and published. It also teaches them that their identities are necessarily enwrapped and implicated in the way they articulate their ideas; it introduces them to another way of becoming familiar with extant research and embarking on studies of their own. One example in the book is Stuart Hall, considered by many to be a cofounder of British cultural studies. *Black Pioneers in Communication Research* traces his life and career and shows how the context conditioned his scholarship. We also talk about how Hall's own indigenous third world cultural identity as a native of Kingston, Jamaica, shaped how he saw colonialist relations and the contradictory human impulses to discuss the real, authentic pains and frustrations of their struggles through a phony, socially manufactured means: mass media entertainment. This mapping of Hall's life, career, ideological influences, and conceptual approach provides rich detail rarely seen in academic texts. Consequently, this book is ideal for instructors of undergraduate and graduate courses in communication, Black Studies, ethnic studies, cultural (media) studies, film, mass media, theatre, and performance, as well as ones that touch upon the world-views of Africana intellectuals and everyday Africana citizens throughout the Diaspora.

❖ EMERGENCE AND SIGNIFICANCE OF THE BOOK

Besides the need to illumine the centrality of Africana scholars and scholarship within the field of communication, the impetus for a book with this focus and approach came from a friend and colleague at Penn State University: criminologist Shaun Gabbidon. In his book, *African American Criminological Thought*, he and his coauthor Helen Taylor Greene presented the backgrounds, lives, and career histories of 10 leading African American scholars of criminology. (Incidentally, the layout of *Black Pioneers in Communication Research* emulates the one found in *African American Criminological Thought*.) Shaun Gabbidon encouraged us to seriously consider pursuing a project similar to his but related to communication pioneers. To assess the interest in such a volume within the field of communication, we solicited the help of two colleagues, Carlos Morrison and Trina Wright, who assisted in the distribution of a survey to members of the National Communication Association's Black Caucus and African American Communication and Culture Division. After receiving almost 50 completed surveys, we perused the list of recommended scholars, looking particularly for recurrent names. Because there was no limit to the number of scholars that any survey participant could mention, the list of nominees, or identified "pioneers," exceeded 50 names. After we identified the 20 most frequently mentioned names, we pared the list down to a manageable number, which we decided would be 16. The project began in 2000. Because of attrition, personal circumstances of the pioneers that prevented interviews, and an imbalance of men and women, we ended up with 12 pioneers, one of whom dropped out late in the process. Because we had already completed all the interviews, transcribed the interviews, and begun writing the chapters, we decided to go with the 11 remaining pioneers rather than initiate another interview and start the process all over again for one more individual.

Black Pioneers in Communication Research has a companion volume, which began at the same time and was published by Sage: African American Communication and Identities: Essential Readings (2004). It provides a set of reprinted articles from more than two dozen Black communication scholars.

The most difficult task in writing the book you hold in your hands was selecting who would be showcased. The relative absence of mainstream appreciation and discussion of African American communication research can easily lead one to presume that Blacks have contributed little to nothing to the field. Quite to the contrary, many scholars could have been included in a volume like this one. However, after reviewing books that included 100 miniature biographies on "influential people," it became clear that such volumes are diluted versions of the current project. They commit the disservice of discussing someone's entire life in two to four pages, which not only limits the use of the materials by readers but also seems a bit insulting to those whose lives are chronicled. Rather than take that route, we chose to do in-depth examinations of each person's life. There is only one pioneer showcased in this book who is deceased: Hallie Quinn Brown. We conducted interviews with the remaining pioneers (with the exception of Stuart Hall because of personal reasons), wrote the chapters about their lives, and let the pioneers read the chapters and make modifications if they chose to do so. Consequently, this book is a true tribute to each of them.

Black Pioneers in Communication Research is important for several reasons. It is the first of its kind in the field of communication. There have been biocritical sourcebooks on rhetors who lived centuries ago, but there has never been a book that exclusively chronicled the lives of both historical and contemporary communication scholars who laid the foundation for several areas of endeavor within the field of communication and beyond. This book is also important because it is a systematic exploration of early contributions to several areas of disciplinary inquiry: intercultural and international communication, interpersonal communication, Black women's gendered communication, media images and representation, critical cultural studies, language and culture research, Black rhetoric, nonverbal communication, communication sciences and disorders, and performance studies. Finally, this book is significant because it offers a resource for students and faculty interested in African American scholarship.

❖ PURPOSE AND RATIONALE

The title, *Black Pioneers in Communication Research*, signifies two things. First, not everyone in the volume is African American (Stuart Hall is Caribbean). Second, the pioneers are not included only for their service or leadership endeavors within professional associations, although almost all of them have contributed quite significantly in this regard. This is a book about contributions to communication *research*, which does not mean that every person presented here is highly prolific. The mere quantity of work does not bespeak the quality of the contribution. It is important to say this because there is a general presumption that African American scholars have merely presented convention papers or haphazard interdisciplinary scholarship over the years rather than scholarship worthy of citation and use within mainstream empirical and conceptual-theoretic communication studies. It is difficult to interpret the exclusion of African American research in any other way. Although professors may feel compelled to adopt this book for courses related to African American communication and ethnic studies, or as a supplement to communication theory, there may also be an interest in having students read this text to better understand the emergence of the performance ethnography work of Joni Jones or the gender and interpersonal communication research of Marsha Houston, for example.

❖ LAYOUT OF THE BOOK
AND REASON FOR INCLUSION

Black Pioneers in Communication Research is organized into 11 alphabetized chapters titled with the names of each of the pioneers: Molefi Kete Asante, Donald E. Bogle, Hallie Quinn Brown, Melbourne S. Cummings, Jack L. Daniel, Oscar H. Gandy, Jr., Stuart Hall, Marsha Houston, Joni L. Jones, Dorthy L. Pennington, and Orlando L. Taylor. Each chapter includes a photo; an introduction; sections covering the pioneer's personal background, academic background, and experience; contributions to the field of communication (sometimes noting outstanding leadership contributions) and contributions to communication theory and research; a conclusion; references, further readings; and a timeline. This easy-to-follow and consistent chronological approach across all the chapters facilitates the reading of and access to various dimensions of the scholars' lives and careers.

It is perhaps a reasonable question to ask why these scholars, in particular, are included in this book beyond the two reasons given thus far: they were peer-selected, and it is generally better to do an in-depth examination of a few scholars than a survey of many. We approached this issue by including here a brief overview of some noteworthy contributions that each scholar has made to the field of communication to provide you with a glimpse of their prodigious works. The synopses of each pioneer's contributions are presented here in alphabetical order, which is the way each pioneer appears in the book.

Molefi Kete Asante has been identified by the *Utne Reader* and the *Chronicle of Higher Education* as one of the "100 most influential thinkers in America," and he is one of the most prolific scholars in the world. Asante is the "father of Afrocentricity," and numerous citations of his work in communication are evidence that he has undoubtedly influenced much of the research on Africana communication experiences. He is internationally renowned, and his work is cited in at least 20 disciplines, although it is probably reasonable to argue that his greatest impact has been in Africana studies. Asante is also the founding chair of the first doctoral program in African and African American studies.

Donald E. Bogle's contributions to communication are primarily in mass media, particularly in film and television. He has written most extensively about the history of Black images and representation in film and TV, and each volume has been enormous in size and importance. When people think of stereotypical Black images and representations, they think almost immediately of the mammy, coon, mulatto, buck, and tom images. Bogle has been almost solely responsible for introducing these images to mainstream mass media scholars and everyday citizens via his books, articles, documentaries, and expert interviews.

Hallie Quinn Brown was an unsung scholar who lived almost 100 years—from 1850 to 1949. Before the field of communication existed as it does today, she studied at the Boston school of oratory and subsequently became a professor of elocution and an orator in her own right. She taught and advocated an "embodied rhetoric," in which rhetors were more than speakers espousing ideas via a well-structured conceptual edifice. Brown was an activist who believed in morally upright, principled, and transformative speech. She wrote seven books during her lifetime and promoted public political participation via her pedagogy.

Many people have become acquainted with Melbourne S. Cummings through her passionate dedication to the National Communication Association, among other academic societies. She has also made important contributions to communication inquiry through her work on famous Black rhetoricians and leaders such as Booker T. Washington, Martin Luther King, Jr., Mary McLeod Bethune, and Andrew Young. Despite her line of inquiry in rhetorical studies, Cummings is perhaps most known for her work in media and communication development. Her 1988 article on the changing image of Blacks in television traced a few patterns of Black images in televised sitcoms such as *227*, *The Jeffersons*, and *Good Times*. Almost seven years later, she edited (with Orlando Taylor and Lyndrey Niles) a collection of original essays about communication development initiatives, strategies, and approaches. It is in that book that the nuanced conceptual work of Oscar Gandy was showcased with the debut of his TrEE model, which we will discuss momentarily.

Jack L. Daniel is known widely for his disciplinary leadership and service, most especially for cofounding the Black Caucus of the National Communication Association, which boasts the largest contingency of Black scholars in the field of communication. His contributions to communication research are also impressive. Daniel's early work related to communication among poor people was one of the earliest communication studies of class in the field, and it became the catalyst for his lifelong critical work concerning oppressed groups, particularly African Americans. He is most famous for his collaboration with Geneva Smitherman-Donaldson on "How I Got Over: Communication Dynamics in the Black Community," which represented a line of research regarding the linguistic carryovers and "deep structures" resident in the Black oral tradition.

Oscar H. Gandy, Jr., the Herbert I. Schiller Term Chair at Annenberg (East) School for Communication, has a very interesting background as a writer, producer, and director of public access television programs.

He is also a prolific scholar whose research spans studies of racial market segmentation, discrimination in information technology, and media privacy and surveillance. Each of these topics, influenced by Gandy's background in sociology, economics, and communication behavior, intersects his work on institutional agenda-setting, public policy, and the submergence of consumer interests. Besides his considerable published scholarship in these areas, Gandy is probably most noted for his TrEE (Transformation, Effectiveness, and Efficiency) model. Gandy argued that for imports (such as technology, food, and resources) to developing nations to be efficient and effective, there must also be some consideration of the transformative potential of these imports.

Stuart Hall, a retired but still-towering scholar in cultural studies, has had monumental significance to the British cultural studies movement. Although he is and always will be known as one of the defining thinkers in cultural studies, Hall is scantly explored in communication research. His work is foundational to the field: As one of the earliest critical studies scholars, Hall has made a mark as an individual who has given cultural studies much of its argot while grappling with ways to explore the confluence of media, Marxist ideology, Diasporic identities, and culture. Within his impressive body of work, Hall introduced a theory known as articulation, which was described earlier.

Marsha Houston (previously Marsha Stanback) is an interpersonal communication scholar whose early work explored asymmetrical relationships among interracial interactants. She was particularly concerned with the kinds of communication strategies employed among individuals with conspicuously different levels of power in a given relationship. This initial line of research led to Houston's continued interest in how varied social cognitions among interracial interactants leads to assumptions about attitudes and behaviors. For the last decade or so, Houston has concentrated primarily on Black feminist studies, and this is certainly where she has made her biggest mark in the field of communication.

Joni L. Jones, who has a doctorate in educational theatre, is a performance ethnographer and scholar who merges production, performance, and praxis in her work. She has written extensively about improvisation as a performance strategy. As with all performance studies, Jones boldly requires that students understand performance as an embodied practice. There is no mind/body split; instead, a duality is intertextually lived and simultaneously affected by everyday experience. Jones is a leading performance ethnographer in communication and continues to work in theatre, communication, and Africana studies.

Dorthy L. Pennington, like Jack Daniel and several others, is a founding member of the National Communication Association's Black

Caucus. Her work has been instrumental in explicating time orientations with respect to African Americans. Pennington is perhaps most noted for this early work—in addition to her research on guilt provocation (discussed earlier). Pennington is one of the forerunners in interracial communication. When Arthur Smith (now known as Molefi Asante) was writing books on interracial communication, Pennington was also exploring the interracial epistemes that interrupt otherwise successful interracial relations.

Amazingly, Orlando L. Taylor wrote his magnum opus—an article about aphasia (the loss of capacity to use words because of brain damage)—by the age of 35. It was from his grant work on aphasia that Taylor published a series of articles linking speech with neurology, and this work became frequently cited. This fascinating research on brain trauma had direct and immediate practical implications, not only for speech capacity but also for memory deficits, language decoding, and loss of language acquisition.

As you can surmise from these brief summaries of their works, the pioneers discussed in *Black Pioneers in Communication Research* are more than deserving of placement in this volume, and, more importantly, acknowledgment and valuation in mainstream intellectual discourse within communication studies and beyond.

❖ A FEW CONCLUDING REMARKS

Even though our initial intention was to provide a volume evenly composed of Black women and men and to demonstrate the significant impact that Black scholars have had on mainstream scholarly communication discourse, *Black Pioneers in Communication Research* still does not represent a comprehensive collection. To do so, it would have to include scholars such as Carolyn Calloway-Thomas, Cecil Blake, Brenda J. Allen, Deborah Atwater, Thurmon Garner, Janette Dates, William Barlow, Fela Sowande, Mark McPhail, D. Soyini Madison, John Baugh, Bishetta Merritt, Sidney Ribeau, Karla Scott, Katherine Hendrix, Jeffrey Woodyard, Olga Davis, Eric Watts, and others. It might also include interdisciplinary scholars such as Carter G. Woodson (historian), Geneva Smitherman (sociolinguist), Aaron Gresson (educational theorist and sociologist), Herman Gray (sociologist), and many others. Of course, a volume of that magnitude would be huge and exceed reasonable publisher constraints.

Beyond the daunting task of selecting the pioneers of communication research among many likely candidates, we also had our share of challenges in the writing of this book. We had a couple of scholars in mind that would have been included, but because of unforeseeable circumstances, they chose not to be involved. In some cases, the pioneers did not authorize personal details and circumstances revealed during interviews. Because of our respect for their wishes and their personal lives, we chose to honor their requests and omit what we initially thought were very pertinent and useful items of information. One consequence of that decision is that there is no clear sense of when every pioneer was born. In some cases, there is scant information about a pioneer's familial or personal relationships, so some chapters ended up being shorter than others. Readers might get the impression that we did not fully consider the personal lives of every pioneer, or that our writing showed bias toward one set of scholars over others because we did not write as extensively or intensively about a given part of their lives. We tried to be balanced and fair, and we can assure you that any imbalanced treatments of or perceived improprieties related to any pioneer's life were not intentional. We sometimes felt loss of control over those dimensions of the project. These challenges of writing the manuscript resulted in the book taking much longer to bring to production than we ever anticipated because of the multiple drafts, rewrites, and omissions within some of the chapters. Nonetheless, we are pleased with the final product and confident that you will also be pleased with the result.

An undeniable facet of Black intellectual life is that Black scholars and Black scholarship have been persistently exposed to a narrowly defined, jingoistic, and self-absorbed—mostly White male—intellectual center. Yet a small but indefatigable legion of communication scholars has devoted itself to correcting the lenses through which the center has been examined—to rescue this other piece of the center from invisibility. When it is suggested that there are classical approaches to rhetoric, language, or communication, we must not think only of Europeans. There are other equally transformative and significant legacies to be considered. *Black Pioneers in Communication Research* demonstrates that, but also it exemplifies a critical and biographical approach to both teaching and writing about communication theories. This is a new beginning. Black scholars and Black scholarship no longer ought to claim a position at the margins when it is so clearly evident that we have always been at the center!

1

Molefi Kete Asante

Afrocentricity is the centerpiece of human regeneration. To the degree that it is incorporated into the lives of the millions of Africans on the continent and on the Diaspora, it will become revolutionary. It is purposeful, giving a true sense of destiny  *based upon the facts of history and experience. The psychology of the African without Afrocentricity has become a matter of great concern. Instead of looking out from one's own center, the non-Afrocentric person operates in a manner that is negatively predictable. It takes no great gift to begin to identify the symbols which will, in their completeness, transform the whole of the African world and necessarily influence European and Asian thought.*

(Asante, 1988, p. 1)

Gramley Library,
Salem College
Winston-Salem, NC 27108

❖ INTRODUCTION

Molefi Kete Asante is the world's foremost expert on the subject of Afrocentricity. As progenitor of the term, Asante has initiated a dialogue about Africanity that has penetrated multiple community levels and has been unmatched throughout the world. Scholars from virtually every field of study have utilized, commented upon, or built careers around the Afrocentric paradigm (Hamlet, 1998; Turner, 1991; Zeigler, 1995). In short, Asante gave the world a new vocabulary for discussing, interpreting, and understanding Africana experiences— one which, as the epigraph states, cautions African Diasporic peoples from "looking out from one's own center" to make sense of and function in the world. Whether people have accepted or rejected the ideas inherent in the paradigm, the fact is that people all over the world have grappled with what it means with respect to how they interpret the human condition.

Asante is among the top 10 most-cited Black scholars, holding company with William Julius Wilson, Cornel West, Henry Louis Gates, Jr., W. E. B. DuBois, Richard Wright, Frantz Fanon, and Martin Luther King, Jr., among others. Although he has been quoted as saying, "I am not pleased with my level of production, because I have far more books in my head than I have energy to produce" (Shea, 1997), Asante has written more than 60 books and 300 articles. He has positioned himself among the elite few who can claim to be the most prolific scholars in the world. More than 4,000 of his published and unpublished papers, as well as personal correspondence, are housed in the Amistad Research Center at Tulane University in New Orleans, Louisiana.

Even though Asante's distinguished career is marked primarily by his association with Afrocentricity, he has accomplished much more. Not only has he developed competency in the Akan, French, Spanish, Arabic, Greek, German, Yoruba, Latin, Swahili, and Middle Egyptian languages but he is also cofounder (with economist Robert Singleton) of the *Journal of Black Studies,* the leading vehicle for refereed, academic discourse concerning Africana peoples. He has been editor of the journal since its inception in 1969. Furthermore, Asante developed and launched (at Temple University) the first departmental doctoral program in African American studies in the nation. As of 2004, there were only two other such programs (at the University of Massachusetts and the University of California, Berkeley). Several other universities offer joint doctorates with African American Studies or doctoral minors and area certificates. Moreover, he cofounded the National Communication

Association (NCA) Black Caucus, the National Afrocentric Institute, and The World University, and was the first president of the Society for International Education, Training and Research (SIETAR). In 1978, he was elected to serve a two-year term as vice president of the International Communication Association, and he served a two-year term as vice president of the National Council of Black Studies from 1988 to 1990.

Asante has been recognized by countless organizations for his commitment to liberatory progress, as exemplified via his research, community service, and teaching. Because of his achievements, he has received many accolades, not the least of which are his doctorates of humane letters from Sojourner-Douglass College and the University of New Haven. He has held endowed chairs and distinguished professorships at several universities, including Howard and Marquette, and served as consultant to many colleges and school districts concerning curricular reform. Asante has also directed more than 120 doctoral dissertations—an impressive record of advisement by any standard.

Although his scholarly presence can be witnessed all over the world, he has concentrated his studies on the African Diaspora, writing and speaking about African descendants in the United States Germany, Sweden, Italy, Mexico, France, China, Japan, Brazil, Senegal, South Africa, Nigeria, Ghana, Jamaica, Trinidad, United Kingdom, Zimbabwe, and Canada. For nearly 40 years, he has built an entire career as an ambassador of social justice and has advocated the reformation of Black Diasporic cultural consciousness. This most serious endeavor has led to his "return" to Ghana, where he was "enstooled as a traditional leader in Ghana in 1993, with the title Kyidomhene of Tafo and the Akyem name Nana Okru Asante Peasah" (Turner, 2002, p. 713). Asante shares this Ghanaian name with a king who granted land for the building of a cultural center in Ghana. He has also established residency in Ghana and returns periodically from his U.S. home. This link has fortified his development of discourses about African-centered experiences.

Indeed, the moment the word *centricity* is discussed, his paradigm of Afrocentricity emerges, not only among academicians but also among people across generations, cultures, and belief systems. Very seldom does any concept borne in academia permeate the public consciousness as has Asante's brainchild, Afrocentricity. *Afrocentric* is an adjective that is used to refer to commercial goods such as clothing and textiles as well as to one's philosophical and cultural orientation to the world. Remarkably, entire corporate marketing campaigns have adopted "Afrocentric" themes to appeal to Black consumers. From Asante's intricate skein of multimethodological but primarily humanistic writings has emerged a standpoint that has been criticized (Lefkowitz, 1996; West, 1993) as much as admired (Ani, 1994; Zeigler, 1995).

Although scholars have written mostly about Asante's academic contributions, this chapter presents a more comprehensive approach by discussing how his life conditioned his scholarship and how his scholarship has helped shape intercultural communication studies. We do this by exploring his personal background, academic experiences, and contributions to the field of communication. This discussion is followed by a conclusion and a list of selected references from his body of writings.

❖   BIOGRAPHICAL INFORMATION

Arthur Lee Smith, Jr., now known as Molefi Kete Asante, was born in Valdosta, Georgia, on August 14, 1942, just 20 miles north of the Florida state line—an area of pinewoods, sandy soil, and Spanish moss. Asante noted, "That [how far it is from the Florida line] is important to say because the line was not a real demarcation of where my relatives lived. They lived throughout southern Georgia and into Florida" (M. K. Asante, personal communication, April 11, 2004). His parents, Lillie Mae Wilkson[1] and Arthur Lee Smith, Sr., both native Georgians, were blue-collar workers, as were the majority of U.S. Blacks in the 1940s. They both came from loving households, but Asante's father's family was slightly better off than the Wilkson family. In the late 1800s, Asante's paternal great-grandfather, Plenty Smith, was a farmer who owned an impressive 150 acres of land in Georgia. Although the revenues from this land did not last three generations (until Asante's childhood), the memories and value of self-determination did; hence, they were impressed upon Asante and his 16 siblings.

Lillie Mae Wilkson, a native of Naylor, Georgia, was a "domestic who cooked and cleaned in White people's homes" (M. K. Asante, personal communication, April 11, 2004). Although she had only a fourth-grade education, she was very wise. Arthur Lee Smith, Sr., originally from Dooley County, Georgia, worked for the railroad until he injured his back and could not work, which only exacerbated the economic hardships his family of 17 children was already experiencing. In an oral history interview with historian and previous doctoral program student Diane Turner, Asante described the modest conditions in which he was raised:

We were poor. Certainly, there were great joys in our family and so on, but the poverty meant that you were denied certain things. I went to school with shoes that had holes in the bottom of them. I experienced poverty in the sense of hunger, of sometimes not having enough food to eat. My parents had a hard time feeding all of us. They were creative in the way they cut the bread, diluted the juices, and used the meat gravies. There were eventually 16 of us. All of them didn't live in the same house, at the same time, but at least 9 children lived in the house at one time. (Turner, 2002, p. 715)

Asante was the fourth child and the eldest boy and had three older sisters. Growing up in the racially segregated south, Asante began picking cotton and laboring in tobacco fields before and after school, until he was 17 years old. He was raised with Christian values and encouraged to have cultural pride and to be hard-working and self-reliant—lessons he learned from both parents. He recalled, "My father was the smartest person I have ever met. He was brilliant. He went to 6th grade, but he read everything. He studied French and German and he took correspondence courses on how to repair radios and watches" (M. K. Asante, personal communication, April 11, 2004). Asante described his mother as being gregarious and loving to be around a lot of people. He surmised, "[T]hey both were an inspiration to me. I guess that is why I love being around people; I love to read and I love critical thinking." His love for reading and critique was evident even as a young student.

❖ ACADEMIC BACKGROUND AND EXPERIENCE

With Molefi Kete Asante's interest in reading cultivated at an early age, he enjoyed composition and literacy throughout school and performed well academically. He attended elementary school in Valdosta, Georgia, until he was about 10 years old. In 1953, at age 11, Asante's parents enrolled him in a boarding school named Nashville Christian Institute in Nashville, Tennessee, operated by the Churches of Christ. He matriculated through Grade 12 and graduated from high school at the Institute. In the summers when school was no longer in session, Asante would return home to work in the fields and earn money before he returned for the fall term. After graduating from the Nashville Christian Institute, he was accepted at Southwestern Christian College in east Texas, where he earned his associate of arts degree. He then attended (and became one of two Black students to integrate) Oklahoma Christian College in Oklahoma City. After receiving his bachelor's degree, he was granted a four-year scholarship to attend Pepperdine University in California. This was a critical juncture in his education because heretofore he had been groomed for the clergy. He made speeches and recited Bible verses in his home church and found that the church congregation responded very well to his oratorical delivery.

At Pepperdine University, Asante was mentored by and took classes from Fred Casmir, whom he described as "one of Hitler's youths" (M. K. Asante, personal communication, April 11, 2004). He meant that Casmir had been recruited to join an organization known as the Hitler Youth, which began in 1926 and soon included more than half of Germany's youth. The Hitler Youth (known in Germany as Hitler Jugend, or HJ) was originally called the youth movement of the German Workers' Party (later named the National Socialist German Workers' Party). Boys and girls could join the HJ at age 10, and the organization functioned as both an early indoctrination of Nazi ideology and an introduction to military training in preparation for becoming a soldier. Somehow, despite Hitler's promilitary and antieducation stance within the HJ, Casmir still became interested in academia. He was particularly intrigued by research concerning persuasion, undoubtedly germinated by his participation as one of Hitler's youths.

Casmir's work in persuasion earned him a national reputation at that time, and Asante was pleased to study with him. In 1965, Asante graduated from Pepperdine with his master's degree in speech communication. He had learned about argumentation, social influence, and public communication strategies, and he was trained well enough to feel comfortable transitioning into a doctoral program. He decided to remain in California and continue his graduate education, and pursued a doctorate at the University of California, Los Angeles (UCLA). His primary mentors at UCLA were Charles Lomas, Ned Shearer, and Paul Rosenthal. Asante's dissertation advisor, Charles Lomas, specialized in revolutionary rhetoric and taught courses aligned with his research interests. Lomas's national reputation was garnered from the speech discipline's embrace of his pioneering work, *Agitator in American Society*. When Lomas left UCLA for a sabbatical leave to Britain, Ned Shearer replaced Lomas as Asante's committee chair and dissertation advisor. Maulana Karenga came to UCLA to give a talk at about this time, and Asante was impressed by the accuracy of his nationalist critiques of European dominance and his thesis that African Americans have too often conceded to European Americans their agency to define themselves culturally. This notion of a displaced sense of agency to define the cultural self stimulated Asante's thinking about worldview and cultural orientation and led to some early unwritten formulations that would later become the paradigm known as Afrocentricity. Asante credits Karenga for having "opened my eyes" (Turner, 2002, p. 718). Shortly thereafter, Asante became president of the local chapter of the Student Nonviolent Coordinating Committee (SNCC).

In 1968, Asante defended his dissertation on Samuel Adams and the rhetoric of agitation during the American Revolution. When he finished writing his dissertation, he simultaneously completed the writing of what would one year later become his first published academic book: *Rhetoric of Black Revolution* (Asante, 1969). This book was soon followed by *Rhetoric of Revolution*, written with Andrea Rich (Asante & Rich, 1970), and *The Voice of Black Rhetoric: Selections*, written with Stephen Robb (Asante & Robb, 1971). Given that 1969 was the latter part of the civil rights movement, the Black Panther Party had been founded in 1966, and Martin Luther King, Jr. had been assassinated in 1968, these themes for Asante's books were not only timely but also cutting-edge for the fields of communication and Black Studies. They were directly aligned with both his educational training as a rhetorician specializing in the discourse of agitation and his developing political and cultural consciousness.

In 1968, aside from his graduation with a doctorate in speech communication, two critical moments occurred in Asante's career. First, Asante convened with a few other Black communication scholars at a Speech Association of America (now the National Communication Association) conference and protested the exclusion of African American communication studies from mainstream disciplinary discourse. Along with Charles Hurst, Jack Daniel, Lucia Hawthorne, Donald Smith, and others, Asante assisted in the development of what is presently known as the Black Caucus of the National Communication Association. Second, Asante began his first job as a tenure-track assistant professor in the Department of Communication at Purdue University. He was the only Black professor at Purdue. Along with Orlando Taylor, who was hired at Indiana University in 1966, Asante was one of the first Black communication scholars teaching at a Big Ten university.

Despite the pervasive presence of racial tensions, Purdue was a great location from which to launch a career because it was a large, well-respected university with great resources. During the one year Asante was there, a White liberal scholar named Robert Kibler befriended him and was one of only a few colleagues who actually engaged him intellectually. This friendship was not enough to keep Asante at Purdue, however. Because living in the Midwest was too uncomfortable for him, he decided to accept an offer to move back to UCLA "under an edict from the chancellor of the campus that all departments should hire African Americans" (Turner, 2002, p. 716). Asante recalled:

> They brought me back for two things: One, to join the speech com-munication faculty as an associate professor with tenure; and two, to direct the Center for Afro-American Studies. They needed a can-didate who could be acceptable to both the Black Panthers and the US Organization, a group created by Maulana Karenga out of the debris of the Watts rebellion. I was the person acceptable to both factions. (M. K. Asante, personal communication, April 11, 2004)

The offer was attractive, so at age 27, Asante took both positions and held them from 1969 to 1973, during which time he also cofounded (with Robert Singleton) the *Journal of Black Studies.* In a personal inter-view with the first author of this book, Asante explained that he and Robert Singleton approached the publisher of Sage Publications in 1969 with a proposal to start the new journal. In the tradition of Black radi-cal activism, Asante and Singleton authoritatively stated, "Look, you don't have any Black journals. You have 12 to 14 journals, and there is nothing on Black people. We want you to publish this journal and give us full editorial rights" (M. K. Asante, personal communication, April 11, 2004). To their surprise, the publisher at Sage accepted their offer immediately and asked Asante to be editor and Singleton to direct the advisory board. The *Journal of Black Studies*, which is published six times per year, maintains the highest circulation, subscription, and citation rates among all Black Studies journals.

In 1972, Asante was a visiting professor at Florida State University before completing his contract term as director of the Center of Afro-American Studies a year later. He also traveled to several countries throughout Africa in 1972 (including Senegal, Ghana, Nigeria, Ethiopia, and Kenya) and had a life-changing experience. After having made this journey, he could no longer ignore the fact that that his cultural and ideological orientations resonated more with ancestral behavioral and cultural traditions of Africa than with those of the United States. Opoku Ware II, an Asantehene, suggested "Asante" as a last name. Asante noted,

> Kete was the name I took from a good friend of mine who was a student at Cal Tech at the time I was at UCLA. His name was Kete Bofah. . . . Molefi was a name chosen in solidarity with the South

African struggle. It's a Southern African name, actually Sotho. (M. K. Asante, personal communication, April 11, 2004)

Molefi means "keeper of the traditions." So Asante shifted from his Anglicized name of Smith to his new, more ideologically satisfying and culturally appropriate name: Molefi Kete Asante.

After his visiting professorship at Florida State University and his trek to Africa, Asante planned to leave UCLA. The Center for Afro-American Studies prospered; however, the speech department did not fare so well. In 1974, the Department of Speech stopped offering a doctoral program and began making financial cutbacks. In 1973, before the downgrading of the speech program, Asante left UCLA to accept a post as professor and chair of the Department of Communication at the State University of New York (SUNY) at Buffalo. This was a major decision because he had a toddler daughter, Kasina Eka, and he had to consider the career of his wife of seven years, Ngena, a St. Louis native who was an economist. She supported the move, and Asante moved the family to Buffalo, New York, where, at the young age of 30, he was promoted to full professor with tenure and appointed to chair of the department.

Asante maintained his position as professor and department chair at SUNY for 12 years, and he was chair of the department of Black Studies for two of those years. He stepped down as chair of the department in 1979 and was divorced from his wife Ngena after 13 years of marriage. He then took a one-year visiting professorship at Howard University. In 1981, Asante married Kariamu Welsh, a choreographer. He and his new wife accepted one-year Fulbright Fellowships to study mass media and dance, respectively, in Zimbabwe. They were formally invited by the deputy minister of communication, Naomi Nhiwatiwa, who also held a doctorate in communication. During their one year of study, they helped to establish two institutions: the Zimbabwe Institute of Mass Communication (ZIMCO) and the Zimbabwe National Dance Company. Shortly after their Fulbright research was completed, they had a son, Molefi, Jr., and in 1984, they decided to move to Philadelphia, Pennsylvania, where Asante was appointed professor and chair of the Department of African American studies at Temple University. He chaired the department until 1996 and has remained at Temple University ever since. In 2002, he married Ana Yenenga, a registered nurse, who serves as his agent for literary and speaking engagements. During the time he has been married to Ana Yenenga, Asante's reputation for scholarship and political activism has increased. He was chosen as one of the 12 African scholars to present plenary sessions at the

African Union's historic meeting of 500 African and Diasporan intellectuals in Dakar, Senegal in 2004. In addition, because of his Afrocentric philosophy, he was selected to write a column for the *Johannesburg City Press*, a paper with a circulation of 3.5 million in South Africa. In October 2004, he was asked to draft the preamble to the constitution of the United States of Africa.

Asante has influenced legions of scholars, yet he finds himself continually inspired by the writings of Cheikh Anta Diop, Marcus Mosiah Garvey, Maulana Karenga, Marimba Ani, Theophile Obenga, and Marcel Griaule. Black rhetorician Charles Hurst's early book, *Effective Expression: A New Approach to Better Speaking (1965)*, was awe-inspiring for Asante because no Black person had authored a mainstream text in communication before. It encouraged him to strive for excellence despite the challenges. Ignoring envious colleagues who admonished him to "slow down" and "not work so hard because you might run out of ideas," Asante has always been a community organizer and has always been a prolific writer, saying,

> When I became a full professor, I decided that I was not going to be like other full professors: that is, not going to produce. I wanted to continue to produce, and I wanted to demonstrate that if you work hard, and if you are consistent, and you are focused, you could really make a major impression on the world. (M. K. Asante, personal communication, April 11, 2004)

Developing Afrocentricity

Afrocentricity is a paradigm that simply promotes the following:

> [A] perspective which allows Africans to be the subject of historical experiences rather than objects on the fringes of Europe. This means that the Afrocentrist is concerned with discovering in every case the centered place of the African. . . [T]he Afrocentric study of phenomena asks questions about *location, place, orientation,* and *perspective* [italics added]. (Asante, 1993, pp. 2–3)

It is an orientation that centralizes Africa in every area of inquiry. The potency of this approach is in its ability to facilitate the retrieval of agency in defining African Diasporic identities, concepts, and worldviews. Its precursor, Negritude, promulgated by Senegalese president Leopold Senghor, never gained the prominence of Afrocentricity. Although it emerged from West Africa, South America, and the Caribbean, it was assigned to the province of a literary paradigm.

For those who are unfamiliar with Afrocentricity, it is important to note that it is a conceptual *and* ideological lens through which one sees the world as an indigenous, collectivistic African. So, for example, an Afrocentric psychologist explores the mind holistically from the perspective of an African with a traditionally collectivistic worldview; therefore, the mind is conceived as part of an interdependent relationship between the mind, body, and spirit. Although other aspects of holistic psychological health (such as spirituality) may be included, from an Afrocentric perspective, the mind or psyche is not detached from the rest of the self. In fact, Okechukwu Ogbonnaya (1994) recommended an Afrocentric remedy to the seemingly static classical psychological perspective that does not account well for an identity in motion. He recommends understanding the person as an *intrapsychic community*. In this community, several selves (or identities) reside, and they must do so harmoniously to avoid chaos and psychological disorder. Each self exists, not in competition with other selves (as happens with an individualistic cultural and conceptual orientation to psychology) but as a collective that appreciates the differences other selves offer. This interplay mirrors the movement and rhythm of life that must be present in any community, and that are necessary for psychological, spiritual, and physical health.

Afrocentricity was conceived while Asante sat in a speech class as a student at UCLA. He heard an instructor discussing the definition of speech as "uninterrupted spoken public discourse" (Asante, 1970a; 1970b). He was baffled by this negligent, grand theoretic notion of speech, which did not apply to his experience as a Black man growing up in a traditional Black church. The call-and-response between an inculcating preacher and engaged congregation and the overlapping affirmation of the message via glossolalia, instrumental rhythms, and oratorical cadence were dynamic facets of speech as exemplified in the experience of the Black church, but they were missing from this professor's explanation of what constitutes public speech. Asante knew this slippage in thinking had to be reconciled, and Black rhetoric had to be accounted for in some way. Then, it dawned upon him, "If we [Black people] had to define speech, our definition would have to include all those 'Amens' and 'That's rights'" (M. K. Asante, personal communication, April 11, 2004). That moment marked the critical turn for Asante, and he subsequently began to critically examine "the location of the African" in every context, whether it was on television, on the radio, in person, or in the curricula. As an Afrocentrist, he continually investigates location, place, orientation, and perspective. There is a distinct difference between an Afrocentric orientation and a Eurocentric one. One unique facet, besides the obvious fact that one sees the world through an African worldview and the other through a European one, is that Afrocentricity is in part marked by sentinel statements. Asante offered an example:

> I turn on the television, for example, and there is Henry Louis Gates, hosting his "Wonders of the African World" series (on the BBC and PBS cable stations). He says, "I may travel to Africa but Harvard is my home." Already, by making that statement, I say, "I can locate him"—I can intellectually locate him by the statement that he has made. These are sentinel statements, and these sentinel statements tell me basically where people are. All of us make them; it just gives you a general idea where people are coming from. So, that sentinel statement allowed me to know exactly where he was. (M. K. Asante, personal communication, April 11, 2004)

Asante contends that Afrocentricity has provided African American studies a critical core it was previously missing. Too often, Asante criticizes, African American studies has become a series of courses as opposed to a set of perspectives concerning the study of people and phenomena. It has become devoid of a focused place where a scholar can build multiple disciplinary [meaning the African American studies discipline] theories that do not replicate course offerings and perspectives in other departments. He posited, "We locate it differently; I mean we can look at the same text, but we do a whole different thing. We do Afrocentric critiques. That's what we began to do and that's critical work that gives you different answers." (M. K. Asante, personal communication, April 11, 2004). By this statement, Asante is suggesting that Afrocentric orientations toward the world are unique in that all phenomena are interrogated with respect to how they fit in a larger, global picture. Rather than accepting that the classical rhetorical canons are invention, organization, style, memory and delivery, for example, the Afrocentrist will ask what other *classical* perspectives there are. If it is evident that *classical* excludes non-Europeans, then the Afrocentrist thinks about the legacies of the Ghanaians, Senegalese, Egyptians, Caribbeans, Chinese, Japanese, and so on. After such a search, it is likely to be discovered that there are *classical* canons outside Europe that predate Aristotle and teach us things Aristotle did not imagine because it was not part of his universe of discourse.

Because of this kind of influence of Afrocentricity, scholars have critiqued Eurocentric international politics and domestic economic policies, for example. Afrocentricity and Eurocentricity are not competing paradigms. Eurocentricity promotes the ideals, perspectives, values, beliefs, practices, and motifs of Europe; Afrocentricity, without replacing Eurocentricity, seeks to promote the ideals, perspectives, values, beliefs, practices, and motifs of Africa.

Afrocentricity has been criticized for being retrogressive with respect to homosexuals and women. The debate about this issue of homosexuality, as it relates to Afrocentricity, emerged after the following statement written by Asante was published:

> Homosexuality is a deviation from Afrocentric thought, because it makes the person evaluate his own physical needs above the teachings of national consciousness. While we must be sensitive to the human complexity of the problem . . . we must demonstrate a real antagonism toward those gays who are as unconscious as other people. . . . The rise of homosexuality in the African American male's psyche is real and complicated. An Afrocentric perspective recognizes its existence, but homosexuality cannot be condoned or accepted as good for the national development of a strong people. (Asante, 1988, p. 57)

This Black nationalistic stance has been interpreted as abrasive and exclusionary. Some readers find this declaration so off-putting that they discount the whole paradigm and write off Asante entirely. For others, this was a risky statement that exemplifies an ideological approach some are afraid to place in writing. In either case, Asante continually refutes the claims that he is homophobic and reiterates the purposes and investigative concerns of the Afrocentric paradigm as being disconnected from patriarchal, dominant interests and in favor of liberation for all Blacks. As he explains why he wrote that statement, he reiterates his concern that homosexuals have relational interests and seemingly consistent individualist orientations that do not always jibe well with the collective interests of the composite, progressive Black Diasporic community.

In spite of the controversy around this paradigm and the beliefs of its progenitor with respect to homosexuals, Afrocentricity remains the most pervasive canonical approach in the fields of African and African American studies. It has affected other fields including communication, sociology, social work, literary criticism, anthropology, sociolinguistics, and many other disciplines.

❖ CONTRIBUTIONS TO COMMUNICATION RESEARCH

Although Molefi Kete Asante has spent the majority of his career maintaining productivity and employed in both communication studies and

African American studies, all his degrees are in communication. Therefore, many of his early writings are in this field. This segment of the chapter explores his contributions to the field of communication as seen in three subdisciplinary areas of inquiry: rhetoric, media and public communication, and intercultural and interracial communication.

Rhetoric

Trained to be a rhetorician specializing in the rhetoric of agitation, Asante wrote about eight articles and three books on the topic within the first three years after graduating from UCLA. Because he had been taught to deconstruct the impetus and exigency of rhetoric, in his first academic book, *Rhetoric of Black Revolution* (Asante, 1969), he systematically uncovered the politically charged practices and objectives inherent in revolutionary discourse. By addressing the strategies, tactics, themes, and audiences of militant rhetoric, he was able to develop a structure for analyzing the nuances of Black and non-Black revolutionary rhetoric (Asante & Rich, 1970a; Asante, 1970b). Asante offered some samples of this type of rhetoric in the first book (Asante, 1969), but then, in the same vein as Carter G. Woodson's (Woodson, 1925) *Negro Orators and Their Orations,* Asante and Robb (Asante & Robb, 1971), introduced 20 famous Black rhetors and their speeches for future rhetorical consideration. The orators included including David Walker, Henry Highland Garnet, Frederick Douglass, Marcus Garvey, Booker T. Washington, Benjamin Mays, H. Rap Brown, Stokeley Carmichael, Malcolm X, and Martin Luther King, Jr.

The release of *Contemporary Black Thought* (Asante & Vandi, 1980) signaled a critical turn in Asante's work. He was no longer concerned principally with just the formation of agitational rhetoric; instead, his focus shifted to the ideology of Black cultural consciousness. He investigated the aspects of rhetoric that influenced Black audiences and began to ask new questions about what inspired them, not necessarily what agitated them. One place where he uncovered unique dimensions of Black rhetoric was within the context of the Black church (Asante, 1970a; 1970b). In examining oratorical features within the Black church, he discovered linguistic practices at work, what are now called tropes or constitutive components of a Black rhetorical canon: repetition, call-and-response, polyrhythm, and epic memory. Repetition refers to the use of the redundancy of themes, phrases, and words to stimulate the audience. Call-and-response, through its interactive form, holds the attention of the audience as the speaker's rhetoric issues the call (to which the audience responds with Amen!, Hallelujah!, Alright! Preach!, or Tell the truth!). The call-and-response can also be nonverbal, as is demonstrated through polyrhythm. The multiple rhythms within the rhetorical episode include the organ, the drums, the speaker's cadence and speech patterns, and the congregation's verbal responses. These parts of the canon are enhanced by epic memory, which refers to the preacher's invocation of ideas that call to mind relevant parts of the congregation's individual and collective experiences.

In the late 1970s, the canon was not so well defined, however. The concept of nommo, or the spoken power of the word, had become well-known, but there was much work to do beyond that. Asante helped to outline several of these rhetorical tropes, but more importantly, he helped to develop an Afrocentric frame in which to understand these patterns. The advent of Afrocentricity came with the 1971 release of his landmark essay "Markings of an African Concept of Rhetoric" (Asante, 1971), which was published in *Today's Speech* (now known as *Communication Quarterly*). Any scholar interested in Afrocentricity will see the subtle and not-so-subtle traces of Afrocentricity in that essay as Asante unravels a critique of western intellectualism while speaking honestly, yet fervently, about African rhetoric and its "concern for coherence and participation, but also in its relationship to the stability of the traditional society" (Asante, 1971, p. 16). His groundbreaking and best-selling books—*Afrocentricity: The Theory of Social Change* (Asante, 1980), *The Afrocentric Idea* (Asante, 1988), and *Kemet, Afrocentricity, and Knowledge* (Asante, 1990)—explored these ideas in depth. Because of Asante's multifaceted program of research, his conceptual work concerning Afrocentricity was being developed in concert with his other adjoining areas of research: Black language, Blacks in the mass media, interpersonal communication, and interracial and intercultural communication. Obviously, these early think pieces on Afrocentricity laid the foundation for his continuing work in Africana studies and communication studies.

Media and Public Communication

Asante's work regarding the mass media and public communication began in the mid-1970s. His first published book (with J. Frye) on this topic was *Contemporary Public Communication* (Asante & Frye, 1976). Throughout his writings, Asante has discussed the effect of televisual images on Black cultural consciousness and argued that television was used as a tool to rally people into the civil rights movement because there were frequent reports on demonstrations, agitational rhetoric, and social justice initiatives. Asante pointed out that television also often showed White storeowners protecting their stores and restaurants, leaving an implicit message that the private interests of White citizens were of more importance than the collective public interests. The effect of television on Black consciousness was multifold. Televised demonstrations in one part of the country could be shown to others in another part of the country, and the result was greater sympathy and a more galvanized set of activists. For some, the images shown "shattered their dreams of a humanitarian society" (Asante, 1976, p. 139). Maintaining this line of inquiry, he coedited *The Social Uses of Mass Communication* with Mary Cassata (Asante & Cassata, 1977), which explored producer constructions and audience consumption of Blackness via public mediated communication. Realizing the need for a companion text explicating the rudimentary aspects of mass communication discussed in their *Social Uses* anthology, Asante and Cassata also coauthored a mass communication textbook (Asante & Cassata, 1979).

Asante's ongoing analyses of U.S. media control of cultural mindsets piqued his curiosity about whether similar issues existed throughout the African Diaspora. So, when he conducted his Fulbright research in Zimbabwe, he decided to address the challenges and disparities of mass communication resources and needs in Zimbabwe, releasing two funded research monographs in 1982: *Media Training Needs in Zimbabwe* (Asante, 1982b) and *Research in Mass Communication: A Guide to Practice* (Asante, 1982a). After articles and books comparing Black and White television, his last monograph concerning mass media was an Afrocentric study, coauthored with Dhyana Ziegler (Asante & Ziegler, 1991) that broadly explored mass media in Africa. Asante's research concerning public communication enveloped critiques and explanations of institutionalized forces at work within a given society. One example of this is his essay with Alice Davis (Asante & Davis, 1985) on Blacks in the workplace. Despite the fact that this work would be presently categorized as organizational communication, it fits the description of public communication as well. By examining it outside of its subdisciplinary habitat, Asante affords us a glimpse at how Afrocentric analyses traverse disciplinary borders and help to illumine habitual practices that serve to subdue the unique cultural voices of institutional members.

Intercultural and Interracial Communication

In much the same way that the preceding research has helped to outline new directions in the field, Asante attempted to do the same

groundbreaking work in intercultural communication, a newly emerging part of the field in the early 1970s. Even as he began to make segues
in this area of endeavor within communication, he was elected as the
first president of the newly forming Society for Intercultural Education, Training and Research (SIETAR). Truly, the nature of his writings
within each line of his research is persistently interdisciplinary. This
partly explains his attraction to Black Studies, which by nature is interdisciplinary. Intercultural and interracial communication scholars have
always admitted and embraced the hybridity of perspectives, methods,
and approaches to the study of race and culture—albeit usually dominated by Eurocentric paradigms, at least within U.S. literature. If there
is a satisfying home for Asante's work in communication, intercultural
communication is it.

There were several influences on Asante's thinking about race. As
previously mentioned, he read and was initially inspired by DuBois,
Garvey, and Karenga. He studied and advocated the teaching of Black
rhetoric (Rich & Asante, 1970) via his research and activism as he
cofounded the NCA Black Caucus. Furthermore, he had resided and
gone to school in Tennessee, Oklahoma, Indiana, and California, and
eventually moved to New York and Pennsylvania. So, he had many
socially and racially different experiences, beginning when he was a
child picking cotton for money in the fields of the racially segregated
south. As a teenager with a job shining shoes, without provocation he
was spat upon by one of his White patrons (Early, 1993), and as an adult
he routinely experienced racism and discrimination within the predominately White institutions in which he has chosen to work throughout
his career. So after years of witnessing and personally experiencing
dehumanizing acts of violence and disregard, "transracial" or interracial communication was a natural, therapeutically gratifying area of
research interest because it gave him a place to psychologically work
through and conceptually articulate the effects of a racially subjugated
people.

His earliest writings, *Toward Transracial Communication* (Asante,
1970c) and *How to Talk to People of Other Races* (Asante, Allen, &
Hernandez, 1971) were sponsored by the Center for Afro-American
Studies and the Transcultural Education Foundation, two organizations with which he closely worked. Subsequently, he landed two book
contracts with well-reputed academic presses to write about interracial
communication—one with Harper & Row and the other with Prentice
Hall. *Language, Communication, and Rhetoric in Black America* (Asante,
1972) and *Transracial Communication* (Asante, 1973) were the two publications (the latter was more well-received). These books set the stage
for other articles and books on African American communication

carryovers (Asante, 1975) and intercultural communication (Asante & Newmark, 1976; Asante, Newmark & Blake, 1979). Eventually, Asante's landmark book, *Handbook of International and Intercultural Communication* (Asante & Gudykunst, 1989), was written. The first edition of this book, published 10 years earlier with Eileen Newmark and Cecil Blake (Asante, Newmark, & Blake, 1979), had modest sales and limited use in the field, but the second edition, coedited with Bill Gudykunst (Asante & Gudykunst, 1989), was *sine qua non*. With insightful chapters written by leading scholars in intercultural studies, the *Handbook* remains a critical source for explications of various paradigms central to the study of race, culture, and communication. Although Asante chose not to coedit the third edition with Gudykunst, he coedited (with Virginia Milhouse and Peter Nwosu) a spin-off of the *Handbook* titled *Transcultural Realities* (Milhouse, Asante, & Nwosu, 2001).

Asante's contributions to communication inquiry can be generally captured in three major lines of research: rhetoric, mass media and public communication, and intercultural/interracial communication. He has also written about the necessity of teaching Black communication in postsecondary institutions (Rich & Asante, 1970). His work has been monumental in the field of communication. In 2002, the National Communication Association awarded him the lifetime achievement award for rhetoric—the Douglas Ehninger Award for Distinguished Rhetorical Scholarship.

Contributions to Africana Studies

Asante is self-trained in the area of Africana studies. Although none of his degrees is in Africana studies, since the beginning of his career, he has established a reputation as a respected researcher, disciplinary leader, and administrative figurehead in the field. When there was no program in which one could attain a doctorate in African American studies, he created one. When there was institutional resistance to funding the program because of doubts about how it would express its disciplinary uniqueness, Asante relieved this ambiguity by developing and refining a solid curriculum based on a unified Afrocentric perspective, which no other department could claim to have. When there was a large body of unsatisfactory Eurocentric reference sources purporting to represent African Diasporic experiences, Asante offered an alternative set of sources: encyclopedias, atlases, high school textbooks, and other source materials. Although he has critics, as all pioneering thinkers do, no one can debate his influence on generations of scholars over the last 35 years. His writings are ubiquitous in Africana studies and cover two major areas of research: (1) philosophical and historical perspectives on Africana experiences, and (2) creative works.

Philosophical and Historical Perspectives on Africana Experiences

Technically, the majority of Asante's writings could fit under this rubric; however, for the sake of simplicity, the discussion in this section focuses on his responses to critics of Afrocentricity and his extensions of the Afrocentric paradigm.

Asante has argued that Afrocentricity is an alternative to a most obvious and hegemonic grand narrative that presupposes Europe as the center of intellectual thought. For example, as mentioned previously, the implication that *classical* (or *traditional*) is a term reserved for Western antiquity is one that mimics the colonialist mentality that African thought is primitive (Jackson, 1995). Although Afrocentricity as metatheory was created approximately 20 years go, there is still much confusion about the concrete objectives of Afrocentricity. A common misconception is that Afrocentrists are anti-White (Lefkowitz, 1996). That is not true; they are anti-oppression. In some respects, Afrocentricity has been resentfully received by the academy as a hostile takeover rather than a movement to construct space for the study and criticism of Black particularity throughout the Diaspora. It is this intellectual xenophobia that has inhibited the progress of cultural models and critical practice within academic institutions.

Although the backlash from both Black (Crouch 1995/1996; Gates, 1993; West, 1993) and White (Lefkowitz, 1996) scholars concerning Afrocentric studies utilizes *essentialism* as an apparatus to justify the critique, essentialist politics and highbrow appropriations of African heritage (in the form of fictitious and historically inaccurate "Middle East" Egyptian studies) have been the catalysts for the present Afrocentric movement. The idea of essentialism presupposes that there is an unchangeable, consistent essence to something, so to say that Afrocentricity is essentialist is to say it tries to argue that there is a single authentic blackness. However, for years Europeanized media have taught television and film audiences that there is only one way to be Black. So Asante's aim is to offer a recuperative set of discourses in which Diasporic Africans are able to retrieve agency to define their own selves.

Asante (1993; 1999) asks us to consider how scholars are to make sense of the ambiguous European canon formations grounded in Egyptian ethics (ma'at) without references to the indigenous cosmology or philosophers that inspired the axiological system. Africanist and Afrocentric scholars such as Chiekh Anta Diop, John Henrick Clark, and Chancellor Williams have been chastised for introducing their cultural orientations and correcting the chronological schedule and historical context in which those orientations are rooted. In fact, Asante introduced a redesignation of the chronological suffix A.D. to a.b.a. (at the beginning again) just to illustrate the antiquity of the world vis-à-vis the European timeline. Each of the previously mentioned scholars, including Asante, have been amid this hostile debate on chronology because it is believed that they have somehow illegitimated European history by countering claims about Greek and Roman primacy in oratorical philosophy. They are not competing so Africa gains one-upmanship over Europe; they are correcting a historiographical error.

The fact is that every culture has its own unique perspective on rhetoric. The Western intellectual tradition must be interrogated and decentralized for other cultures to locate where their cultural legacies and sensibilities fit in the epistemological structure of the world in general, and rhetorical studies in particular (Asante, 2000b). So, to some degree, Afrocentricity is just one step in the demythologization of "classical" rhetoric (Hamlet, 1998). This does not mean that we should avoid celebration of Greek and Roman intellectual traditions, but those traditions should not be considered as the final arbiter of excellence. The Chinese (Kowal, 1995; Lu & Frank, 1993), Native American (Basso, 1970), and African (Asante & Abarry, 1996) cultures each has its own classical rhetoric. Without these cultural rhetorics in major theory and criticism texts throughout various disciplines, we are left with a void in the study of those respective disciplinary traditions (Asante, 2002a; Asante & Asante, 1985). These are the central epistemological, ontological, and axiological concerns Asante has raised via his numerous research studies of both Black rhetoric and Ebonics.

Creative Work on Black Community Consciousness

As a corrective measure for omissions and oversights of African cultural legacies, Asante has developed many reference and pedagogical materials for secondary- and post-secondary level readers, as well as for general audiences. A partial list includes the following: *Historical and Cultural Atlas of African Americans* (Asante & Mattson, 1991),

Classical Africa (Asante, 1993), *African American History: A Journey of Liberation* (Asante, 1995), *African Intellectual Heritage* (Asante & Abarry, 1996), *Classical African Activity Book* (Asante & Mitchell, 1996), *Teacher's Guide for African American History* (Asante, Harris-Stewart, & Mann, 1997), *African American Atlas* (Asante & Mattson, 1999), *The Egyptian Philosophers* (Asante, 2000a), *Customs and Culture of Contemporary Egypt* (Asante, 2002a), and *100 Greatest African Americans* (Asante, 2002b). *Egypt vs. Greece in the American Academy*, edited by Asante and the Afrocentric theorist, Ama Mazama (Asante & Mazama, 2002), added to the discourse on history for general audiences as well as scholars. These reference sources are extensions of Asante's existing Afrocentric works that have sought to equip his readers with sources of pride in African ancestry and cultural traditions. Perhaps what are most innovative for a college professor are his African and African American history textbooks and ancillary materials developed for high school teachers and students. Each of these texts is published with Peoples Publishing Group under the "Asante Imprint," and they hold the distinction of being the only existing historical high school textbooks written from an African-centered perspective.

Asante is also a novelist, painter, and poet. Because of his support of Black publishers, he has consciously chosen to have his creative written works published by Sungai Books, African American Images, and Peoples Publishing Group. Whether it is a book of African (Asante, 1991) or African American names (Asante & Muntaqim, 1997), or an historical novel such as *Scattered to the Wind* (Asante, 2001a), Asante works hard to develop varied sources of pride for African American people. In fact, he confesses that the writing of the historical account of the legendary Mzilikazi of South Africa's sojourn to Zimbabwe found in *Scattered to the Wind* represents "the hardest work I've ever done" (Turner, 2002, p. 729). His poetry, as demonstrated in his book *Love Dance* (Asante, 1996), is also a lyrically creative way to express his endearing commitment to community and unbridled love for one's total self—culturally, socially, and personally. In 2003, Ama Mazama translated his book *Afrocentricity* (Asante, 1980) into French, and it was published in Paris by Menaibuc under the name *L'Afrocentricité* to great fanfare when more than 200 people came out to a book signing and presentation at the Sorbonne.

❖ CONCLUSION

Asante has written extensively about both historical (Asante & Abarry, 1996) and contemporary concerns (Asante, 2001b). His work can be found intercontinentally and has influenced countless scholars. Every facet of his career has been marked by social, cultural, and intellectual activism. He has unabashedly spoken on behalf of Africans throughout the Diaspora. He has shown us that although no human being is flawless, the best we can do as human beings is to love one another and enhance the morally impoverished conditions in which we live. His undying love and commitment to African Diasporic communities is unquestionable.

The Utne Reader identifies him as one of the "100 Leading Thinkers in America." Through his Afrocentric and Africological studies, it is no exaggeration to say Molefi Kete Asante has made a significant impact on world consciousness. He has certainly left and continues to leave an indelible imprint on the field of communication because almost every study of African American communication is either based on or addresses his work. His pioneering efforts, prolific record of research, and nurturing relationships with his students and community are an inspiration to us all.

❖ REFERENCES

Ani, M. (1994). *Yurugu: An African-centered critique of European thought and behavior.* Trenton, NJ: Africa World Press.

Asante, M. K. [Arthur L. Smith]. (1969). *Rhetoric of black revolution.* Boston: Allyn & Bacon.

Asante, M. K. [Arthur L. Smith]. (1970a). Some characteristics of the black religious audience. *Speech Monographs, 37*(3), 207–211.

Asante, M. K. [Arthur L. Smith]. (1970b). Socio-historical perspectives of black oratory. *Quarterly Journal of Black Speech, 56*(3), 264–270.

Asante, M. K. [Arthur L. Smith]. (1970c). *Toward transracial communication.* Los Angeles: UCLA Center for Afro-American Studies.

Asante, M. K. [Arthur L. Smith]. (March, 1971). Markings of an African concept of rhetoric. *Today's Speech,* 13–18.

Asante, M. K. [Arthur L. Smith]. (1972). *Language, communication, and rhetoric in Black America.* New York: Harper & Row.

Asante, M. K. [Arthur L. Smith]. (1973). *Transracial communication.* Englewood Cliffs, NJ: Prentice Hall.

Asante, M. K. (1975). *African and Afro-American communication continuities.* Buffalo, NY: SUNY Center for International Affairs.

Asante, M. K. (1978). *Epic in search of African kings.* Buffalo, NY: Amulefi.

Asante, M. K. (1980). *Afrocentricity: The theory of social change.* Buffalo, NY: Amulefi.

Asante, M. K. (1982a). *Research in mass communication: A guide to practice.* Harare, Zimbabwe: ZIMCO.

Asante, M. K. (1982b). *Media training needs in Zimbabwe*. Harare, Zimbabwe: Mass Media Trust and Friedrich Naumann Foundation.

Asante, M. K. (1988). *The Afrocentric idea*. Philadelphia: Temple University Press.

Asante, M. K. (1990). *Kemet, Afrocentricity, and knowledge*. Trenton, NJ: Africa World Press.

Asante, M. K. (1991). *The book of African names*. Trenton, NJ: Africa World Press.

Asante, M. K. (1995). *Malcolm X as cultural hero and other Afrocentric essays*. Trenton, NJ: Africa World Press.

Asante, M. K. (1996). *Love dance*. Trenton, NJ: Sungai Press.

Asante, M. K. (2000a). *The Egyptian philosophers*. Chicago: African American Images.

Asante, M. K. (2000b). *The painful demise of Eurocentrism*. Trenton, NJ: Africa World Press.

Asante, M. K. (2001a). *Scattered to the wind* [Novel]. Princeton, NJ: Sungai Books.

Asante, M. K. (2001b). Criminal archetypes in the 2000 presidential election: How Black votes were stolen. *Black Scholar, 31*(2), 30–32.

Asante, M. K. (2002a). *Customs and culture of contemporary Egypt*. Westport, CT: Greenwood Press.

Asante, M. K. (2002b). *100 greatest African Americans*. Buffalo, NY Prometheus Books.

Asante, M. K., & Abarry, A. (Eds.). (1996). *African intellectual heritage*. Philadelphia: Temple University Press.

Asante, M. K. [Arthur L. Smith], Allen, A., & Hernandez, D. (1971). *How to talk to people of other races*. Los Angeles: Transcultural Education Foundation.

Asante, M. K., & Cassata, M. (Eds.). (1977). *The social uses of mass communication*. Buffalo, NY: SUNY Communication Research Center.

Asante, M. K., & Cassata, M. (1979). *Mass communication: principles and practices*. New York: Macmillan.

Asante, M. K., & Davis, A. (1985). Black and White communication: Analyzing work place encounters. *Journal of Black Studies, 16*(1), 77–93.

Asante, M. K., & Frye, J. (1976). *Contemporary public communication*. New York: Harper & Row.

Asante, M. K., & Gudykunst, W. B. (Eds.). (1989). *Handbook of international and intercultural communication*. Newbury Park, CA: Sage.

Asante, M. K., Harris-Stewart, C., & Mann, A. (1997.) *Teacher's guide for African American history*. Maywood, NJ: Peoples Publishing Group.

Asante, M. K., & Mann, A. (1997). *Activity book for African American history*. Maywood, NJ: Peoples Publishing Group.

Asante, M. K., & Mattson, M. (1991). *Historical and cultural atlas of African Americans*. New York: Macmillan.

Asante, M. K., & Mattson, M. (1999). *African American atlas* (2nd ed.). New York: Simon & Schuster.

Asante, M. K., & Mazama, A. (Eds.). (2002). *Egypt vs. Greece and the American Academy*. Chicago: AA Images.

Asante, M. K., & Mitchell, J. (1996). *Classical African activity book*. Maywood, NJ: Peoples Publishing Group.

Asante, M. K., & Mitchell, J. (2001). *Discovery essays for teachers.* Philadelphia: Ankh.

Asante, M. K., & Muntaqim, R. (1997). *African American names.* Maywood, NJ: Peoples Publishing Group.

Asante, M. K., & Newmark, E. (1976). *Intercultural communication: Theory into practice.* Alexandria, VA: Speech Communication Association.

Asante, M. K., Newmark, E., & Blake, C. (Eds.). (1979). *Handbook of intercultural communication.* Beverly Hills, CA: Sage.

Asante, M. K. [Arthur L. Smith], & Rich, A. (1970). *Rhetoric of revolution.* Durham, NC: Moore.

Asante, M. K. [Arthur L. Smith], & Robb, S. (1971). (Eds.). *The voice of Black rhetoric: Selections.* Boston: Allyn & Bacon.

Asante, M. K., & Vandi, A. S. (Eds.). (1980). *Contemporary Black thought.* Beverly Hills, CA: Sage.

Asante, M. K., & Ziegler, D. (1991). *Thunder and silence: The mass media in Africa.* Trenton, NJ: Africa World Press.

Basso, K. (1970). To give up on words: Silence in western Apache culture. *Southwestern Journal of Anthropology, 26,* 213–320.

Crouch, S. (Winter 1995/1996). The Afrocentric hustle. *Journal of Blacks in Higher Education,* 77–82.

Early, G. (Ed.). (1993). *Lure and loathing: Essays on race, identity and the ambivalence of assimilation.* New York: Viking/Lane Press.

Gates, H. L. (1993). *Loose canons : Notes on the culture wars.* Oxford, UK: Oxford University Press.

Hamlet, J. (Ed.). (1998). *Afrocentric visions: Studies in culture and communication.* Thousand Oaks, CA: Sage.

Hurst, C. G. (1965). *Effective expression: A new approach to better speaking.* New York: Merrill.

Jackson, R. L. (1995). Toward an Afrocentric methodology for the critical assessment of rhetoric. In L. A. Niles (Ed.), *African American rhetoric: A reader* (pp. 148–157). Dubuque, IA: Kendall-Hunt.

Kowal, K. (1995). Reading Lao Tzu as rhetoric. In W. Covino & D. Jolliffe (Eds.), *Rhetoric: Concepts, definitions and boundaries* (pp. 125–132). Boston: Allyn & Bacon.

Lefkowitz, M. (1996). *Not out of Africa: How Afrocentrism became an excuse to teach myth as history.* New York: Basic Books.

Lomas, C. W. (1968). *Agitator in American society.* Englewood Cliffs, NJ: Prentice Hall.

Lu, X., & Frank, D. (1993). On the study of ancient Chinese rhetoric/Bian. *Western Journal of Communication, 57,* 445–463.

Milhouse, V., Asante, M. K., & Nwosu, P. (Eds.). (2001). *Transcultural realities.* Thousand Oaks, CA: Sage.

Ogbonnaya, A. O. (1994). Person as community: An African understanding of the person as an intrapsychic community. *Journal of Black Psychology, 20,* 75–87.

Rich, A., & Asante, M. K. [Arthur L. Smith]. (1970). An approach to teaching interracial communication. *Speech Teacher, 19*(2), 138–144.

Shea, C. (1997). Prolific professors take pride in prodigious activity. *Chronicle of Higher Education, 35,* A13.

Turner, D. (2002). An oral history interview of Molefi Kete Asante. *Journal of Black Studies, 32*(6), 711–734.

Turner, R. (1991). Afrocentrism: Affirming consciousness. In J. C. Everett (Ed.), *Child welfare: An Africentric perspective* (pp. 32–49). New Brunswick, NJ: Rutgers University Press.

West, C. (1993). *Keeping faith.* New York: Routledge.

Woodson, C. G. (1925). *Negro orators and their orations.* New York: Russell Press.

Ziegler, D. H. (1995). *Molefi Kete Asante and Afrocentricity: In praise and criticism.* Nashville, TN: James C. Winston.

Further Reading

Asante, M. K. [Arthur L. Smith]. (1964). *Break of dawn.* Philadelphia: Dorrance.

Asante, M. K. (1989). *Umfundalai: Afrocentric rites of passage.* Philadelphia: National Afrocentric Institute.

Asante, M. K. (1993). *Classical Africa.* [Part of the Asante Imprint series of high school textbooks.] Maywood, NJ: Peoples Publishing Group.

Asante, M. K. (1995). *African American history: A journey of liberation.* [Part of the Asante Imprint series of high school textbooks.] Maywood, NJ: Peoples Publishing Group.

Asante, M. K., (1999). *Scream of blood.* Princeton: Sungai Books.

Asante, M. K., & Asante, K. W. (Eds.). (1985). *African culture: The rhythms of unity.* Westport, CT: Africa World Press.

Asante, M. K., & Mazama, A. (2005). *Encyclopedia of black studies.* Thousand Oaks, CA: Sage.

Min, E. J., & Asante, M. K. (Eds.). (2000). *Social conflict between African Americans and Korean Americans.* Alexandria, VA: University Press of America.

Note

1. This is not the same name given by Turner (2002) in her 2002 interview with Asante. Turner's notation was incorrect, perhaps because of a transcription error. Wilkson is the name Molefi Asante gave to the authors of this book on November 8, 2004.

Molefi Kete Asante

Photo courtesy of Molefi K. Asante

1942	Born as Arthur Smith in Valdosta, Georgia.
1960	Received high school diploma from Nashville Christian Institute.
1964	Received bachelor of arts degree from Oklahoma Christian College.
1965	Received master of arts degree from Pepperdine University.
1968	Received doctorate from UCLA.
1969	Published *The Rhetoric of the Black Revolution.*
	Served as associate professor, Department of Communication and as director of Afro American Studies.
1971	Served as president of the Transcultural Education/ Communication Foundation (1971–1981).
1972	Published *Language, Communication, and Rhetoric in Black America.*
1973	Changed name to Molefi Kete Asante, which means "keeper of the traditions."
	Published *Transracial Communication.*
	Became professor and chair of the Department of Communication at SUNY, Buffalo (1973–1982).
	Became charter member of The World University (1973–1982).

1975 — Served as president of the Society for Intercultural Education, Training, and Research (SIETAR).

1976 — Published *Intercultural Communication: Theory into Practice*, with Eileen Newmark.

Received doctorate of humane letters from the University of New Haven, New Haven, Connecticut.

1977 — Served as professor and chair of the Department of Black Studies at SUNY, Buffalo (1977–1979).

1979 — Became curator for the Museum of African and African American Art and Antiquities, Buffalo, New York (1979–1984).

1980 — Published *Contemporary Black Thought*, with A. Sarr Vandi.

Published *Afrocentricity: The Theory of Social Change*.

1981 — Consulted with the Zimbabwe Institute of Mass Communication.

1984 — Became Ralphe Metcalfe Chair for Distinguished Scholars, Marquette University, Milwaukee, Wisconsin.

Served as professor and chair of the Department of African American Studies at Temple University. Continues to teach and remained chair until 1996.

1985 — Became UNESCO reviewer for International Scholarly Books.

1987 — Created the first doctoral program in African American Studies at Temple University.

1988 — Published *The Afrocentric Idea*.

Served as vice president and vice chair of the National Council of Black Studies (1988–1990).

Served as vice president of the International Communication Association (1988–1990).

1989 — Became president of the National Afrocentric Institute (1989–1991).

Published *Handbook of International and Intercultural Communication* with William B. Gudykunst.

Founded the National Afrocentric Institute and was named president (1989–present).

1990 — Published *Kemet, Afrocentricity, and Knowledge*.

1991 — Published *Historical and Cultural Atlas of African Americans*, with Mark Mattson.

Received doctorate of humane letters from Sojourner-Douglass College, Baltimore, Maryland.

1993   Founded Asante Imprint Books, Peoples Publishing Group for Afrocentric Infusion.

1995   Served as Walter Annenberg Chair for Distinguished Scholars, Howard University School of Communication.

Published *Malcolm X as a Cultural Hero and other Afrocentric Essays.*

Published *African American History: A Journey of Liberation.*

Received the Morgan State University College of Arts and Sciences Award for Distinguished Academic Service.

1996   Published *African Intellectual Heritage* with Abu Abarry.

2000   Received the Nguzo Saba Award for Scholarly Initiative (NAKO).

Served as president of the African Writers Endowment Foundation.

Published *The Painful Demise of Eurocentrism.*

2001   Published *Scattered to the Wind.*

Published *Transcultural Realities* with Virginia Millhouse and Peter Nwosu.

Lectured at many schools, including Columbia University, Dartmouth University, Harvard College, Howard University, Penn State University, Princeton University, University of Manchester (UK), University of Leeds (UK), University of Michigan, and University of Pennsylvania.

2005   Published the *Sage Encyclopedia of Black Studies* with Ama Mazama.

2

Donald E. Bogle

The idea [of the book Toms, Coons, Mulattoes, Mammies & Bucks: An Interpretive History of Blacks in American Films] *was to examine those things that had been so important and of such great interest to me during my early formative years—African American movie history and the*  *contributions of African American actors and actresses to Hollywood cinema . . . In those early decades, there had been no Black writers, no Black directors, and no Black producers. So, what audiences were shown often were these stereotyped images of African Americans, but I felt that there were these messages that were coming through in the performances by African American actors and actresses. So, I wanted to deal with those things that I had seen in a movie like* Carmen Jones *and really articulate all of that and explore it mainly for myself. Once I started researching the book and learned more about*

early independent Black cinema—race movies—I also wanted to examine this movement. I was especially fascinated by a race movie like the silent film Scar of Shame *and of course, the body of work of Oscar Micheaux. Always, though, I understood the significance of Black actors and actresses in Hollywood. Often working without sensitive scripts or directors, the actors and actresses struggled to create unique characterizations within the stereotyped conceptions of their roles. . . . These things compelled my attention, and I wanted the language I used to articulate these concerns to be direct and accessible. In a way, it was me against the world (or the prevailing opinions) to set the record straight. I had this burning conviction to explore past Black movie history as much as possible. It was challenging and very difficult because I was breaking new ground. Yet ultimately it was very rewarding.*

—D. Bogle (personal communication,
November 20, 2004)

❖ INTRODUCTION

Nationally acclaimed author of three award-winning books, Donald E. Bogle is possibly the nation's most prodigious African American film historian and critic. He is certainly the most cited (Anderson, 1997; Bates & Garner, 2001; Cripps, 1993; Dates & Barlow, 1990; Harris, 1999; Means-Coleman, 2001; 2002; Orbe & Strother, 1996; Toll, 1974). Despite having a modest goal of exploring Black performances just for his own understanding, as the opening quotation suggests, Bogle's work has transcended those ambitions and gained him considerable recognition. He has appeared on such television programs as *Good Morning America, The Today Show, Nightline, The Charley Rose Show, Entertainment Tonight, Donahue,* and Showtime's *It's Black Entertainment*; he has lectured across the United States at hundreds of colleges, universities, and civic organizations; and he has written for popular magazines such as *Film Comment, Ebony, Essence,* and *Spin.* Bogle was a commentator for the HBO special *Mo' Funny: Black Comedy in America* (Bogle, 1990c) and the recent American Movie Classic (AMC) channel documentary on African Americans in the movies: *Small Steps, Big Strides* (Bogle, 1997b).

Bogle has been a commentator for several televised specials and documentaries while also curating film retrospectives for museums and theaters that pertain to African American film history as diverse as the careers of Sidney Poitier and Dorothy Dandridge to blaxploitation cinema and the images of African American women throughout Hollywood history (Bolden, 1999). He has conducted public interviews of such figures as Sidney Poitier, Cicely Tyson, Spike Lee, and Morgan Freeman. Film director Lee proclaimed, "Mr. Bogle continues to be our most noted Black-cinema historian" (Lee, 1992, p. ix). At Lee's request, Bogle also wrote the introduction—a look at the depiction of Black jazz musicians in movies—for Lee's companion book for his film *Mo' Better Blues* (Bogle, 1990b).

Although he has a strong background in literature and a host of experiences working in print media (for *Ebony* and Doubleday Books), from an early age Bogle embarked on a rigorous course of independent study of film history and criticism that led to the publication of his first book. Even as a child, he was no stranger to media, especially print journalism. His father, John D. Bogle, was vice president and advertising director of *The Philadelphia Tribune,* the nation's oldest continuously published African American newspaper. Growing up in a large family (that included an extended family of aunts, uncles, and cousins in neighboring communities), Bogle and his siblings heard their parents discuss social, political, and cultural issues at the breakfast and dinner table. At large family gatherings, there would be conversations about any number of African American dignitaries—Langston Hughes, Jackie Robinson, Dorothy Dandridge, W. E .B. Dubois, or Billie Holiday, among others. He occasionally accompanied his father to the office on Saturdays to browse through the *Tribune's* library. He was reared to appreciate the arts, media, African American culture, and ongoing social and political concerns of the Black community.

In some respects, Bogle believed he had a typical childhood. He enjoyed baseball, but never felt he was as good at it as he wanted to be. His favorite sport was basketball, yet he never had any illusions about being a great basketball star because of his height. Bogle suffered from severe asthma attacks (and later debilitating migraine headaches), so he spent hours in front of the television watching all types of programs. He was particularly fascinated by old films, especially those in which African American performers appeared. In fact, in the late 1950s, he decided "to run away from home and go to live at the movies" (Bogle, 2002, p. xx). That day, he saw (in Technicolor) Dorothy Dandridge and a host of other African American stars in Otto Preminger's Black-cast musical *Carmen Jones*. For the young asthmatic Bogle, moviegoing (whether in theaters or in front of the television) was a journey, perhaps an escape into a different world. Bogle withdrew into another sphere where, as he revealed in a personal interview, "I thought movies were real" (D. Bogle, personal communication, November 20, 2004). Bogle discovered that screen images were not only compelling but also instructive. The movies seemed to be creating a series of narratives about race, culture, and relationships. He decided to see every movie in which Black actors and actresses were shown. He later committed to chronicling and critiquing the vast array of cinematic and televisual depictions of Blacks and has since dedicated his life toward that end.

Bogle's book, *Toms, Coons, Mulattoes, Mammies & Bucks* (Bogle, 1973), was named Best Film Book of the Year by the Theatre Library Association, which hosted an intimate literary ceremony at Lincoln Center's Library of the Performing Arts. In 1987, he wrote and executive-produced (with Joerg Klebe of German Education Television) the four-part, four-hour PBS television series *Brown Sugar: Eighty Years of America's Black Female Superstars* (Bogle, 1987), which he adapted from his book of the same title (Bogle, 1980). The series was awarded the American Women in Radio and Television Award of Excellence. In 2001, *Primetime Blues* (Bogle, 2001), was celebrated with the American Library Association Black Caucus' Image Award. Bogle received an honorary doctorate degree from his alma mater, Lincoln University in 1998. To date, Bogle has edited a three-part book series titled *Black Arts Annual: 1989–1990* (Bogle, 1990a) and has authored six books. The sixth and latest one, *Bright Boulevards, Bold Dreams: The Story of Black Hollywood* (Bogle, 2005), systematically examines the various challenges and issues confronted by Black Hollywood actors and actresses from the early years of the twentieth century through the late 1950s and mid-1960s.

While developing his passion for film history, Bogle worked with one of the nation's premier film directors: Otto Preminger, director of *Carmen Jones* and *Porgy and Bess*. Bogle interviewed scores of Black actors and actresses, including Fredi Washington (an actress featured in *Imitation of Life* and *Emperor Jones*), Mantan Moreland, Eddie Anderson, Vivian Dandridge (Dorothy Dandridge's sister), Cicely Tyson, and Morgan Freeman. Each of these experiences has helped Bogle in his search for knowledge about African American film history.

As a professor at both New York University and the University of Pennsylvania, and as an occasional freelance writer for popular magazines, Bogle has established an impressive interdisciplinary presence in academe and beyond. As a leading authority on Black film and television history, he frequently speaks to varied audiences on the lecture circuit and does media commentary concerning screen representations of Blacks. Although the archetypes of toms, coons, mulattoes, mammies, and bucks were discussed in early studies of Black film history, Bogle's comprehensive examination of these stereotypes has introduced these character profiles to several generations of Americans.

❖ BIOGRAPHICAL INFORMATION

Donald E. Bogle was born in Philadelphia in the early 1950s and grew up in a suburb outside of Philadelphia (D. Bogle, personal communication, November 20, 2004). He is the son of the late John D. Bogle, who was vice president and advertising director of *The Philadelphia Tribune*, and Roslyn Woods Bogle, who was a homemaker and very active in community affairs. John Bogle was a college-educated, Washington, D.C. native, born of a middle-class background. He attended Virginia Seminary and later earned his bachelor of arts degree in history from Langston College. Shortly thereafter, he began working for the *Baltimore Afro American* newspaper and later moved to Philadelphia to help run *The Philadelphia Tribune*, the newspaper of which Donald's older brother Robert Bogle is now publisher. John Bogle was known to be a dynamic speaker and a highly charismatic man determined to fight for the rights of African Americans.

Bogle's mother, Roslyn Woods Bogle, was raised in an upper-class family in Virginia, part of the Black southern elite. Her father, Robert

Clisson Woods, was president of Virginia Theological Seminary. Perhaps because of her father's public and community roles, Roslyn Woods Bogle developed a strong appreciation for the arts and *high culture* at an early age. Conversant in such wide-ranging topics as politics, current events, social issues and concerns, and literature, she also paid close attention to American popular culture, as did her husband. At the same time, she was a down-to-earth, deeply spiritual individual who, although known for her civic activities, was quite a private person who enjoyed reading. In this respect, Bogle feels a similarity to his mother. Although he has been fascinated by the personal histories of so many people he has met over the years, he very rarely feels comfortable discussing his own life.

The youngest of six children of Robert Woods Bogle and his wife Nellie Hunter Woods, Roslyn never knew her mother (she died when Roslyn was only a year old). She was raised by her paternal grandmother and aunt until her father remarried. Her father and his new wife, Nellie Hunter Woods, had three more children. As a child, Roslyn was a voracious reader. She excelled in Latin, mathematics, and literature. Yet because she was a true free spirit, she decided not to pursue a college education—a decision motivated by her elopement with John Bogle while still a teenager. Both wanted a large family. After having children, Roslyn consistently encouraged each of them to pursue an education. She always believed that a solid foundation came from reading as much as possible on any number of subjects and that reading was the beginning of one's personal intellectual growth and the first step in a life of independent study.

At a young age, Bogle was excited to learn that his mother had been well-connected to community leaders and dignitaries of her day, such as the poet/critic Sterling Brown and Alain Locke. In October 2004, Roslyn Woods Bogle's civic contributions and love for literature and the arts were recognized by Lincoln University in Pennsylvania with the establishment of the Roslyn Woods Bogle Reading Room. Bogle's parents were, of course, the most important influences on his formative development and interests in media.

Bogle was born during the post–World War era, when television was a brand new technological innovation and Hollywood movies were in a period of transition. Blacks had been in films since the Black character Mungo appeared in the 1769 production of *The Padlock*. During the years of silent motion pictures, when Hollywood itself was just taking shape and when Black roles were sometimes played by Whites in blackface, African Americans gradually found a place in the film industry, usually by playing comic servant roles. After the talkie (i.e., talking film) era began in the late 1920s, more African Americans were seen playing actual roles in films—especially during the Depression era, when performers such as Stepin Fetchit, Hattie McDaniel, Louise Beavers, Paul Robeson, and Eddie "Rochester" Anderson became well-known to mainstream audiences. Yet, more often than not, Black actors were still saddled with stereotyped roles. In the late 1940s and 1950s, however, films such as *Home of the Brave*, *Pinky*, *Carmen Jones*, and *The Defiant Ones*, which featured performers such as James Edwards, Dorothy Dandridge, and Sidney Poitier, redefined the cinematic landscape with the depiction of controversial themes. Audiences saw more sympathetic portrayals of Black characters than ever before. Indeed, as Bogle posited,

> During and after World War II, American films—and American audiences—changed and lost their innocence. A world war had been fought in part against fascism abroad. Now some believed there was a battle to be fought at home. At this time many Americans underwent their first pangs of guilt. Many people experienced a "liberal" urge to right old wrongs. Sometimes in films the Negro was used as a metaphor for social inequities and injustices. With Sidney Poitier, mainstream audiences saw the rise of the Negro as social symbol. Often at the movies old wrongs were corrected in a patronizing or condescending manner. But significant changes did come about . . . The new opportunities benefited the entertainers while paving the way for the emergence of sympathetic Negro character roles in feature films . . . these new Negro characters were used for social statements, and they often paid homage to the democratic way of life. (Bogle, 2002, p. 137; D. Bogle, personal communication, January 28, 2005)

The late 1940s and early 1950s signaled a critical juncture, not only for the film industry but also for the United States, which was in the midst of a racial crisis marked by civil unrest and court battles leading to school desegregation (e.g., *Brown v. Board of Education* and James Meredith's integration of the University of Mississippi). Despite this historical epoch, Bogle had a relatively uneventful childhood, consisting primarily of his undying thirst for knowledge about Blacks in film.

❖ ACADEMIC BACKGROUND AND EXPERIENCE

Bogle attended predominately White schools until college, when he enrolled at Lincoln University in Pennsylvania. His elementary and secondary school experiences were not memorable, but Bogle distinctly recalls having an excellent elementary English teacher named Ms. Daly and a wonderful high school literature teacher named Ms. O'Neal, who energized his interest in writing. Having teachers who were fair and open-minded was significant for Bogle because although his elementary and high school educators prided themselves on being "liberal," many of the racial attitudes and perspectives of White teachers were still heavily affected and tempered by the sociopolitical climate of the late 1950s and 1960s. These two teachers facilitated Bogle's already growing passion for literature. To major in film studies still was not possible at most colleges and universities; therefore, Bogle knew he would major in literature. Although he planned not to go to college at one point, Bogle's parents insisted that he enroll. It took some coaxing before Bogle could willingly accept the idea of going to college, but after his visit to the Lincoln University campus, he was so enamored with what he saw of campus life that he decided almost instantly to attend. He remembered,

> My parents felt that going to a Black school would be very important for my development, and they were right. It was one of the best experiences I have ever had. I was particularly excited about the fact that learning did not stop outside the classroom. We often saw our professors outside of the class. Sometimes we would have coffee with them in the Student Union Building. Or some professors invited students to their homes for dinners with their families. (D. Bogle, personal communication, November 20, 2004)

Literature professors H. Alfred Farrell and Edward Groff and dramatic literature professor Lou Putnam had a profound impact on Bogle's understanding of dramatic writing. In fact, Groff encouraged Bogle's interest in film history and criticism as an area of study. Because of Groff's vast knowledge of movie history, Bogle consulted with him often while writing his first book, *Toms, Coons, Mulattoes, Mammies, & Bucks: An Interpretive History of Blacks in American Films* (Bogle, 1973). Emery Wimbish, Director of Lincoln University's Langston Hughes Memorial Library, was also important to Bogle's development. Wimbish frequently ordered special books from other collections at Bogle's request and kept the library well-stocked with important periodicals. Seemingly casual conversations with these professors—about films, literature, or current events (especially those focusing on the growing civil rights and Black Power movements)—proved meaningful for Bogle.

After graduating with honors from Lincoln University, Bogle decided to pursue his master's degree, with a focus on creative writing, at Indiana University. He received some mentoring from creative writing professor William Wilson and found most of his literature classes stimulating, but he was often the only African American in his classes, especially his writing courses. Bogle found the atmosphere at the university a rather isolating environment in which to study and he yearned to learn more about film history. At Indiana University, he was fortunately able to view a number of old films, and although he formed a number of friendships with other students on campus, he chose not to return after his second year of study. He briefly took time off and then took graduate courses at Columbia University, although he never completed his master's degree.

Bogle chose not to allow graduate school aspirations to dictate the course of his life. Because of his ever-growing interest in Black film history, Bogle briefly worked at *Ebony* magazine and (in New York) for Otto Preminger, the acclaimed director and producer of such films as *Carmen Jones* (Bogle's favorite childhood film) and *Porgy and Bess*. To get the job with Preminger, Bogle sent him a letter describing his interest in and enthusiasm for the film industry. Miraculously, Preminger gave him a chance to work as a story editor, reading books and scripts to help Preminger decide which film projects to pursue. This was late in Preminger's career, and it was an excellent opportunity for Bogle—working alongside such an esteemed and celebrated member of an elite group of movie producers. An added benefit was working in Preminger's executive office suite on Fifth Avenue in New York City. Furthermore, because Preminger had worked with Dorothy Dandridge (whom Bogle had seen on-screen when he was young), Bogle could get detailed responses to questions he had about Dandridge's life and career—answers and insights that only an insider would have. Through Preminger, Bogle also met and interviewed Dorothy Dandridge's older sister Vivian, who proved immensely important to Bogle when he pieced together Dorothy Dandridge's life for his book, *Dorothy Dandridge: A Biography* (Bogle, 1997a).

After working for Preminger, Bogle returned briefly to graduate work. He was dissatisfied with his studies, however, because he still could not study the history and contributions of African Americans in motion pictures. So he embarked on an ambitious and demanding period of independent scholarly research. He recalled,

> When I look back on that time in my life, I still see it as exciting and invigorating. I put myself on a tough, rigorous schedule of reading just about everything I could on general film history as well as volumes of film criticism and countless biographies and

autobiographies. At the Schomburg Center for Research in Black Culture, I began digging through their files and Black periodicals to unearth information on African Americans in films. I did the same at Lincoln Center's Library of the Performing Arts. In time, I drew up extensive lists of old films that I sought to find and view. I would see films wherever possible. I'd check the television listings each week to see what films were scheduled. In this era before the advent of VCR's, I'd sometimes get up at two or three in the morning to view an old film in which an African American appeared. It might be *The Mad Miss Manton* with Hattie McDaniel or *Buck Benny Rides Again* with Eddie "Rochester" Anderson or *Show Boat* with Paul Robeson and Hattie McDaniel. (D. Bogle, personal communication, November 20, 2004)

Bogle went to screenings at the Museum of Modern Art and viewed old films at revival houses in New York. Despite not being able to locate every film in the Library of Congress that he wanted to see, he found himself viewing films from private collections to uncover more information about Black actors and actresses who worked in films. He interviewed performers living in New York who had worked for Oscar Micheaux and eventually traveled to Los Angeles, where he met with and interviewed King Vidor (director of the 1929 Hollywood Black-cast film *Hallelujah*) and actors Mantan Moreland and Clarence Muse, among others. Bogle became increasingly fascinated by the responses of African American audiences to films, particularly the covert messages they detected in the performances of certain actors and actresses. He interviewed older relatives and friends about films they saw in the past and questioned contemporaries about their reactions to more recent movies. Bogle was influenced by film critics Pauline Kael and Andrew Sarris and read everything Kael wrote. He admitted, "I was stimulated by her clarity, her energy, her extraordinary insights, her knowledge of movie history, her lack of pretentiousness, her honesty, and her humor" (D. Bogle, personal communication, November 20, 2004). Bogle discovered the critical observations of Black critics such as Sterling Brown and L. D. Reddick, who were navigating uncharted waters by taking the images of African Americans in literature or film seriously, long before it was intellectually fashionable to do so. This was an intense period of reading, viewing films, interviewing, and reflecting that was rich and rewarding. In fact, Bogle asserted, "It laid the foundation for my first book, *Toms, Coons, Mulattoes, Mammies, & Bucks: An Interpretive History of Blacks in American Films*" (D. Bogle, personal communication, January 28, 2005).

❖ CONTRIBUTIONS TO COMMUNICATION RESEARCH

When contemporary communication scholars think of the nature and scope of communication inquiry, film studies often are assigned to another school, college, or department. Nonetheless, many of the nation's most well-trained film specialists, producers, directors, writers, critics, and performers were educated in mass communication departments comprised of print, radio, television, and film studies. Others came from a host of other disciplines such as English, business, sociology, and political science. Bogle was trained in literature and he now teaches at the University of Pennsylvania and New York University's Tisch School for the Arts. Despite his literature background, Bogle has influenced countless communication scholars intrigued by stereotypical images of Blacks on television and in cinema. To effectively capture the simultaneous breadth and focus of his work, this segment of the chapter accents five of his most pivotal works: *Toms, Coons, Mulattoes, Mammies & Bucks: An Interpretive History of Blacks in American Films* (Bogle, 1973), *Brown Sugar: Eighty Years of America's Black Female Superstars* (Bogle, 1980), *Blacks in American Films and Television: An Illustrated Encyclopedia* (Bogle, 1988), *Dorothy Dandridge: A Biography* (Bogle, 1997a), and *Primetime Blues: African Americans on Network Television* (Bogle, 2001).

Toms, Coons, Mulattoes, Mammies & Bucks: An Interpretive History of Blacks in American Films (1973)

As the epigraph for this chapter suggests, Bogle began his line of research on Black performers' roles and representations in film as a result of a childhood curiosity about the making of cinema. Although some cinemagoers were entertained by the acting, narrative coherence, or visual effects, Bogle found himself so thoroughly engrossed in the screen images that he felt he was actually "living" the film. He maintained,

As a kid, I felt the movies were really real and I guess a lot of other kids have felt that way. I couldn't understand how people on movie screens got their faces blown up the way they did, and how they got to these Olympian sizes. And I saw afterwards you could go back and meet them. That, I thought was compelling. And when I talk about television [in my work], I would see a lot of old movies on television. That was when I first became interested in African Americans in movies, because the old films you might see on TV were ones like the Shirley Temple movies where you would see Bill Bojangles Robinson or the old Charlie Chan movies with Mantan Moreland and so forth. I began watching them and I couldn't understand why I wasn't seeing more of the Black performers. And, when they were offscreen I would always wonder, "Well, where are they?" (D. Bogle, personal communication, November 20, 2004)

While being drawn to these images, identifying with the Black performers, and having these interrogations, Bogle pursued the answers to his own questions. When asking his elementary schoolteachers and peers about Black thespians, he noticed their constantly dismissive responses. After completing high school and then college at an early age, he decided to investigate the careers and lives of these "larger-than-life" actors and actresses.

In the fourth edition of *Toms, Coons, Mulattoes, Mammies & Bucks* (2002), Bogle uncovered more than 90 years of film history in 10 chapters and a little more than 450 pages filled with cast posters, still shots, and portraits. Each chapter, beginning with the early 1900s, represents a decade of films. The book ends with a discussion of films of the 1990s and into the new millennium. The idea was to chronicle and critically explain the development and perpetuation of stock minstrel characters presented as meek and kowtowing uncle toms; groveling, bulging-eyed coons; light-skinned, tragic mulattoes; nurturing mammies; and brutal, maniacal bucks.

Bogle poured all his energies into the research for this book. As he recalled,

When I received the final copy of this book, it looked like it had shrunk tremendously. I had imagined it to be a manuscript that was at least ten feet high, because my first draft was very, very long. It was very difficult to write because there was virtually nothing else available at the time [to use as a resource]. I had to make a place for myself, because no one was really talking about Black popular culture. Now, there is plenty. (D. Bogle, personal communication, November 20, 2004)

After the release of this book, Bogle received many invitations for speaking engagements and was pleased to know that he had a receptive audience despite being steadfast in completing the project primarily as a way to satisfy his own interests. *Toms, Coons, Mulattoes, Mammies & Bucks* has become what the publisher HarperCollins calls "a classic study of African American movie images" (HarperCollins.com, 2004).

It is the first volume of its kind to assemble an interpretive history of facts, films, performers, and performances. (In this context, *interpretive* refers to both Bogle's method and critical-reflective writing process.) As with most of his books, Bogle not only viewed films but also interviewed as many people as possible. No one was really talking about Black popular culture and the effects of its images on audiences, although much more is being written today. Nonetheless, Bogle felt he had to make a place for himself. It is evident via the content, approach, and style of his writing that Bogle did that by viewing every film he could and taking copious notes about the total production of the films, including plot lines, climaxes, genres, behaviors, and quirks. His underlying philosophic approach was that of a critical film ethnographer interested in exploring the unspoken and unwritten nuances in the films. Critical ethnography is about identifying experiences, exploring semantic changes in meaning over time, and implicitly advocating social change.

Initially, Bogle hoped to provide some documentation (at least a mention) and interpretation of every film in which an African American appeared in a significant role. As he toured the United States for book signings and speaking engagements, Bogle was often asked about African American women in popular culture—not only those women who appeared in films but also women such as Josephine Baker, Bessie Smith, Billie Holiday, and Ethel Waters. These women made occasional or one-time-only film appearances, but they were known primarily for their successful careers in music or on the stage. Bogle became interested in focusing on images of African American women in popular entertainment: films, theatre, music, and television. This research led to the writing of *Brown Sugar: Eighty Years of America's Black Female Superstars* (Bogle, 1980).

Brown Sugar: Eighty Years of America's Black Female Superstars (1980)

Brown Sugar: Eighty Years of America's Black Female Superstars was an extension of Bogle's cartography of Blacks in films to include other areas of popular culture. He wanted to explore the unique challenges and issues facing African American female entertainers and to reveal the particular achievements of those women who challenged the male-dominated (usually *white* male-dominated) world of show business. In fact, as the title of *Toms, Coons, Mulattoes, Mammies & Bucks* implies, even the roles of women in film were different. No matter whether the roles were played by Ethel Waters, Fredi Washington, Josephine Baker,

Marian Anderson, Billie "Lady Day" Holliday, or Dorothy Dandridge—they were different from the roles of male actors. Black female performers in films expected to be typecast as either a mulatto or a mammy. But what intrigued Bogle most, as he recounted, was the following:

> At hundreds of college campuses across the country, I spoke on Black film history . . . What always impressed and sometimes surprised me most were the great number of questions asked about Black female entertainers—in movies and out. The questions were endless. How did Josephine Baker's career begin? Why had Baker never been as great a sensation in the States as she was in Europe? . . . What did Ethel Waters do before she became the prototypical Black matriarch in films? . . . Why hadn't Dorothy Dandridge made more movies? Who were Bessie Smith and Ma Rainey? (Bogle, 1980, p. 11)

Bogle realized that African American women in music and nightclubs had far more control over their images than film actresses who had to work with a script. He became fascinated by the way female musical performers created their own personae. This interest sparked another line of inquiry that was still aligned with his writing trajectory because he had always been enthralled by Dorothy Dandridge in particular. When Bogle embarked on the project, he discovered an endless well of information about the films and the personal lives of the performers. In some cases, he had to be selective about how much to say about their public and/or private lives. The first draft of the book ended up being a gigantic manuscript that had to be cut in half before going to press. In keeping with the first book, the result was an illustrative chronology of Black female superstars (not only in film but also in other areas of popular entertainment) from 1900 to the late 1970s. He explicated their personal backgrounds, the sociopolitical climate of the entertainment industry, their performer personae, and any industry challenges they encountered. Each decade was introduced as an era. For example, the second chapter, which covers 1900 to 1920, was titled "Beginnings," the fourth chapter, which covers the 1930s, was titled "Pop Myths," and the final chapter, which examines the 1970s, was titled "Survivors." Bogle addressed three motifs of Black female representations: sex symbol, social symbol, and political symbol. (These motifs were also true for Black male performers.) Bogle's exploration of entertainers as divas was varied as he explained that divas were not just well-fit and curvaceous women; they were overweight. Despite depictions of divas as nonmaternal, Bogle contended that even a youthful and shapely Ethel Waters was billed as Sweet Mama Stringbean. Black female entertainers of the 1920s and 1930s were superstars, not only because of what they endured but also because they possessed other talents besides acting. They had to be quintessential performers. The film profiles of early blues-singing artists such as Josephine Baker, Ethel Waters, Bessie Smith, Ma Rainey, Ida Cox, Alberta Hunter, and many others proved that these women known for their lucrative "race records" were exceptional. These women, almost all of whom grew up in the lower class, were entertainers who were stylistically innovative, had uncompromising talent, and knew how to move audiences emotionally. Black actresses were appropriately known more broadly as entertainers who were dancers, singers, instrumentalists, comedians, and socialites. They had to be more than sex symbols and entertainers; they were social and political symbols as well. As social symbols, their celebrity was an amenity few other Blacks enjoyed and despite the challenges with racism, sexism, racial segregation, and exclusion, Black female entertainers were more privileged than most Blacks. Their high-profile status placed heavy demands on them from their local and cultural communities. Much like today's entertainers, they were expected to be role models and (more importantly) political symbols who would without hesitation stand up and fight for social justice, racial progress, and cultural parity.

Bogle confronted a serious problem (that he rarely discussed) while writing *Brown Sugar*. He suffered from debilitating migraine headaches that could last for four or five days, during which time he could not work. He remembered,

> I couldn't have any lights on. Nor could I have loud music. Just nothing. With migraines, you usually just stay in a dark room, hoping the darn things will pass. For a time, too, I could not commit to social engagements because I never knew when a migraine might put me out of commission. I learned to work my way around the headaches as much as I could. (D. Bogle, personal communication, January 28, 2005)

Despite the headaches, Bogle persevered and continued his long hours of work on the book. Upon completing *Brown Sugar*, Bogle had hoped to write a companion volume on African American male images in popular culture, which would include an examination of images of Black athletes and music stars. But literary agents and publishers expressed little interest in the subject, and Bogle felt those reactions were very telling. *Brown Sugar* has been celebrated as a book and as a

PBS television series. While developing the show, Bogle spent an inordinate amount of time researching and gaining access to film footage (in addition to traveling back and forth from New York to Los Angeles to do interviews). It was a labor of love that was a culmination of his years of activities engaged in the film industry. The four-part, four-hour series that aired in 1987 was executive-produced by Bogle and Joerg Klebe of German Education Television. The series instantly won rave reviews, and Bogle was honored that year with a special award from the American Women in Radio & Television for the series.

Blacks in American Films and Television: An Illustrated Encyclopedia (1988)

While Bogle was completing *Brown Sugar: Eighty Years of America's Black Female Superstars*, he was invited to do an encyclopedia about Blacks in American films by Jeff Conrad, a friend and previous colleague from Doubleday Books (who had moved to Garland Publishing). Although not part of his future writing plans, Bogle was flattered by the offer and decided to pursue the project. He had to immediately begin working on it after he completed production of the television series *Brown Sugar: Eighty Years of America's Black Female Superstars*, which was difficult because he was used to taking breaks between projects.

The encyclopedia was an all-consuming project that required numerous screenings of films that Bogle had never seen or films that he wanted to screen again. As he had done with *Toms, Coons, Mulattoes, Mammies, & Bucks*, he screened old films at the Library of Congress as well as on television, at film festivals, at movie revival theatres, and through private collectors. Bogle saw the book as a very important contribution to the literature concerning Blacks in film and television. In fact, his encyclopedia would be the first of its kind.

Bogle's tasks included cataloguing and offering a critique of the films and television shows plus discussing their origins (if from a book or theatrical play), production, directing, scriptwriting, casting, release dates, and storyline. With films and then television shows presented in alphabetical order, the book permitted Bogle to tie his various works together in one place as a resource for film *and* television enthusiasts. Rather than end the book with descriptions of the television shows, Bogle added bonus materials that featured brief biographies of nearly 125 performers, including Bill Bojangles Robinson, Mantan Moreland, Oscar Micheaux, Ossie Davis, Ruby Dandridge, Hattie McDaniel, Cicely Tyson, and Pam Grier.

Dorothy Dandridge: A Biography (1997)

After reviewers heralded the book and award-winning television series *Brown Sugar: Eighty Years of America's Black Female Superstars*, Bogle was surprised that publishers were so dismissive of his prospectus for a book on Dorothy Dandridge. Because most editors at major publishing houses were not familiar with Dandridge (who was remembered primarily only within the African American community), they did not understand the importance of her life and career. Several major publishing houses passed on Bogle's book proposal before a small, Black-owned publishing house, Amistad Press, expressed interest in the project. Not only was Bogle excited that Amistad was supportive of the biography but was even more impressed by the staff's awareness of Dandridge's then unacknowledged icon status in movie/cultural history. Bogle had waited a very long time to do this book, and it proved not only challenging to write but became a favorite writing project as well. He noted in an interview, "There was never a moment I did not want to go to the computer to write about Dorothy Dandridge" (D. Bogle, personal communication, November 20, 2004).

The writing of *Dorothy Dandridge: A Biography* began long before any words were written. It began the day Otto Preminger spoke at length with a young Donald Bogle about Dorothy Dandridge as an entertainer, as a woman, and as an actress in *Carmen Jones*. It continued when Bogle interviewed Dorothy Dandridge's sister, Vivian Dandridge, and when he worked hard to gain access to old newspaper clippings, memorabilia, and even to the homes Dandridge owned. During a period of five years, Bogle, with the assistance of an excellent researcher Phil Bertelsen (now a film director), meticulously researched the book. Bogle traveled back and forth from his home in Manhattan to his "second home" in Los Angeles. Years were spent interviewing Dandridge's friends, acquaintances, and professional associates. Years were also spent going through microfilm of old newspapers and magazines at various libraries on the east and west coasts. Of great importance was material Bogle found at the Academy of Arts and Sciences Library in Los Angeles. He also did research at the Schomburg Center for Research in Black Culture at New York Public Library and at Lincoln Center's Library of the Performing Arts. Bogle also searched everywhere for photographs of Dandridge. Today, he has an excellent and extensive personal archive of photos and print material on Blacks in films and television and, of course, an extensive collection of material on Dandridge. Bogle's complete collection is one of the best in the country and he hopes that someday it will go to a university or museum.

Dorothy Dandridge, a Cleveland, Ohio native, was described as having a "razor-sharp intensity," "haughty glamour," and "breathtaking beauty" (Bogle, 1988, p. 375). Her performances in *Carmen Jones* and *Porgy and Bess* were testimony to all these characteristics. Dandridge was talented, bright, witty, and humorous both on-screen and offscreen, which made her death all the more disturbing. Bogle explains that with 32 movies and short films to her credit, Dandridge died of a drug overdose at the young age of 42, eclipsing a career that was prolific but still in its beginning stages. She had already reached stardom and was an icon to young Blacks all over the United States. Bogle remembers,

> My parents spoke of Dandridge much as they did Jackie Robinson: as someone distinct and pioneering; someone who was altering mainstream conceptions of what Black Americans could or could not do. From what I gathered, Dandridge was an altogether unique and unprecedented cultural phenomenon: a successful Black dramatic actress in Hollywood and perhaps Black America's first bonafide movie star, already a glowing figure of legend and glamour. (Bogle, 1997a, p. XIII)

Dorothy Dandridge: A Biography is an amazing, 613-page fitting tribute to the Dandridge family. The book explores Dorothy Dandridge's life from before her birth, through the day of her untimely death, and to the weeks and months after as news-reporting agencies scrambled to make sense of her overdose. Bogle takes time to offer painstaking details about Dorothy being born into a "broken" family and what that meant for her life and her search for identity. Indeed, after reading the book, it is difficult not to see Dandridge as a phenomenon who overcame many obstacles throughout her life. She will always be remembered as the first Black woman to be nominated for the Best Actress Award by the Academy of Motion Pictures Arts and Sciences for her performance as self-titled character in the film *Carmen Jones.*

Dorothy Dandridge: A Biography is segmented into three parts that cover her childhood, early career, and height of stardom, respectively. It is a highly sensitive treatment of her family life, love life, and professional proclivities—even examining the intricacies of her experience in nightclubs, and of course Hollywood, as places very unwelcoming to Blacks during her lifetime. Bogle was careful to present readers with a comprehensive snapshot of her personality, whims, attitudes, and perspectives via sundry correspondences, photographs, movie stills, interview excerpts, newspaper articles, and personal conversations with her family. Although Bogle's other books provided compendia filled with trivia about Black film history, this biography was also an important contribution to communication studies (along with *Toms, Coons, Mulattoes, Mammies & Bucks*) as a narrative exemplar.

Prime Time Blues: African Americans on Network Television (2001)

The writing of *Prime Time Blues* came on the heels of Bogle's completion of *Dorothy Dandridge: A Biography*. Bogle had just finished composing an introduction for a book titled *A Separate Cinema: Fifty Years of Black Cast Posters* (Bogle, 1992), which put the spotlight on John Kisch and Edward Mapp's (Kisch & Mapp, 1992) movie posters. Bogle was approached by the publishers of Kisch and Mapp's book (Farrar, Straus, & Giroux) to do a volume about Black representations on television. Bogle already wrote several books chronicling Blacks in film and created an encyclopedia that included Blacks in television, but he had never treated television as a totally separate topic for a book. This was his opportunity. He signed the contract and began writing immediately, but it was a different writing experience because he was still a bit exhausted from having just completed *Dorothy Dandridge: A Biography* (a manuscript that was more than 1000 pages long in draft form).

Nonetheless, Bogle was enchanted with the idea of doing a book about Blacks on network television. Because the decade-by-decade chronological approach worked well in previous books, Bogle maintained that same organizing structure. *Primetime Blues* offers an impressive array of descriptions and critiques of Black televisual images. As one critic notes,

> Taken simply as a catalogue of appearances by African Americans on television over the past sixty years . . . Bogle seems to have watched every episode of every TV show that ever featured Blacks, from *Beulah* and *Amos n' Andy* in the early days, to the slew of UPN shows now, with stops along the way for hits like *Julia*, *Sanford and Son*, and *The Cosby Show* and the many all too brief series like *Get Christie Love*. He discusses all of them, not just the shows in general, but individual episodes, plus TV movies and Black themed episodes of White shows. (BrothersJudd.com, 2004)

Primetime Blues was somewhat risky for Bogle because his forte has always been primarily film. He arduously worked to bring film and television texts to bear with a critical, scholarly lens. It has never been an easy task, but it has been a rewarding one. In 2001, Bogle received the

American Library Association's Black Caucus Distinguished Book Award for this book. Although Bogle has been criticized for not bringing enough scholarly interpretation and analysis to his examination of Blacks in film history, he is indisputably America's most significant film historian chronicling screen images of Blacks. *Primetime Blues* is another piece of evidence that proves his importance to this area of inquiry.

❖ CONCLUSION

Donald Bogle has always been unafraid to delve into the affective domain of everyday living rather than having a purely scientized and detached way of thinking about life. His worldview has been influenced by what he has understood over the years to be the principal function of cinema—to cause people to emote and to reconsider how they live. Bogle passionately believes that scholars should avoid allowing the scientific to inhibit and interfere with the emotive habitat in which human beings find themselves most often. He also remains committed to observing the responses and needs of African American audiences as to what they see on the big and little screens. So in all of his books, Bogle attempts to strike a balance between an objective critical examination and a more personal biographical look at cinematic and televisual performances. The significance of this is its experiential return to a basic understanding that we are all citizens who live in a world with people who maintain competing identities and contradictory impulses. These inner tensions and social ambiguities are hard to capture purely via empirical studies or personal biographies alone.

Bogle's latest book, *Bright Boulevards, Bold Dreams: The Story of Black Hollywood* (Bogle, 2005) gives more evidence of Bogle's point of view: It offers a behind-the-scenes, critical exploration of Black Hollywood actors and actresses of the 1910s through the mid-1960s, describing the way they lived and socialized. He notes what their lives were like onscreen and off-screen, paying attention to the intricacies of their everyday lives and how that affected their careers. The period between 1910 and the late 1950s is what Bogle identifies as the "old Black Hollywood," a time when Black performers still struggled to get positive roles and still lived in segregated enclaves in the exurbs of Los Angeles. The book also provides a portrait of Los Angeles itself, which in some respects was a segregated city. Nonetheless, *Bright Boulevards, Bold Dreams* points out that a vibrant, exciting social scene flourished in Black Los Angeles, with Black nightclubs, theatres, and grand hotels such as the Dunbar on Central Avenue (the great Black thoroughfare).

It was a time when stereotypes were broken and more Black independent filmmakers began to emerge. It was also a time of economic and racial strife. During the beginning of the Great Depression and after the stock market crash, Black actors and actresses had a hard time getting work and could hardly be selective about the parts they received if they chose to maintain theatrical performance as their primary occupation.

The end of the "old Black Hollywood" era was also the beginning of widespread television viewing in American homes (shows such as *Beulah* began to make it on the air). It was also an era that saw Black stars—such as Nat "King" Cole, Sammy Davis Jr., and Dorothy Dandridge—function in a more integrated movie capital, live in areas previously closed to African Americans, and socialize more with the larger Hollywood community. In a review, *Library Journal* wrote this about *Bright Boulevards, Bold Dreams*: "[I]t's the story behind the camera, the tales of nightclubs, agents, and the social scene, that makes this work stand out . . . no other work is as encompassing of the social scene" (*Library Journal*, 2004). And *Entertainment Weekly* selected the book as its Editor's Choice, writing that it is "meticulously researched" and "engrossing." "Shameful, funny, enlightening, and sobering, this tale of movieland's dark side is a must-read for any student of film history" (Sinclair, 2005).

With the addition of this latest book, Bogle continues to be the nation's leading Black film and television historian. He has tirelessly chronicled the appearance, roles, and dispositions of Blacks in film and on television. He has offered an exhaustive range of interpretations and perspectives on the images of Blacks, and as one book critic who reviewed *Primetime Blues* put it, "[E]very snippet of TV history is held up and examined like an important fossil in the hands of a paleontologist" (BrothersJudd.com, 2001). Recently, Bogle served as a consultant and the author of the chapter on film history in the *Creative Fire* volume of Time-Life's ambitious and lauded three-volume set on African American history and culture, *African Americans: Voices of Triumph* (Bogle, 1993).

Bogle has also curated a number of important film series in New York, including a major retrospective on the career of Sidney Poitier at the American Museum of the Moving Image. He interviewed Poitier as part of that series. He conducted a similar public interview with Spike Lee for the Museum's retrospective on the filmmaker's career. Bogle has also both curated and co-curated major series at New York's Film Forum: *Black Women in the Movies: Actresses, Images, Films*; *Blacks in the Movies: Breakthroughs, Landmarks, Milestones*; the successful *Blaxploitation, Baby!* in the summer of 1995; and the highly publicized Dorothy Dandridge retrospective.

Bogle's pioneering historical work concerning Blacks in film and television is unparalleled and his contributions as a film and television historian-critic and a chronographer have been indispensable to communication research. He has toiled to leave to posterity a comprehensive history, complete with photos, exploration of scenes and episodes, and informed criticism.

❖ REFERENCES

Anderson, L. M. (1997). *Mammies no more.* Lanham, MD: Rowman & Littlefield.

Bates, B., & Garner, T. (2001). Can you dig it? Audiences, archetypes, and John Shaft. *Howard Journal of Communications, 12,* 137–157.

Bogle, D. (1973). *Toms, coons, mulattoes, mammies & bucks: An interpretive history of Blacks in American films.* New York: Viking Press.

Bogle, D. (1980). *Brown sugar: Eighty years of America's Black female superstars.* New York: Harmony Books.

Bogle, D. (Producer). (1987). *Brown sugar: Eighty years of America's Black female superstars* [Television series]. New York: German Education Television.

Bogle, D. (1988). *Blacks in American films and television: An illustrated encyclopedia.* New York: Fireside.

Bogle, D. (1997a). *Dorothy Dandridge: A biography.* Philadelphia: Amistad Press.

Bogle, D. (Documentary Expert Commentator). (1997b). In V. Cato. (Director), *Small steps, big strides: The Black experience in Hollywood* [Television broadcast]. Jericho, NY: American Movie Classics.

Bogle, D. (2001). *Primetime blues: African Americans on network television.* New York: Farrar, Strauss and Giroux.

Bogle, D. (2002). *Toms, coons, mulattoes, mammies & bucks: An interpretive history of Blacks in American films* (4th ed.). New York: Continuum.

Bogle, D. (2005). *Bright boulevards, bold dreams: The story of Black Hollywood.* New York: Valentine books.

Bolden, T. (1999). *Strong men keep coming: The book of African American men.* Hoboken, NJ: Wiley.

BrothersJudd.com (2001). *Primetime blues: African Americans on network television.* Retrieved November 4, 2004, from www.brothersjudd.com/index .cfm/fuseaction/reviews.detail/book_ id/58/Prime%20.

Cave, J., & Britten, L. (Eds.) (1993.) *African Americans: Voices of triumph.* New York: Time-Life Books.

Cripps, T. (1993). *Making movies black.* New York: Oxford University Press.

Dates, J., & Barlow, W. (Eds.). (1990). *Split image: African Americans in the mass media.* Washington, DC: Howard University Press.

HarperCollins.com (2004). *Donald Bogle: Biography.* Retrieved November 4, 2004, from www.harpercollins.com/global_scripts/product_catalog/ author_xml.asp?authorid=19.S.

Harris, T. (1999). Interrogating the representation of African American female identity in the films "Waiting to Exhale" and "Set It Off." *Popular Culture Review, 10*(2), 43–53.

Kisch, J., & Mapp, E. (1992). *A separate cinema: Fifty years of Black cast posters.* New York: Farrar, Straus and Giroux.

Lee, S. (1992). Preface. In J. Kisch & E. Mapp, *A separate cinema: Fifty years of Black cast posters* (pp. iii-vii). New York: Farrar, Straus and Giroux.

Library Journal (2004, December). Book review. [Review of *Bright boulevards, bold dreams*]. Retrieved November 4, 2004, from http://www.libraryjournal .com/index.asp?layout=searchResults&content=all&text=bright+boule vards.

Means-Coleman, R. (2001). *African American viewers and the Black situation comedy.* New York: Garland.

Means-Coleman, R. (2002). *Say it loud!: African American audiences, media and identity.* New York: Taylor & Francis.

Orbe, M., & Strother, K. (1996). Signifying the tragic mulatto: A semiotic analysis of Alex Haley's *Queen. Howard Journal of Communications, 7,* 113–126.

Sinclair, T. (2005, January 28). Book Review. [Review of *Bright boulevards, bold dreams.*] *Entertainment Weekly* [electronic version]. Retrieved November 4, 2004, from http://www.ew.com/ew/article/review/book/0,6115, 1019240_ 5_0_,00.html.

Toll, R. C. (1974). *Blacking up: The minstrel show in nineteenth century America.* New York: Oxford University Press.

Further Reading

Bogle, D. (1990a). (Ed.). *Black arts annual: 1989–1990.* New York: Garland.

Bogle, D. (1990b). Foreword. In S. Lee & L. Jones (Eds.), *The mo' better blues book* (pp. 15–30). New York: Simon & Schuster.

Bogle, D. (Documentary Expert Commentator). (1990c). In R. Pryor (Director), *Mo' funny: Black comedy in America* [Television broadcast]. HBO.

Bogle, D. (1992b). Introduction. In E. Waters & C. Samuels, *His eye is on the sparrow* (pp. 1–9). New York: De Capo Press.

Donald E. Bogle

**Photo courtesy of photographer Gasper
Tringale, taken from *Primetime Blues:
African Americans on Network Television*.**

Early 1950s	Grew up in a suburb of Philadelphia, Pennsylvania.
Late 1950s	First viewed director/producer Otto Preminger's *Carmen Jones* and saw Dorothy Dandridge in the title role. He immediately became fascinated with the lives and filmic images of Black entertainers.
1960s	Received a bachelor's degree in literature from Lincoln University before pursuing a master's degree in creative writing at Indiana University and taking additional graduate courses at Columbia University.
Early 1970s	Worked at *Ebony* magazine before taking a job as story editor for famed director/producer Otto Preminger.
1973	Published popular work, *Toms, Coons, Mulattoes, Mammies, & Bucks*.
1980	Published *Brown Sugar: Eighty Years of America's Black Female Superstars*.
1987	Wrote and executive-produced four-part, four-hour PBS television series, *Brown Sugar: Eighty Years of America's Black Female Superstars* (adapted from his book of the same title).
1987–1990	Edited three volumes of the *Black Arts Annual*.
1988	Published *Blacks in American Films and Television: An Illustrated Encyclopedia*.

1990s	Began teaching at New York University's Tisch School for the Arts in its dramatic writing program. Later accepted a faculty position as lecturer at the University of Pennsylvania.
1990	Served as expert commentator for the HBO documentary *Mo' Funny*, a chronicling of Black humor.
1992	Wrote an introduction for the book *Separate Cinema: Fifty Years of Black Cast Posters,* highlighting John Kisch and Edward Mapp's movie posters.
	Wrote the introduction to the autobiography of Ethel Waters, *His Eye is On the Sparrow.*
1995	Curated a major series at New York's Film Forum. Highly successful *Blaxploitation, Baby!* appeared in the summer of 1995.
1997	Published *Dorothy Dandridge: A Biography.*
1999	Appeared as a celebrated writer in Tonya Bolden's book, *Strong Men Keep Coming: The Book of African American Men.*
2001	Published *Primetime Blues: African Americans on Network Television.*
2005	Published *Bright Boulevards, Bold Dreams: The Story of Black Hollywood,* a behind-the-scenes critical exploration of Black Hollywood actors and actresses of the 1910s through the late 1950s and the mid-1960s.

3

Hallie Quinn Brown

(1850–1949)

We believe that the right thinking White American will soon realize that he cannot afford to ignore twelve million loyal citizens of color. It is sadly true that unjust laws are enacted and cruel discriminations made against the Negro. He is held aloof by every other group forming a part of this nation. He is regarded by  *many as a liability rather than an asset in promoting the value of American life.*

(Hallie Quinn Brown,
as quoted in McFarlin, 1975, p. 180)

❖ INTRODUCTION

Hallie Quinn Brown was a professor of elocution, lecturer, and civil rights activist during the end of the nineteenth and beginning of the twentieth centuries. Despite the fact that her literary and oratorical works gave voice to thousands of disenfranchised people of her era and that she "produced pedagogical materials confronting important issues that educators still grapple with today," her contributions to the field of rhetorical communication are seldom mentioned in noteworthy writings on elocutionary theory (Kates, 1997, p. 59). Much of this negligence is because of the limited social roles women and African Americans could take on at the time. Even today, Brown's work goes unrecognized in most scholarly discussions of elocutionary theory. In the article, "Hallie Quinn Brown: Black Woman Elocutionist," Annjennette McFarlin noted:

> Although "Miss Hallie" as she was known by all, was recognized as one of the greatest elocutionists on two continents, Europe and America, she never made a history book, nor have any of her speeches ever appeared in any speech anthologies. (McFarlin, 1980, pp. iv)

As "one of the first colored ladies to take up elocution as a profession," Brown taught thousands of African Americans about the power of the spoken word during a period in history when they were not expected to, or welcomed to, be a political force (Daniel, 1970, p. 298). As described in *Notable Black American Women*, she was indeed "one of the most important black leaders ever to emerge" (Smith, 1992, p.116). In this chapter, her role in transforming mainstream elocutionary practice and instruction to acknowledge African American linguistic traditions is spotlighted in an effort to add her contributions to communication research with those of popular mention.

❖ BIOGRAPHICAL INFORMATION

Hallie Quinn Brown was born the fifth of six children in Pittsburgh, Pennsylvania, on March 10, 1850. Her parents, Thomas Arthur Brown and Frances Jane (Scoggins) Brown, were former slaves. Thomas Brown, who was born into slavery in Frederick County, Maryland, purchased his freedom on his twenty-fifth birthday. In 1834, he purchased the freedom of his sister, brother, and father from his owner and mother, a Scottish woman. Frances Scoggins, Brown's mother, was freed by her White owner and maternal grandfather from his plantation in Winchester County, Virginia, after the Revolutionary War. Frances Scoggins and Thomas Brown got married right after Frances turned 22 years old in 1840. They resided in Pittsburgh in their homestead on Hazel Street until 1864. At the time of Brown's birth, her father worked as a steward and express agent for riverboats traveling between St. Louis and New Orleans, with a stop in Pittsburgh (Strom, 1999). He had been a porter and conductor previously. The Brown family enjoyed a life of relative privilege because the couple had accumulated a considerable amount of real estate before the Civil War. With their savings, the parents strived to provide their children with the educational opportunities they never had.

Brown's early years, however, were not spent distanced from the plight of her less-fortunate contemporaries. The Brown home often served as a station of the Underground Railroad, a haven for fugitive slaves traveling in search of freedom. Prior to arriving at the Brown home, many of these slaves had been waiting to be transported to Canada (Baker, 1987; Hine, 1993). The Browns also provided space in their home as a headquarters for ministers of the local African Methodist Episcopal (AME) church. In fact, "Ministers frequented the Brown's family home so often that one room was known as the 'Bishop's Room'" (McFarlin, 1975, p. 15). These early connections to members of her community helped establish Brown's sensitivities for education and human rights, which later drove her activist efforts.

In 1864, because of the mother's poor health, the Brown family relocated to Chatham, Ontario, Canada, where the father became a farmer. Brown was 14 years old when she began her education there, and she remained there as a student until 1870 (Fisher, 1993). At that time, the family moved again to Wilberforce, Ohio, where they built a house, Homewood Cottage, and sent Brown, along with her younger brother John, to Wilberforce College, an AME church institution (Davis, 1933).

❖ ACADEMIC BACKGROUND AND EXPERIENCE

Hallie Quinn Brown began her education in elocution on her family's farm in Chatham, Ontario, Canada. She sharpened her early skills by delivering addresses to the cows, sheep, and birds there. Almost daily, Brown would inquire about the health of the animals and climb onto a tree stump or old log to discuss the important issues of her day (McFarlin, 1980). While in Canada, Brown was influenced in ways that shaped her life ambitions. One early event that she recalled into adulthood was the moment that encouraged her to proclaim that she would one day meet Queen Victoria of England. In her book, *Tales My Father Told, and Other Stories,* Brown wrote of a parade her family attended in honor of the Queen's birthday:

> The twenty-fourth day of May was Queen Victoria's birthday, and it was befittingly celebrated with pomp and splendor throughout the Dominion of Canada. On one such occasion our family went to Chatham to participate in the festivities. Soldiers in gorgeous uniform marched through the streets which were decorated with many fluttering flags. Bands bore a large banner upon which was imprinted the face of the Queen. My eyes were fastened on that banner and I was unable to banish the picture from my mind. (Brown, 1925a, p. 15)

To see a woman (of any race) held in such high regard was a first for young Brown. This event taught her that women could do much more than her immediate circumstances had shown. Brown was determined to enlighten others in much the same way as she had been on that day—yet for her it would occur from the podium.

Brown navigated her way through many life challenges. After two happy years in Canada, the Brown family home was destroyed by a fire that came from post–Civil War hostilities. Her sister Mary was killed in the tragedy, and her family was forced to sell much of their Pittsburgh property to rebuild and sustain Homewood Cottage. During this time of financial hardship, Brown worked on the family farm as a farmhand. She grew to see the benefits of hard work and learned that women could stand up to almost any challenge.

In addition to educational experiences on the farm, Brown and her younger brother attended public school in Canada, where they experienced "racial prejudice and humiliation" (McFarlin, 1975, p. 19). Brown's parents decided that she and her brother would attend a college built to educate Blacks, as older sister Belle had. Thus, Brown became a student at Wilberforce College, where she was introduced to what she often called the "Art of all Arts": rhetoric. Brown was immediately attracted to the energy of campus life, and after one term at Wilberforce, she realized that her passion for the spoken word would be fostered there. She wrote of instruction from one of her first mentors— Daniel Alexander Payne, who was a family friend and an AME bishop, as well as the founder, owner, and president of Wilberforce College— in the following words:

> Bishop Payne, in the classroom and at home, guided me in speech, taught me to be articulate, how to pronounce, to modulate, taught

me to read. I read to him daily. He was a typical teacher. I grew in
knowledge and understanding. (McFarlin, 1975, p. 20)

Brown received a bachelor's degree from Wilberforce University,
where she was one of seven graduates. In 1873, she delivered her first
public speech as salutatorian of her graduating class (Smith, 1992).
Thereafter, Brown taught at several schools—such as the Senora
Plantation school in Mississippi and Allen University in Columbia,
South Carolina—and eventually became the dean of Allen University
from 1875 to 1887. During the summers, she attended the American
Chautauqua Lecture School, a notable literary and scientific circle, and
graduated from there in 1886. At the Chautauqua School, Brown was
influenced by Professor Robertson of the Boston School of Oratory.
Brown took a summer course with Professor Robertson, "The Art of
Speech and Oratory," which spoke to her passion to become an effective public communicator. After completing the course, Brown's career
as an instructor of elocution was launched. In 1890, just four years after
graduating from the Chautauqua School, Brown received an honorary
master's degree; much later (in 1936), she received an honorary doctorate of laws degree from Wilberforce University. For a year, beginning in 1892, she served as dean of women at Tuskegee Institute. After
her stint at Tuskegee, Brown returned to Dayton, Ohio (on the border of
the small town of Wilberforce), to teach classes to adult migrant workers in the Dayton public schools. She continued teaching at Wilberforce
University until Central State University and Wilberforce University
split in the late 1920s or early 1930s. She decided to remain with the
institution dedicated to public education, so she transitioned across the
street to Central State University.

Brown, the Educator

Brown's early experiences as a classroom teacher were quite challenging. Her first teaching assignments were at plantation schools
in the South. During these times, she endured the strain of dilapidated
living conditions, severely inadequate teaching facilities, and a shock-
ing degree of illiteracy among both children and adults. Of this early
time in her teaching career, Brown recalled, "Surrounding me was
desolation, poverty and want glared at me" (McFarlin, 1975, p. 32).
For example, after several attempts to seek repairs for the Senora
Plantation school in Mississippi (a building with no windows and
many cracks in the mortar) to no avail, Brown undertook the repairs

herself (Smith, 1992). Rather than withdrawing from the disappointing conditions, Brown's steadfast character motivated her to improve the conditions of her immediate environment.

Despite the challenge of teaching with limited resources, Brown strived to educate and empower her students to realize the transformative value of public address. She firmly believed that with proper instruction in elocution, any motivated person could impart significant social influence. Brown's pedagogy centered on the role of education as a social tool that deemed the holder responsible for using it to improve society for those who otherwise had few opportunities to do it for themselves. As a result, she successfully taught large numbers of children and some adults to read and speak with diction.

Brown returned to Ohio in 1887 to teach in the Dayton public school system and remained there for four years. Her success as a teacher soon caught the attention of the Tuskegee Institute, where she was paid $60 per month plus complimentary housing to become the lady principal (i.e., dean of women) for a year, from 1892 until 1893, under the direction of Booker T. Washington. Although Brown was offered an appointment as professor of elocution at her alma mater, Wilberforce University, in 1894, she did not accept the offer until 1906 because of her blossoming travel schedule with both the Lyceum and the Wilberforce (later renamed Stewart) Concert Company as a reader.

During her travels, Brown sojourned in Germany, France, Switzerland, England, and other parts of Europe—lecturing, singing, and reciting (a combination of more than 90 memorized pieces) in major cities of Great Britain (Davis, 1933). She had a repertory comprised of works such as "Shakespeare and Mark Twain . . . political activist poems and speeches (like Frances Watkins Harper's 'The Dying Bondman'), and dialect humor (Irish, German, Negro)" (Donawerth, 2002, p. 173). Brown was especially adept at interpreting the poetry of Paul Lawrence Dunbar.

While in Great Britain, Brown was presented twice (in 1897 and 1899) to Queen Victoria at Windsor Castle as a guest and notable elocutionist (Stetson, 1983). In fact, through her established networks in England—and because of how impressed the Queen was with her—Brown was asked to help establish the first British Chautauqua in North Wales in 1895. Unlike the American Chautauqua School, British Chautauqua was a traveling education and entertainment group akin to the Lyceum. After a five-year sojourn in Europe, Brown assumed the position of professor of elocution at Wilberforce University (Logan & Winston, 1982).

Brown, the Lecturer

Brown was a magnificent public speaker. Her expertise was widely noted in newspapers, pamphlets, and serials throughout the United States and Europe. For instance, the *African Methodist Episcopal Church Review* noted her ability to defy popular convention with extreme success:

> Miss Brown may be thought to gesticulate too frequently in some of her didactic selections; but right here is shown that she discards the rigid rules of the books and follows nature, for she possesses an ardent temperament, and nearly every sentence she utters in private conversation is made emphatic or impressive by a gesture or variation of the facial expression. Miss Brown possesses a voice of "wonderful magnetism and great compass." At times, she thrills by its intensity; at times, it is mellow and soothing. She seems to have perfect control of the muscles of her throat, and can vary her voice as successfully as a mocking-bird. (Unknown, 1890, p. 259)

Brown moved audiences in ways that few other elocutionists could. She left an impression on listeners that preceded other successful African American women speakers by nearly a century.

Brown's conviction and firm belief in an "embodied rhetoric" that was located within African American communities and vernacular led her to travel extensively as a lecturer, reciter, and elocutionist before both American and international audiences (Kates, 1997; Logan & Winston, 1982). One organization she traveled with was the Lyceum, a well-known band of traveling educators, performers, and entertainers (Wright, 1906). Although Brown's activities with the Stewart Company ended two years after they began (the company disbanded in 1884 because of financial difficulties), her reputation soon reached another acclaimed African American speaker of the era: Frederick Douglass.

Douglass helped sponsor Brown's second trip to Europe in 1894. She decided to make the trip to England to raise financial support for a campus library at Wilberforce. Before her departure, Douglass wrote a moving letter of introduction to present Brown to "his British friends" (McFarlin, 1975, p. 120). Brown's relationship with the Douglass family remained strong even after Douglass' death. After six years of extensive fund-raising and touring, Brown was able to return to the United States with England's support for the Frederick Douglass Memorial Library.

Brown's ties to Europe remained strong and she eventually returned there as a representative to the Women's Missionary Society of the African Methodist Conference in Edinburgh, Scotland. She remained on a European lecture tour for seven months to raise additional funds for Wilberforce at the request of the board of trustees. Her exceptional efforts resulted in the construction of Emery Hall, a dormitory named after the mother of Julia Emery, a London philanthropist. In 1906, she returned to Wilberforce on a full-time basis as professor of elocution. She spent many years in the English department there and became a member of the board of trustees.

A critic from the *Indianapolis Times* wrote of Brown's reception as an elocutionist in the following words: "Miss Hallie Q. Brown, the elocutionist with the company, was loudly applauded. Many credit Miss Brown with being one of the best elocutionists before the public" (McFarlin, 1975, p. 42). With her career as an elocutionist established, Brown was asked to address several groups throughout the southern United States and one in Europe to raise financial support for Wilberforce. Brown's success also afforded her the unique opportunity to teach public speaking to White ministers. Her acceptance in this capacity was proof that she had established herself as one of the premier elocutionists of her time (McFarlin, 1980).

Brown, the Leader and Activist

In addition to her interests in education and public lectures, Brown's concern for civil rights was bolstered during her time at Wilberforce. Many times in her writing, she recalled hearing Susan B. Anthony present her ideas about civil liberties for women to the students of the university. Anthony's convictions regarding women's suffrage led Brown to become an organizer and crusader in the women's Christian temperance movement (Kates, 2001). In 1893, along with five other Black women leaders of African American women's organizations, Brown was selected to speak before the World's Congress of Representative Women, a forum connected with the Columbian Exposition in Chicago, Illinois (Wertheimer, 1997). The other Black women invited to speak to the all-White delegation were Anna Julia Cooper, Fannie Jackson Coppin, Sarah J. Early, Frances Watkins Harper, and Fannie Barrier Williams. The issues that emerged ranged from Whites' intellectual imperialism and perception that Blacks were inferior, to Black women's rights to sexual autonomy, to (as Anna Julia Cooper put it) the way that "Black women of the south have to suffer and struggle and be silent" (Leeman, 1996, p. 44). Realizing the need for a national organization to support Black women in America, Brown established the Colored Woman's League of Washington, D.C., in 1894.

The league was a predecessor of the National Association of Colored Women (NACW). The impetus for Brown's efforts stemmed from the exclusion of Black representatives from most social and political decision-making circles (Smith, 1992). She also lectured in support of the British Women's Temperance Association early in her career. From 1905 to 1912, Brown was president of the Ohio Federation of Colored Women's Clubs. Still unsatisfied with her contributions, she became president of the NACW from 1920 to 1924. During her term as president, Brown initiated two major programs: the preservation of the Frederick Douglas Home in Washington, D.C. and the institution of a scholarship fund for women pursuing higher education. She served as chairperson of the scholarship committee and was pleased when the fund was named in her honor years later (Hine, 1993).

Brown held several leadership positions in the early 1920s. In 1924, she spoke at the Republican convention in Cleveland, Ohio, in support of the Republican party's nomination and campaign for fellow Ohioan Warren Harding to the U.S. presidency and also seized the opportunity to speak up for civil rights by promoting an antilynching bill. She also spoke fervently on behalf of the nomination of Herbert Hoover in 1932.

Brown was clearly very engaged in holding prominent leadership positions as an activist speaking on behalf of women's rights in many political arenas. Among these positions were her roles as vice president of the Ohio Council of Republican Women and director of Colored Women's Activities at the Republican national campaign headquarters in Chicago. Much like her popularity as an educator and lecturer, her reputation as a strong political voice grew. On May 6, 1925, her activism was reported in *The New York Times* when she and a group of other NACW members walked out of the International Council of Women's Conference because they were instructed to sit in a racially segregated section of the conference venue, the Memorial Continental Hall in Washington, D.C. Brown publicly criticized the Daughters of the American Revolution (DAR) for refusing to allow the conference to be held at a location with desegregated seating arrangements (Smith, 1992). Her challenges to the racial and gendered ideologies of the time provided a public voice for the thousands of women and African Americans who were silenced by the oppression of their social world (Davis, 1933).

Brown remained an active lecturer, fund-raiser, and political advocate until her death on September 16, 1949 at the age of 99. She was the longest-living member of her immediate family, although her mother lived to the age of 95. Although she never married or bore any children, she maintained regular correspondence with her niece, Frances Hughes, during the later years of her life. Letters to Hughes have helped to provide details about the last 24 years of Brown's life. Within them, Brown wrote of her "three loves": Wilberforce University, the AME church, and the NACW (McFarlin, 1975). Two buildings memorialize Brown's life and extraordinary achievements: the Hallie Quinn Brown Community House in St. Paul, Minnesota, and the Hallie Q. Brown Memorial Library at Wilberforce University.

Brown left numerous writings about the accomplishments of historical African American men and women and the need for them to have a political voice as her legacy. Her pedagogical efforts focused on the empowerment of African Americans and women in the hopes that her students would develop the desire and acumen to speak to the nation on behalf of their communities in a way that produced change. In essence, Brown's goal was to teach her students to be vocally active participants in the new political climate that shaped post-reconstruction America.

❖ CONTRIBUTIONS TO COMMUNICATION RESEARCH

In addition to her work as a lecturer-elocutionist, Hallie Quinn Brown authored and edited eight books comprised of instructional texts and anthologies designed to educate citizens about the art of oratory and about the notable achievements of Blacks in American history: *Bits and Odds: A Choice Selection of Recitations for School, Lyceum, and Parlor Entertainments* (Brown, 1880); *Elocution and Physical Culture: Training for Students, Teachers, Readers, and Public Speakers* (Brown, 1910); *First Lessons in Public Speaking* (Brown, 1920); *The Beautiful: A True Story of Slavery* (Brown, 1924); *Tales My Father Told, and Other Stories* (Brown, 1925a); *Our Women: Past, Present and Future* (Brown, 1925b); *Homespun Heroines and Other Women of Distinction* (Brown, 1926, 1988); and *Pen Pictures of Pioneers of Wilberforce* (Brown, 1937). Henry Louis Gates, in the introduction to the 1988 edition of *Homespun Heroines and Other Women of Distinction*, published by Oxford University Press, even cited another book titled *Michile—The African*, but no publication date was given. Brown self-published the first two books in the preceding list, noting "Homewood Cottage" as the publishing company. When discussing her contributions to communication, it is important to note the two specific texts that offered detailed instructions on how to successfully execute a public presentation: *Bits and Odds: A Choice Selection of Recitations for School, Lyceum, and Parlor Entertainments* and *Elocution and Physical Culture: Training for Students, Teachers, Readers, and Public Speakers*. Donawerth (2002) explored each of these two texts extensively and even provided excerpts from both books. A third text, *Homespun Heroines and Other Women of Distinction*, will be discussed here as well to highlight Brown's extensive contributions, even beyond language and elocutionism or public speaking.

In *Bits and Odds: A Choice Selection of Recitations for School, Lyceum, and Parlor Entertainments*, Brown wrote, "True expression is a simple interpretation of nature. Elocution is the art of expressing thoughts and sentiments in the most natural manner. But elocution is also a science. It embraces a study of the respiratory system and the construction and management of the vocal organs" (Brown, 1880, p. 23). She further explained that elocution is distinctive. It is not a synonym for oratory, but rather a unique extension of oratory that is meant to convey ideas to a listening audience. She noted that elocution evokes emotion and represents the embodiment of a text by a speaker. So it is not merely the responsibility of the speaker to talk but also to do several other things: (1) to cause affect and effect among the audience; (2) to be rhythmic and harmonious; (3) to be stylistically appropriate [rate, pitch, volume, tone, etc.]; (4) to offer ethical content; (5) to express herself naturally [verbally and nonverbally]; (6) to express immediacy or a sense of sympathy with the audience without being overly emotional or out of control; and (7) to clearly interpret her message to the listening audience in a way that can be easily understood. This cogent articulation of elocution is parallel to the most celebrated *classical* texts. Brown provided clear instructions and elaborated each point. This first book, published in 1880, would not be followed by another for 30 years.

In 1910, the book (which appeared more as a pamphlet), *Elocution and Physical Culture: Training for Students, Teachers, Readers, and Public Speakers*, was published by Brown's own publishing company: Homewood Cottage (Brown, 1910). What is perhaps most significant about this book is that it appeared when she was 60 years old, and after she had traveled and lectured extensively. Brown was not only more polished as a speaker but she also realized that a text of this nature was needed for instructors. This book was indicative of the whole elocutionary movement in communication studies because it was a step-by-step guide on what to do when delivering a speech.

After reading *Elocution and Physical Culture: Training for Students, Teachers, Readers, and Public Speakers*, it is easy to recall some of the early public speaking texts, in which 100 faces were shown on a page and students were required to identify which emotion correlated with which facial expression. This was one of the predominant paradigms for teaching public speaking in the early 1900s.

Brown's text included precise instructions for instructors teaching elocution to students. Many dimensions were covered—such as hand gestures and total body motions including neck, torso, arm, hand, wrist, finger, foot, and toe movements—in addition to positioning the body in front of the audience. Brown even covered dress, attitude, and walking. This information was all in Part I of her 15-part lesson guide. In the remaining parts, she pointed out rules for speaking successfully. These guidelines included functions of the human anatomy; proper use of voice and diction; and use of colors, Bible reading, and hygiene of the voice. This latter section indicated when and how to use the voice. As Brown explained:

> Never use the voice immediately after eating; the most suitable time for practice is in the morning before breakfast. No *exercise* must be taken on a full stomach. Hot and cold drinks are injurious. Avoid vigorous vocal exercises when suffering from a cold. Do not force the voice beyond its normal strength. Take plenty of outdoor exercise. . . . Tobacco is also detrimental to the voice . . . Smoke should not be inhaled through the lungs nor blown through the nostrils. This practice produces irritation, dryness, and congestion of the mucous membrane. (Donawerth, 2002, p. 192)

These practical facets of public presentation were certainly heuristic in the 1910s and are still quite useful today. Brown then wrote *First Lessons in Public Speaking* (Brown, 1920), which was an important and contributory follow-up to her last text. It also gave practical instructions, but this time the audience was both instructors and students. Public speaking and elocution were not her only interests. In fact, many knew Brown just as much for her speaking as for her political activism (Shoemaker, 1913).

In 1926, at the age of 76, Brown edited a volume titled *Homespun Heroines and Other Women of Distinction* (Brown, 1926, 1988). In that anthology, Brown contributed 21 of the 60 biographies. There were 28 contributors in total, and the chapters covered the lives of many unsung heroines of her time: Phillis Wheatley, Sojourner Truth, Sara Allen, Fannie Jackson Coppin, Lucy Smith Thurman, Harriet Tubman, Catherine Delany, Frances E. W. Harper, Sara Garnet, and Madame C. J. Walker. The professions of these women included physicians, nurses, lawyers, entrepreneurs, journalists, poets, teachers, activists, church leaders, homemakers, and elocutionists. This book was one among many such chronicles of Black lives, including *Who's Who in Colored America* (1927), which became an annual listing from 1927 until 1950.

Brown's work embraced African American culture and situated it within American rhetorical history. During a time when White editors sought to marginalize the literary contributions of African Americans and women, Brown used her texts as a vehicle to teach students about the numerous contributions African Americans have made to American society and about their opportunities to speak out against the injustices they saw every day. She wrote to, and through, African American post–Civil War communities in a way that no other writer had done before her time.

After emancipation, African American communities struggled to find a place and voice in American society. Gilyard described the intellectual milieu of the time in the following excerpt:

By the end of slavery, the three most powerful influences on African American consciousness and rhetorical practice were (1) the *Black church,* with its urgent sermons galvanizing and voicing the aspirations of the people, (2) the *slave narratives* and their incessant message of literacy for freedom, and (3) the *African American jeremiad,* a primary vehicle of secular protest. (Gilyard, 1999, p. 627).

Brown viewed elocutionary instruction as a progressive means to address the social ills stifling minority communities. Her unorthodox approach to elocutionary instruction was an outgrowth of both her personal experiences as a plantation school instructor and her belief that the plight of African Americans would be improved only with education and social action. Brown often spoke of the social obligations that accompanied freedom for African Americans. In her speech, *Not Gifts but Opportunity,* she offered the following argument:

If the Negro Race is to come to real freedom and true spiritual power and progress; if he is to enter that larger sphere of life which is not meat and drink—there must be a body of God's elect—men and women trained to large knowledge, broad vision and lofty spiritual purpose, who, as teachers and moral leaders, shall lift the standard and lead our people into a larger life. The upward pull through trained leadership; the character-begetting power of strong personalities, the inspirations to higher ideals, to self master, to efficient service through genuine leadership must be recognized. Where there is no vision the people perish. Without such teachers, helpers, and leaders, the schools and colleges must fail and the race sink to lower levels. No stream can rise higher than its source. (McFarlin, 1975, p. 176)

With the larger goals of equality and prosperity for women and African Americans in mind, Brown considered oratory the most available means to promote social change. Almost 100 years before her time, she recognized the need for African Americans to be literate and articulate if their voices were to ever be heard by White America. Thus, she departed from traditional elocutionary instruction, which taught the following to students:

> Detailed analyses of all the movements of head, hand, arm, and body; minute descriptions of shades of facial expression; intricate calculations of the uses of the human voice; and all these embroidered and beset with innumerable rules allegedly derived from nature. (Thomas, 1943, p. 206)

Instead, Brown envisioned elocution as a means to an important end—social uplift and economic independence. In contrast to previous scholars who taught elocution as a form of public performance, Brown taught it as a form of political participation (S. Kates, personal communication, 2003). She saw elocutionary instruction as "education that can be translated into action" (McFarlin, 1988, p. 175).

During Brown's life, instruction and training in the art of elocution were often restricted to the formal academy. Aside from the few elite, learning the art of public speaking was out of reach for most African Americans. Although various reciter texts were available during this time, access to such materials required a degree of affluence that newly emancipated slaves simply were not afforded. Brown found that the elocutionary movement itself offered many opportunities for instruction in breathing, gesture, and pronunciation, whereas little to no instruction was available in the use of public address to inspire marginalized audiences. She observed that the fundamental ideologies of the movement itself neglected the importance of audience culture and linguistic heritage (S. Kates, personal communication, 2003). This need for cultural inclusion in elocutionary instruction was of pressing concern for Brown as she developed her expertise.

Brown was determined to provide the tools necessary for African Americans to establish and utilize their political voice to promote social change and inform others of *their* responsibilities in the effort. According to Susan Kates (1997), "Brown lived in a time when a black woman educator did not have the opportunity of articulating all of the social and political implications of her work for her community" (p. 61). Thus, she sought to enlighten others so that they might be able to speak to these concerns candidly and effectively in the future. Kates (1997) described the goal of Brown's pedagogy as an "embodied rhetoric," "a rhetoric located within, and generated for, the African American community" (p. 59).

Brown's scholarly and pedagogical contributions were best illustrated in her written work. According to Kates (1997), Brown altered common elocutionary pedagogy in three specific ways. First, many of her works included selections written in African American vernacular English. An example from her reciter text, *Bits and Odds: A Choice Selection of Recitations* (Brown, 1880) illustrated this practice:

> Well you know dat de apple tree was the sacred vegetable ob de garden ob Eden till de sly an insinuvating sea-serpent crawled out ob de river on Friday mornen, bit off an apple, made "apple-jack," handed de jug to Eve, she took a sip, den handed it to Adam. Adam took anoder, by which bofe got topseycated an' fell down de hill ob Paradise, an' in consequence darof, de whole woman race an' human race fell down casmash, like speckled apples from a tree in a stormado. Oh! What a fall war dar, my hearers, when you an' me, an' I, an' all drapt down togedder, an' de serpent flapped his forked tongue in fatissaction. (Kates, 1997, p. 12)

Brown endorsed pride in African American linguistic traditions by using the language of African American communities to advance the ideals of Black intellectualism and sociopolitical inclusion. Certainly, as a college graduate and activist who had spoken before many decision-making national polities, she did not speak this way in most public forums.

Brown reclaimed important moments in African American history and literature. Her work frequently referred to African American contributions that were neglected in tales of American history. For instance, her book, *Bits and Odds* (Brown, 1880) included a poem by George H. Boker that brought to light the important contributions of African American soldiers in the Civil War:

> Dark as the clouds of even,
> Ranked in the western heaven,
> Waiting the breath that lifts,
> All the dead mass, and drifts
> Tempest and falling brand
> O'er a ruined land;-
> So still and orderly,
> Arm to arm, knee to knee,
> Waiting the great event
> Stands the black regiment. . . .
> "Now," the flag-sergeant cried,

"Through death and hell betide,
Let the whole nation see
If I were fit to be free
In this land; or bound
Down like the whining hound–
Bound with red stripes of pain
In our cold chains again!"
Oh! what a shout there went
From the Black regiment!

(Kates, 1997, p. 65)

As evidenced in this selection, Brown's text critiqued the incomplete history of America told in mainstream texts and anthologies.

Brown's view of the social role of elocution differed from that of common theorists. Prior to her influence, elocutionary instruction was thought of as a means to intellectual refinement and economic prosperity. In contrast, Brown saw the value of instruction in elocution as a means to achieve social and moral transformation (S. Kates, personal communication, 2003). Brown's work made rhetorical instruction available to post-emancipation African Americans.

Brown's scholarship provided her contemporaries with opportunities to study writing and speaking. From *within* the African American experience, she was able to share the power of the spoken and written word. Although *Bits and Odds* is one of her more noted works, Brown left a seven-volume legacy of books before her death. All her books described the transformative nature of rhetorical study and fully embodied the "Lifting as We Climb" principle that was so much a part of Black social movements at the turn of the century (Kates, 1997, p. 69).

In the book *Women Builders*, Sadie Daniel (1970) summarized Brown's contributions as follows:

The causes for which she worked, racial uplift, equality for women, temperance, political improvement, the church, educational advancement, Women's clubs, excellence in the arts—the Scholarship Fund, and the institutions which bear her name, all attest to a century of building a better more perfect humanity by Hallie Q. Brown. Few women of any period, race, or creed have equaled her versatility, her loyalty, her purposefulness, her acumen, and the wide range of her contributions to progress in the world. She built in many areas and in each one she left a residue of inspiration, a foundation of courage and intent for young people to continue moving, lifting as they climb. (p. 307–308)

Brown's contributions were multifaceted. She was a teacher, author, lecturer, entertainer, and activist. Her career was marked by multiple successes and her contributions to communication were made manifest through her writing of three books about public speaking: *Bits and Odds: A Choice Selection of Recitations for School, Lyceum, and Parlor Entertainments* (Brown, 1880), *Elocution and Physical Culture: Training for Students, Teachers, Readers, and Public Speakers* (Brown, 1910), and *First Lessons in Public Speaking* (Brown, 1920). At a time when Black voices in communication were subdued, Brown was a pioneer who helped to define the parameters of the field of speech and rhetoric. She deserves her rightful place in history alongside the early forerunners in communication research.

❖ CONCLUSION

Hallie Quinn Brown spent her entire life speaking in support of women's suffrage, civil rights, and higher education. Her work served as a foundation for the development of other "embodied" scholarship, such as that which is chronicled throughout the remainder of this text. Brown was a diligent humanitarian, political activist, and educator. Although her contributions to elocutionary theory have received almost no mention in most rhetorical texts, it is hoped that her contributions to the field of communication will be better recognized in years to come. She is an inspiring example to us all as a champion for social justice and personal success.

❖ REFERENCES

Baker, H. (1987). *Modernism and the Harlem renaissance*. Chicago: University of Chicago Press.

Brown, H. Q. (1880). *Bits and odds: A choice selection of recitations for school, lyceum and parlor entertainments*. Xenia, OH: Chew Press.

Brown, H. Q. (1910). *Elocution and physical culture: Training for students, teachers, readers, and public speakers*. Wilberforce, OH. Homewood Cottage.

Brown, H. Q. (1925a). *Tales my father told, and other stories*. Xenia, OH: Eckerle.

Brown, H. Q. (1925b). *Our women: Past, present, and future*. Xenia, OH: Eckerle.

Brown, H. Q. (1926). *Homespun heroines and other women of distinction*. New York: Oxford Press.

Daniel, S. I. (1970). *Women builders*. Washington, DC: Associated Publishers.

Davis, E. L. (Ed.). (1933). *Lifting as they climb*. New York: G. K. Hall.

Donawerth, J. (2002). *Rhetorical theory by women before 1900: An anthology*. Lanham, MD: Rowman & Littlefield.

Fisher, V. (1993). Brown, Hallie Quinn. In D. C. Salem (Ed.), *African American women: A biographical dictionary* (pp. 68–71). New York: Garland.

Gilyard, K. (1999). African American contributions to composition studies. *College Composition and Communication, 50*(4), 626–644.

Hine, D. C. (1993). *Black women in America: An historical encyclopedia.* New York: Carlson.

Kates, S. (1997). The embodied rhetoric of Hallie Quinn Brown. *College English, 59*(1), 59–71.

Kates, S. (2001). *Activist rhetorics and American higher education, 1885–1937.* Carbondale: Southern Illinois University Press.

Leeman, R. (Ed.). (1996). *African-American orators: A bio-critical sourcebook.* Westport, CT: Greenwood Press.

Logan, R. W., & Winston, M. R. (1982). *Dictionary of American Negro biography.* New York: Norton.

McFarlin, A. S. (1975). *Hallie Quinn Brown: Black woman elocutionist.* Unpublished doctoral dissertation, Washington State University, Pullman.

McFarlin, A. S. (1980). Hallie Quinn Brown: Black woman elocutionist. *Southern Speech Communication Journal, 46*(1), 72–82.

Shoemaker, J. W. (1913). *Practical elocution: For use in college and schools by private students.* Philadelphia: Penn.

Smith, J. C. (1992). *Notable Black American women.* Detroit: Gale Research.

Stetson, E. (1983). Black feminism in Indiana, 1893–1933. *Phylon, 44*(4), 292–298.

Strom, C. (1999). Hallie Quinn Brown. In J. Garraty & M. Carnes (Eds.), *American national biography* (pp. 676–677). New York: Oxford University Press.

Thomas, O. (1943). The teaching of rhetoric in the Unites States during the classical period of education. In W. N. Brigance, *A history and criticism of American public address* (pp. 206–207). New York: McGraw-Hill.

Unknown. (1890). Sketch of the life of Miss Hallie Quinn Brown. *African Methodist Episcopal Church Review, 6*(3), 257–261.

Wertheimer, M. (Ed.). (1997). *The rhetorical activities of historical women.* Columbia: University of South Carolina Press.

Who's Who in Colored America (1927). New York: Who's Who in Colored America.

Wright, A. A. (1906). (Ed.). *Who's who in the Lyceum.* Philadelphia: Pearson Brothers.

Further Reading

Brown, H. Q. (1906). Folklore [delivered in 1873 at the Lyceum in England]. In A. A. Wright (Ed.), *Who's who in the Lyceum* (pp. 44–50). Philadelphia: Pearson Brothers.

Brown, H. Q. (1920). *First lessons in public speaking.* Xenia, OH: Eckerle.

Brown, H. Q. (1924). *The beautiful: A true story of slavery.* Wilberforce, OH: Homewood Cottage.

Brown, H. Q. (1937). *Pen pictures of pioneers of Wilberforce.* Xenia, OH. Aldine.

Hallie Quinn Brown

**Photo courtesy of Central State University
Archives, Wilberforce, Ohio**

1850	Born in Pittsburgh, Pennsylvania, on March 10.
1864	Began her education in Chatham, Ontario.
1870	Attended Wilberforce University.
1873	Received a bachelor's degree from Wilberforce University.
1880	Published *Bits and Odds: A Choice Selection of Recitations*.
1886	Attended the American Chautauqua Lecture School.
1887	Returned to Ohio to teach in the Dayton public school system.
1890	Received an honorary master's degree from Wilberforce University.
1893	Became dean of women at Tuskeegee Institute under Booker T. Washington.
1894	Established the Colored Woman's League of Washington D.C.
	Traveled throughout Europe as a reader with Wilberforce Concert Company.
1895	Spoke in London at the third biennial convention of the World's Woman's Christian Temperance Union.
1897	Served as a representative to the International Congress of Women.
1905	Began her service as president of the Ohio Federation of Colored Women's Clubs.

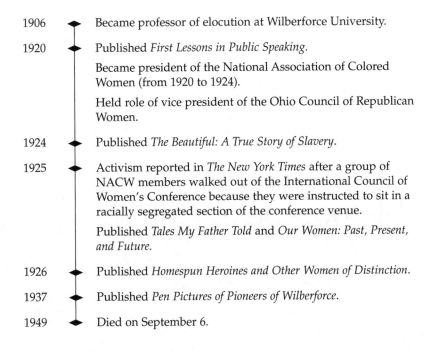

1906 — Became professor of elocution at Wilberforce University.

1920 — Published *First Lessons in Public Speaking.*

Became president of the National Association of Colored Women (from 1920 to 1924).

Held role of vice president of the Ohio Council of Republican Women.

1924 — Published *The Beautiful: A True Story of Slavery.*

1925 — Activism reported in *The New York Times* after a group of NACW members walked out of the International Council of Women's Conference because they were instructed to sit in a racially segregated section of the conference venue.

Published *Tales My Father Told* and *Our Women: Past, Present, and Future.*

1926 — Published *Homespun Heroines and Other Women of Distinction.*

1937 — Published *Pen Pictures of Pioneers of Wilberforce.*

1949 — Died on September 6.

4

Melbourne S. Cummings

More than 800 African lan-
guages, various European and
Asian languages, and innumer-
able pidgins and creoles await
students of African communica-
tion. . . . No amount of cultural
chauvinism can deny African
cultural continuities around the
world. Given the many linguistic
codes that are used in Black communication, it follows that
the ethnography of Black communication is an equally
diverse and complex matter.

(Cummings, quoted in
Cummings & Daniel, 1997, p. 361)

❖ INTRODUCTION

Melbourne S. Cummings, a graduate of University of California, Los Angeles (UCLA), is one of the first Black females to have graduated with a doctorate in communication and to become active in research and service within well-known national communication venues. She shares this distinction with Dorothy Pennington and Lucia Hawthorne. Cummings has written extensively about themes that traverse the areas of African American communications: rhetoric, pedagogy, poetry, song, comedy, and television. As noted in the preceding epigraph, she has advocated the inclusion of Black rhetoric and linguistic codes as meaningful areas of communication study. Moreover, she teaches courses that span several disciplinary perspectives and include topics related to rhetoric and public address, as well as nonverbal and intercultural communication. Cummings has served on major planning, organizational, and policy boards in regional, national, and international communication associations. She also has traveled widely in Africa, Europe, and Asia as part of intercultural exchanges in communication, international education, and religion.

Within the 30-year span of her career, Cummings has been the recipient of numerous accolades. On November 22, 2002, she was honored with the National Communication Association Mentor Award, a distinction that signifies lifelong professional achievement and active mentorship of others who have gone on to achieve success. She was the first African American scholar to receive this award, and rightfully so, because she is among a handful of scholars who have assisted in ushering more than 50 doctoral recipients in the last 30 years into our field. Several of them have become professors and have had a significant impact on both national and international communities. Cummings's genuineness, honesty, forthrightness, and savvy ability to get things done when the bureaucracy would have it otherwise are a few among many personal qualities that have facilitated endless mentor–protégé relationships throughout her extensive career. For some professors, mentoring is an accessory to the other things they do as a teacher. Cummings places emphasis on mentoring as part of her purpose in academia, as well as her ongoing research, teaching, and professional service.

Cummings has been broadly influential throughout the discipline. More specifically, she has worked arduously to guide scholars toward establishing heuristic research in the field. As immediate past chair and faculty member of the Department of Communication and Culture at Howard University, she sat at the helm of an institution that continues to boast of having trained and graduated the vast majority of African

Americans with doctoral degrees in the United States. It is not an exaggeration to say that more than half of African American communicologists who are members of the National Communication Association (NCA) are graduates or affiliates of Howard University's graduate school and the John H. Johnson School of Communications—and have thus been directly influenced by the mentorship of Cummings. She is also a founding associate editor of the *Howard Journal of Communications* and has been an editorial board member of several academic journals inside and outside of the field of communication.

Testament to the way Cummings's continued commitment to the advancement of the profession and her students is valued came with her honors in 1987 and 1995, respectively. First, she was presented with the NCA's Robert J. Kibler Memorial Award, which recognizes commitment to the profession, demonstrated valuation of diversity, and vision for the possibilities of progress. Second, Cummings received the NCA Black Caucus's Distinguished Service Award. This award is particularly significant because she is considered one of the early pioneers of the Black Caucus, being the first person of record to solely preside over the caucus during its initial years of development. In the mid-1990s, the Black Caucus facilitated the emergence of the NCA African American Communication & Culture Division, a unit whose primary foci are the production and promotion of scholarship about African American communication. Today, the Black Caucus has more than 400 members and its membership produces almost all scholarship in the field of African American rhetoric and communication.

The development and impact of Cummings's research has been important to the foundations of African American communication studies. Early in her career, she received a National Defense and Foreign Language (NDFL) grant for African Studies, which was to be used for her studies in East Africa. She has since studied, toured, and resided in more than a dozen countries in Africa. In fact, she devised and developed (with Orlando Taylor and Lyndrey Niles) an organization whose mission was to bring together international communication scholars for discussion, sharing, and collaboration of their African and African Diaspora research, interests, and experiences at international conferences. The initial name of the organization was the World Congress on Black Communications Planning Conference (later changed to the World Congress on Communications and Development in Africa and the African Diaspora because it was deemed more appropriate by Kenyan scholars in Nairobi). The organization hosted four conferences—in Bellagio (Italy), Nairobi (Kenya), Barbados, and Senegal, respectively—before it was disbanded because of lack of funding (Daniel, 1995). Each of the conferences was sponsored or cosponsored by the Rockefeller Foundation and/or Howard University. One of the important conceptual advances that originated from this conference was the notion of "orature" as a term that better described the writings that came out of Africa or its Diaspora. The term was created and introduced at the Nairobi conference by Kenyan scholars Micere Mugo and Ngugi wa Thiong'o. The research presented at these conferences culminated in a book, edited by Cummings, Niles, and Taylor (1992), titled *Handbook of Communications and Development in Africa and the African Diaspora.*

Cummings has been a guest lecturer at approximately 35 high schools, colleges, and universities, sharing her research concerning African Diaspora communicative experiences.

Cummings has distinguished herself as one who genuinely cares about the well-being and success of her students and the vitality of the profession. Her vision, forthrightness, commitment, and dedication represent the best to which all academicians may aspire.

❖ BIOGRAPHICAL INFORMATION

On September 18, 1942, Melbourne S. Cummings was born as Melbourne Jean Stenson in Monroe, Louisiana, some 20 miles from her home in the small town of Rayville, Louisiana. Her parents were Theolis Stenson, from Greenwood, Mississippi, and Emma Virginia Elizabeth Brown Stenson, from Wisner, Louisiana. Theolis grew up in a small "shotgun" house and was part of a large family, for which work, even among children, was extremely valued. The family's work expectations for him were apparent even when he attended elementary school. In fact, he was forbidden to go to school beyond the third grade because the family needed him to work. This and other pressures motivated Theolis to leave home at age 11. He ended up in a migrant camp in Louisiana, where he met Emma, his wife-to-be. She was about 14 years old when she visited the camp (her mother worked as the camp cook) and met Theolis. Unlike Theolis, Emma was raised to embrace education. Although her upbringing was not marked by the despondency experienced by her husband-to-be, she lived a modest lifestyle as a child. Besides their southern background, Theolis and Emma found they had a lot in common and enjoyed one another's company. They married a year later—Emma was only 15 years old, and Theolis was 20. They decided to settle in Rayville, Louisiana, not far from Emma's childhood home.

Raised in an era of Jim Crow segregation, Theolis and Emma earned only a modest living. He began working in the town's cotton gin, but the earnings from that job were insufficient to support his wife and eight children. He decided to become a pipe layer, which paid much more, but the job took him from Rayville to Houston, Texas. Although his family continued to live in Rayville, Theolis spent the majority of his time working in Houston. He would come home only on holidays and special occasions such as birthdays and graduations. Cummings, who was five when her father left home to work in Houston, recalled:

> He would always come home on the holidays and bring mason jars full of pennies he had saved for us. I remember he would also buy us big gifts for special occasions. There was one instance where my mother told him I wanted a leather coat, since a lot of the kids had leatherette coats in my neighborhood. He surprised me by bringing home a leather coat he purchased from Neiman Marcus. I didn't understand the significance of that until much later. I think that was his way of reminding us he was still there and he loved us. (M. S. Cummings, personal communication, May 11, 2004)

Emma was a cook—as her mother was. Her primary role was to raise her kids and to supplement her husband's financial support of the family. Emma attended school through the 11th grade, and education was very important to her, so she made sacrifices to see that her children went to school. Religion and spirituality were also very important. Emma and all her kids were very active in one of the local churches—Mt. Zion Baptist Church. In fact, the Stenson family lived next door to the church, and Cummings played piano for the children's choir.

Cummings's parents were very influential, instilling values of hard work, creativity, open-mindedness, honesty, and self-motivation. Some evidence of many of these traits is exemplified in Cummings's musical instrument training. She enjoyed the luxury of playing the piano, beginning at age four and continuing until she reached college, so she never had to work in the cotton fields during the summer, as her siblings and friends had to do. She also played the clarinet and the bell lyre in the high school band. The family lived modestly, as did most of the families in Cummings's close-knit community, but Emma was quite well-known and respected.

Cummings was the fourth of eight children. In a personal interview, she explained:

They used to say that she [my mother Emma Stenson] had two sets of children because of the age differences, and so I'm the middle child even though I'm the fourth, since there are eight. My sister, whom I'm next to, is five years older than I am. The one whom she is next to is six years older than she. They assumed that I was the last. However, after I was born, the children continued to be born: four more came just about every two years. So, they say that I am the youngest of the first set and oldest of the second set of children—a very special place in the family. I am sort of everybody's favorite. (M. S. Cummings, personal communication, May 11, 2004)

Cummings's siblings, in order from eldest to youngest, were Theolis, Zeofious Lee, Susie Pearl, Henry James, Emma Jo, Dennis Coley, and Lillian Faye. All are still living except Theolis, who died of a stroke just three months after his mother passed. Emma had a long bout with diabetes and eventually succumbed on April 19, 1996—her 81st birthday. Cummings recalled:

It was a beautiful passing. It was quiet and peaceful. It seemed as if we could see the pain leave her face. We were sort of content with that. Everybody sort of played his or her part in her life and she in theirs, since she had been such a warrior for us. She was an absolutely wonderful mother. (M. S. Cummings, personal communication, May 11, 2004)

Although the town of Rayville was as racist as any other southern town, Cummings remembers that most parents attempted to shelter their children from most of the negative effects of racism. She remembers feeling no real sense of exclusion or any negative effects of the ill treatment that usually attends racism. She revealed:

My mother was a cook, and, at one time, she worked in houses, cleaning houses and taking care of Whites' children. And so, in one of the families for whom she worked, the woman of the house was a seamstress—actually, a tailor—and she liked me for some reason. She didn't really know me that well, but she knew my mother, and my mother would always talk about her children. Because I excelled in school, she always made dresses for me. So, sometimes when I had things that were special that I had to do—like, if I had to go to a State Fair or something like that, she would make me a dress. I didn't have really terrible experiences with Whites. (M. S. Cummings, personal communication, May 11, 2004)

Cummings told a story about going to the home of a White family to pick up her sister's housecleaning wages. Having no qualms about approaching anyone, she went straight to the front of the house and knocked on the door. She did not know that "colored people" had to go around to the rear of White people's homes. The White gentleman of the house opened the door ever so slightly and kindly explained that she had to go around back because he could not let the air conditioning out. Cummings had never heard of air conditioning, but it sounded feasible, so she obliged by going to the rear of the home. In retrospect, Cummings reasoned that he had his (White) code of conduct to uphold, and she had to do what she was expected to do. It was the code of the South. The gentleman gave her the money and a piece of candy from the back door and then sent her on her way. In retrospect, Cummings appreciated the care he had taken to not damage her self-esteem. (M. S. Cummings, personal communication, May 11, 2004)

According to Cummings, Blacks and Whites in Rayville, although clearly segregated, lived generally as civilly as the times permitted. In fact, several Blacks were local business owners. Cummings noted,

Of course, we had many White businesses, but we also had a few Black decently paid professionals: morticians, grocery store owners, teachers, dry cleaning business owners, bar and nightclub owners, carpenters, repairmen, as well as beauty and barber shop owners. (M. S. Cummings, personal communication, May 11, 2004)

Blacks still enacted routine deference to Whites. Black men were still called "boys" and were expected to address White girls as "Miss" after they reached a certain age. As a 12-year-old child, Cummings, who was affectionately known to family and close friends as "Peaches," discovered that one of the deacons in her church was calling all the teenaged Black girls "Miss." The kids made fun of him, and Cummings recalls thinking that he was ridiculous, until her mother said to her, "What you don't understand is that he is required to call little White girls 'Miss' and he feels that if he has to call them that, then he should grant the girls of his own race the same respect." These three anecdotes bespeak the kind of upbringing Cummings remembers having. She acknowledges that her perceptions were not called into question until her interactions in college with northern Blacks. (M. S. Cummings, personal communication, May 11, 2004)

❖ ACADEMIC BACKGROUND AND EXPERIENCE

Melbourne S. Cummings attended Rayville Rosenwald School, a K–12 school named after a White southern philanthropist who endowed southern schools for Blacks to attend. The high school was later renamed Eula D. Britton High School to honor the Black principal of the school. Cummings's education took place in a regular school with several buildings that were very similar to the White school buildings—except that the White school was made of brick and had the latest equipment and school supplies. Rayville was the parish seat, so it fared a little better than surrounding school districts. The four women who had the greatest influence on Cummings during her school years were Mrs. Stevens, Mrs. Mansfield, Mrs. Smith, and Mrs. Austin. Mrs. Austin taught Cummings how to write effectively. Mrs. Mansfield taught math, and Mrs. Smith taught a broad range of courses in eighth grade. Mrs. Stevens introduced her to the library and taught her how to use it. Cummings also went to the town's "colored" public library, which had a fairly extensive collection, despite not having many of the most up-to-date books. The library contained the classics and many of the old discarded volumes from the White library. Cummings's initial interest in writing and writers was piqued during these library visits.

After graduating from high school at age 17 with a 4.0 grade point average, Cummings enrolled as an English major at Southern University in Baton Rouge, Louisiana. There was never a doubt in her mind—or in the minds of her family, teachers, and community members—that she would go to college. Cummings chose Southern University because it had a solid academic program and had a reputation as the largest and one of the best Black schools in the United States. Its enrollment included students from all over the world, several of whom were from Africa. Cummings thoroughly enjoyed her collegiate experience and was self-motivated to be a model student. Although several of her siblings went to college, Cummings was the only one in her family to graduate from college. She was mentored in college by Dr. Blydon Jackson and Dr. William Couch, both of whom coincidentally moved to North Carolina—Dr. Jackson went to the University of North Carolina, and Dr. Couch moved to North Carolina Central University (NCCU). At about the same time, Cummings left Southern University for NCCU. A year after she earned her bachelor's degree in English at age 20, Cummings went on to earn her master's degree, also in English, from NCCU.

The primary area of research for Cummings's master of arts degree program was dramatic literature, with a specific focus on Eugene

O'Neill. At that time, much of the entire program of study in dramatic literature was centered on British literature (O'Neill was an exception). Although Black literature was far outside the curricula, Dr. Couch was a specialist in it, so he taught interested students outside of the formal classrooms. He also generated Black literature reading lists. This had a profound effect on Cummings's thinking, and Dr. Couch became her master's thesis advisor.

Just before graduating from NCCU in 1964, Cummings met her husband-to-be, Robert Cummings, who had received a full scholarship to NCCU from the state of Florida. During this time, Blacks were discouraged from attending White colleges by receiving full scholarships to attend any school located outside of the state. Black students applied to a White state university and received a scholarship to attend the out-of-state school of their choice. The state would not reject Black students in writing; it would just invite them to attend a predominantly Black state school with a scholarship. For this reason, Robert decided to attend NCCU. He had been taking classes in graduate school for a while, teaching high school during the school year and matriculating through his graduate program only during the summers. Robert met Melbourne Jean Stenson at NCCU in 1964. Six months later—on his birthday, December 22, 1964—they were married while he was completing his master's degree in history. Cummings had just completed her thesis, "Critical Analysis of Selected Dramatic Plays of Eugene O'Neill." Shortly after the wedding, Melbourne and Robert Cummings moved to his home state of Florida, where they lived separately (she in Fort Lauderdale; he in Dade City, near Tampa) for a year and saw one another only on weekends. She taught English and chaired the English department at Crispus Attucks High School. The following year, she taught at Florida Agricultural & Mechanical University (FAMU) before returning with her husband to North Carolina to teach English at Winston-Salem State University. Cummings taught at Winston-Salem State University for three years, from 1966 to 1969, and subsequently moved with her husband to California to pursue doctorates at UCLA. Cummings's doctorate was to be in African literature. The decision to move to UCLA was based on a State Department Fulbright-Hayes grant that Robert received to institute African Studies into "teacher education" institutions. So Robert's proposed idea for the funded award was to attend UCLA, which had a thriving African Studies Center, to get ideas for instituting African Studies. After touring parts of Africa, Robert would then return to his home institution and implement the strategies and suggestions.

Upon her arrival at UCLA in 1969, Cummings quickly learned that the study of African literature was neither a pursuit the English

Department respected nor intended to support. Her only options were to stay in the program to study Shakespeare and Chaucer or to find another program. Although Cummings was trained in British literature, it was not her primary interest, so she took classes in the English graduate program while actively searching for another program of study. A year later, Cummings heard about Arthur L. Smith (now known as Molefi Kete Asante), a new young professor in the Speech Communication department. She discovered that his teaching and research interests were aligned with hers, so she transferred to the Speech Communication department, using her accumulated credits in English from the previous year to fulfill her cognate requirements. Although they were the same age, Arthur Smith became Cummings's professor, mentor, advisor, and lifelong friend. Andrea Rich, a White scholar and research collaborator of Smith's, also became a major formative influence in terms of Cummings's understanding of interracial communication. As a graduate teaching assistant, Cummings taught interracial communication and rhetoric courses. She was one of three Black graduate students in the program—the other two, who were master's degree students at the time, were Shirley Weber and Marcia Clinkscales. With Smith's guidance, Cummings specialized in Black rhetoric, graduating in 1972, with a Ph.D. in Speech Communication from UCLA. Her dissertation, which she wrote under Smith's direction, was titled, "The Rhetoric of Bishop Henry McNeal Turner, Leading Advocate of the African Emigration Movement, 1868–1907."

Immediately after graduation, Cummings and her husband moved to Kenya for the required research year as part of his program of study for the Ph.D. Two years later, on August 19, 1974, Cummings gave birth to the first of their two sons, Samori. By this time, they changed their plans of returning to Winston-Salem and instead took positions in Miami, Florida. Cummings had a position at Florida International University as assistant professor in English and Communications, and Robert was director of African American Studies at the University of Miami. They stayed in Miami for three years and then moved in 1976 to Washington, D.C., where Cummings became an associate professor in the Howard University Department of Communication Arts and Sciences at the age of 33. Her husband was appointed director of Howard's African Studies Center. At the time of Cummings's appointment, Orlando Taylor was department chair of the School of Communications, and Lyndrey Niles was its associate dean. Taylor and Niles launched significant programs of research in Black communication studies and were active participants in founding the Speech Communication Association Black Caucus. On May 10, 1978, within two years of arriving at Howard University,

Cummings's second son, Samir, was born. She had just become director of Graduate Affairs and served a six-year term, beginning in 1980, as associate dean of the School of Communications before becoming department chair in 1993. Cummings found the environment at Howard to be comfortable and conducive to her research and personal interests. Cummings was mentored by the vice president of Academic Affairs, Lorraine Williams, and this relationship was one of her most fruitful academic mentoring experiences.

The combination of being at Howard University, the nation's leading historically Black university, and being a mother of two young children significantly affected Cummings's lifestyle and cultural consciousness. She had been wearing her hair natural as an afro for at least 10 years before her second child was born, which signified a sense of cultural pride indicative of the civil rights activism of the 1960s and 1970s. Cummings was trained by Arthur Smith (Molefi Asante) and was working alongside Orlando Taylor, a speech pathologist who, in collaboration with Gloria Walker, founded the Black Caucus of the American Speech and Hearing Association and the Speech Communication Association.

❖ CONTRIBUTIONS TO COMMUNICATION RESEARCH

Early in her tenure at Howard University, Melbourne S. Cummings sharpened her awareness of the issues confronting not only Blacks in the field of communication but also the study of Black rhetoric. The entire field of communication was founded around the turn of the 20th century, but it really began to flourish in the 1920s. With the exception of a very few works, such as historian Carter G. Woodson's catalogue of speeches, *The Negro and His Orations* (Woodson, 1925), it was not until the late 1960s that nondeprecating literature concerning Black communication and rhetoric finally emerged. Although there was much to study, many White scholars chose to study European-American discursive experiences from Eurocentric perspectives. When there were studies of Blacks, the discussions often centered on eugenicist views of the intellectual and behavioral incapacity of Blacks—or their so-called heathen dispositions. This racist portrayal of Blacks severely impoverished the study of Black communication, so before any analysis of rhetoric could begin, there was a constant underlying imperative to reconcile depictions of Black rhetoric and to claim a space where it could be celebrated.

Besides Cummings, many Black scholars took part in the emergence and celebration of Black communication research at this time:

Arthur Smith, Lucia Hawthorne, Charles Hurst, Fela Sowande, Dorothy Pennington, Jack Daniel, Orlando Taylor, Gloria Walker, Marcia Clinkscales, and others. Cummings's research was pioneering and heuristic because of its nuanced insistence that extant rhetorical traditions include *Black* rhetorical traditions, especially in the study of Black rhetors. To fully comprehend the significance of Cummings's scholarship, it is necessary to explore the programmatic areas of her research, which covered three primary themes: constituting Black rhetoric, Black public address, and Black popular culture.

Constituting Black Rhetoric

Like a lens zooming in and out to get a panoramic view of its surroundings, Cummings sought both to study Black rhetoric and to question why Black rhetoric had been absent from disciplinary conversations in the first place. She remarked:

> As we took classes, we realized there was not a whole lot of stuff that we could put our hands on, except for a speech by Frederick Douglass or Booker T. Washington–one, two of those. We saw how very difficult it was for people to just accept Black literature, Black rhetoric, and etcetera, in my classes. They would say things like, "That's good, but everything you do is about black people." And my response, just initially was a sort of angry response: "Everything you do is about white people, but at least what I do is about black people all over the world." So, that was one of the things that I wanted to do—in my contributions—I wanted to teach students to know about their heritage. (M. S. Cummings, personal communication, May 11, 2004)

Cummings's first article was a review essay published in the *Journal of Black Studies* titled "Problems of Researching Black Rhetoric" (Cummings, 1972). In this article, she said, "Most established (White) rhetoricians have found only Black speakers such as Booker T. Washington and Martin Luther King, Jr. acceptable for rhetorical study, and even these studies have been, for the most part, cursory, superficial, and conventional" (Cummings, 1972, p. 503). Given that Cummings's postsecondary intellectual development and cultural consciousness were heavily influenced by the sociopolitical context in which the civil rights movement flourished, exercising voice and agency were very important acts. To have one's voice suppressed and disenfranchised was due cause for any citizen to protest against the establishment.

Although the historical records have consistently chronicled protests at colleges and universities, intellectual battles were also being waged by academicians against universities for promoting culturally exclusive and homogeneous curricula. Cummings's strategy was to point to and develop a set of resources that would be readily available as a reply to those who would claim that Black rhetoric and communication could not be taught because they were systematized areas of inquiry. The first step in implementing this strategy was to note up-front the challenges of gaining access to public address source materials. Some of these challenges included referencing speeches by Black dignitaries that were delivered extemporaneously without notes; finding media information about nontranscribed speeches such as letters, newspaper reports, and family memoirs; locating books by Blacks that are either out of print or were initially published with low print runs; and critically assessing sources reporting speeches to ascertain any political and/or social bias.

These challenges have pervaded the study of Black rhetoric since the early 1970s. Nonetheless, Cummings and Daniel (1992) wanted to note the paradigmatic consistencies found in Black rhetorical texts. To do so, the authors turned their attention to interdisciplinary approaches to Black rhetoric, from anthropology and sociolinguistics to literature and psychology. In explicating the distinct oratorical features of Black rhetorical texts, they could more easily distinguish between varying speaking styles exposed in, for example, the Melville Herskovits and E. Franklin Frazier debate or the philosophical dialogues of Booker T. Washington and W. E. B. Dubois. Cummings and Daniel's study also called for an advanced understanding of Black texts as not simply speeches to be collected or deserving of only a cursory scholarly glance but also speeches that should be systematically studied to uncover the rhetorical strategies and cultural nuances employed. Moreover, they wanted readers to know that the sermonic tradition, as seen via traditional Black preaching, is a site richly enhanced by variations in tonality, pitch, rate, pauses, and dynamic interplay between speaker and audience. Clearly, this oral tradition was classical in its own right, but distinct from White classical rhetorical paradigms. The argument developed in Cummings's studies of Black rhetoric is that the criteria for oratorical effectiveness are different for Black audiences and communities, so if scholars are to analyze Black orators, they ought to be aware of the cultural context and criteria that impinge on the speaker. She has consistently called for comparative studies that explain and constitute the Black communication genres throughout the African Diaspora and within multiple communal contexts (Cummings,

1982; Cummings, 1992; Cummings, 1995a; Cummings & Daniel, 1992; Cummings & Roy, 2002).

Black Public Address

Public address is often considered an extension or rubric of rhetoric. In fact, some have alternatively named it podium rhetoric. As mentioned earlier, Cummings was trained as a rhetorician at UCLA under the tutelage of Arthur Smith (Molefi Asante), who was director of the Center for Black Studies and associate professor of communications. His research was primarily concerned with revolutionary rhetoric at the time, and this was filtered throughout the rhetoric classes he taught. Much of Cummings's Black public address research emerges out of this tradition. Throughout her career, she has studied the speeches of such prominent orators as Booker T. Washington (Cummings, 1977), Andrew Young (Cummings, 1979), Bishop Henry McNeal Turner (Cummings, 1982), Martin Luther King, Jr. (Cummings & Niles, 1991/1992; Cummings, 1995b), and Mary McLeod Bethune (Cummings, 1996).

Cummings analyzed Booker T. Washington's "compromise" speech—he was asked to share the speaking platform with White southerners while speaking to an interracial audience. Cummings asserted, "He admonished Blacks that they should stop seeking social and political equality, and begin working to attain economic respectability" (Cummings, 1977, p. 77). This "pull-yourself-up-by-your-own-bootstraps" industrial education approach became famously associated with Washington's philosophical stance, and he quickly became known as an accommodationist. He also produced results as he attempted to mend racial relations, however, and wherever he spoke, White supporters would donate money and sundry items to his cause—industrial education for Blacks. This agrarian ideal was attractive to Whites who were still resistant to formal education in the classroom, so they supported Washington because he seemed to understand that school was no place for Blacks. At the same time, he brought hope to Black sharecroppers by promising them that the time was ripe for seizing commercial opportunities in the South.

Like Washington, Andrew Young was also a bridge builder for race relations in the South, but he lived in a different era. Young was a Congregationalist preacher (Cummings, 1979) and a politician who benefited from his association with a loyal support base in the southern Black church. He also enhanced his political clout as "Martin Luther

King, Jr.'s lieutenant . . . and chief mediator" responsible for "organizing the church structure to achieve racial equality in areas such as jobs, education, and public accommodation" (Cummings, 1979, p. 228), as well as by establishing a liaison between the Black and White communities. Although he was soft-spoken, Young was always honest, morally righteous, and direct with his constituencies, whether it was as minister of the church or as United Nations ambassador. Cummings described how this created problems in his political roles yet enhanced his respectability in the church. Nonetheless, Cummings maintained that Young agreed to become the United Nations ambassador because he could see the potential he had in this position to use it as a pulpit—and he did that well.

Although Martin Luther King, Jr., had no political aspirations, he was a Baptist minister whose oratory was respected for "its vivid imagery, its fluid style, its piercing truths, and its inspiring admonitions" (Cummings & Niles, 1991/1992, p. 49). King is perhaps the most studied orator of all time, but Cummings (1995b) managed to find something heuristic to discuss when exploring King's references to death in his speeches. Cummings and Niles (1991/1992) noted:

> King personally believed that he was carrying out the will of God as he worked tirelessly to obliterate injustices in the United States and then the world . . . After 1965, his speeches became even clearer testaments of an almost eerie closeness with God. Even now when one listens to recordings of his late speeches, one is likely to feel simultaneously chilled and calmed by his passionate pleas. (p. 54)

Rather than simply chronicle the moments leading up to his death, Cummings and Niles (1991/1992) analyzed King's speeches within their rightful spiritual, social, political, and cultural contexts.

Cummings had an attraction to rhetors who were revolutionaries. She enjoyed studying the speeches of people who established or participated in countermovements. Bishop Henry McNeal Turner, the subject of her dissertation, was one such individual. He was a Methodist Episcopal minister who became an African Methodist Episcopal (AME) minister and bishop. Cummings's analysis of Turner's oratory demonstrated a shift in his perspective over the years, from accommodationist to Black nationalist-separatist. Turner consistently worked in the "back to Africa" movement, trying to convince Blacks that they had no other alternative except to leave the country if they wanted to find freedom and manhood. He experienced some backlash from Blacks about his emigrationist perspective, but he was steadfast in his convictions, claiming that because Blacks are descendants from Africa, they would be returning home. Despite the drawbacks related to declines in physical health, "Turner's rhetoric grew in intensity with each adverse argument presented to him" (Cummings, 1982, p. 462). He was in search of respect and freedom, which he believed would never be granted to Blacks in America.

Cummings's research concerning Black rhetoric and public address illustrates a theory-to-method approach. In her early career work, she concentrated on explicating the need to research, teach, theorize about, and maintain Black rhetorical traditions. Her subsequent research has applied the early theorizing about Black idiom and Black rhetorical tropes to the rhetorical analyses of prominent Black leaders. Although Black rhetoric and public address are Cummings's two primary lines of research, she has also dabbled in studies of Black popular culture.

Black Popular Culture

In 1988, Cummings wrote an article for the *Journal of Popular Culture* that explored the "The Changing Image of the Black Family on Television" (Cummings, 1988). In this insightful essay, she examined stereotypical media representations, or what Donald Bogle (1973) named the "pantheon"—toms, coons, mulattoes, mammies, and bucks. She discussed a wide range of televised Black images and roles—from variety shows such as *Ed Sullivan's Toast of the Town* to the *Amos 'n Andy Show* to *227*, *The Jeffersons*, *Good Times*, and *The Cosby Show*—with particular attention to the perpetuation, disintegration, and/or amelioration of Black images. Noticing the continued patterns of pantheon figures spanning television programs, Cummings asserted, "For every positive feature of *The Jeffersons,* the character of George had at least two negatives. He was not only loud and boisterous, he was ostentatious, ignorant, a bigot, and a chauvinist" (Cummings, 1988, p. 79). She continued to point out the underlying tensions between stereotype and saving grace and concluded that although TV executives appear responsive to the public outcry for more progressive images, they seemed unrelentingly tied to retrogressive and pathologized representations of Blacks. Of all the shows discussed, she maintained that *The Cosby Show* appeared least problematic.

Because of this interest in mass-mediated effects of stereotypical images on children, Cummings and Roy (2002) coauthored a study of the manifestations of Afrocentricity on rap music. In this study, they investigated the various facets of the Afrocentric communication paradigm as latently expressed in hip-hop music. After analyzing the lyrics of several popular rap songs, they discovered that the objectives of rap music appear aligned with Afrocentric rhetorical notions of "balance, harmony, and transcendence in community" (Cummings & Roy, 2002, p. 59).

The three themes Cummings has explored throughout her career are Black rhetoric, Black public address, and Black popular culture. Each is linked to her developed interests in investigating organized responses to constraints on freedom of expression. Each openly critiques the strengths and limitations of these resistance efforts, but acknowledges that the fundamental goal of revolutionary rhetoric is to retrieve agency over self-definition. With that in mind, Cummings's research can be characterized as a set of visionary and transformative perspectives concerning social justice and cultural inclusiveness.

❖ CONCLUSION

Melbourne S. Cummings is a pioneer of communication, not only because of the magnitude or quantity of her publications but also because of her total contributions to the field of communication in leadership, mentoring, teaching, and research. As the quintessential teacher, even her research and leadership instruct us. She has worked steadily toward enhancing the placement and respect of paradigms related to Black rhetoric and public address so that following generations will not have to. Cummings did not create a new theory. Instead, she left her mark on the field of communication by developing a line of inquiry that directly challenged mainstream communication scholarship and provided a set of studies that exemplified how one might analyze Black rhetoric, with particular attention to constituent aspects of a Black rhetorical canon. Her legacy teaches communication scholars that there are multiple cultural standards, models, and discourses worthy of attention and inclusion. As a community organizer and proud mother of two sons—Samori is a physician, and Samir is a lawyer—Cummings has maintained that her family life "stands as a testament that success is possible despite the odds" (M. S. Cummings, personal communication, May 11, 2004), that society can structurally stack against marginalized communities. She has also taught us that although some scholars (Black and non-Black) offer knee-jerk reactions to systematic exclusion from curricula, leadership, and full disciplinary participation, a well-structured proactive response—exemplified via research, teaching, and service—yields more effective results. Finally, the greatest mentoring lesson her life and career can teach us is that as we maintain family balance, professional integrity, and moral convictions, we must also continue to lift as we climb!

❖ REFERENCES

Bogle, D. (1973). *Toms, coons, mulattoes, mammies & bucks*. New York: Continuum.

Cummings, M. S. (1972). Problems of researching black rhetoric. *Journal of Black Studies, 2*(4), 503–508.

Cummings, M. S. (1977). Historical setting for Booker T. Washington and the rhetoric of compromise, 1895. *Journal of Black Studies, 8*(1), 75–82.

Cummings, M. S. (1979). Andrew Young: A profile in politico-religious activism. *Western Journal of Black Studies, 3*(4), 228–232.

Cummings, M. S. (1982). The rhetoric of Bishop Henry McNeal Turner. *Journal of Black Studies, 12*(4), 457–467.

Cummings, M. S. (1988). The changing image of the Black family on television. *Journal of Popular Culture, 22*(2), 75–85.

Cummings, M. S. (1992). Teaching the African American rhetoric course. In L. Niles (Ed.), *African American communications: An anthology in tradition and contemporary studies* (pp. 239–245). Dubuque, IA: Kendall-Hunt.

Cummings, M. S., & Daniel, J. L. (1997). The study of African American rhetoric. In J. L. Golden, G. F. Berquist, & W. E. Coleman (Eds.), *The rhetoric of western thought* (pp. 360–385). Dubuque, IA: Kendall-Hunt.

Cummings, M. S., & Niles, L. (1991/1992). King as persuader: Facing the ultimate sacrifice. *Journal of Religious Thought, 48*(2), 49–56.

Cummings, M. S., Niles, L., & Taylor, O. (1992). (Eds.) *Handbook of communication and development in Africa and the African Diaspora*. Boston: Ginn Press.

Cummings, M. S., & Roy, A. (2002). Manifestations of Afrocentricity on rap music. *Howard Journal of Communications, 13*(1), 59–76.

Daniel, J. L. (1995). *Changing the players and the game: A personal account of the Speech Communication Association Black Caucus origins*. Annandale, VA: Speech Communication Association.

Daniel. J. L., & Cummings, M. S. (1992). African American linkages to Africa through oral discourse. In M. S. Cummings, L. Niles, & O. Taylor (Eds.), *Handbook of communication and development in Africa and the African Diaspora* (pp. 17–24). Boston: Ginn Press.

Woodson, C. G. (1925). *Negro orators and their orations*. New York: Russell Press.

Further Reading

Cummings, M. S. (August, 1995). The speech communication profession and how it relates to the Black experience. *Proceedings of the Summer Conference on Defining the Field of Communication*, Annandale, VA, 24–28.

Cummings, M. S. (1995). A comprehensive assessment of scholarly writings in Black rhetoric. In L. Niles (Ed.), *African American rhetoric: A reader* (pp. 87–116). Dubuque, IA: Kendall-Hunt.

Cummings, M. S. (1996). African American orators: Mary McLeod Bethune. In R. Leeman (Ed.), *African American orators: A bio-critical sourcebook* (pp. 1–9). Westport, CT: Greenwood Press.

Melbourne S. Cummings

Photo courtesy of Melbourne S. Cummings

1942	Born as Melbourne Jean Stenson in Monroe, Louisiana, on September 18.
1963	Graduated from North Carolina Central University.
1964	Married Robert Cummings on December 22.
	Taught English and chaired the English department at Crispus Attucks High School (1964–1965).
1965	Taught at Florida Agricultural & Mechanical University (FAMU).
1966	Taught English at Winston-Salem University (1966–1969).
1972	Wrote the article, "Problems of Researching Black Rhetoric" for the *Journal of Black Studies*.
	Received a doctorate in Rhetoric from UCLA. Her dissertation was titled, "The Rhetoric of Bishop Henry McNeal Turner, Leading Advocate of the African Emigration Movement, 1868–1907."
1973	Taught English and speech at Florida International University (1973–1976).
1974	Gave birth to first son, Samori, on August 19.
1976	Became associate professor in the Howard University Department of Communication Arts and Sciences.
1978	Gave birth to second son, Samir, on May 10.

1980	◆	Became associate dean of the Howard University School of Communications (1980–1986).
1987	◆	Received the National Communication Association's Robert J. Kibler Memorial Award.
1988	◆	Published the "Changing Images of the Black Family on Television" in the *Journal of Popular Culture*.
1991/1992	◆	Wrote article about Martin Luther King, Jr., "King as Persuader: Facing the Ultimate Sacrifice" in the *Journal of Religious Thought*.
1992	◆	Wrote *Handbook on Communications and Development in Africa and the African Diaspora* with Orlando Taylor.
1993	◆	Became department chair of the School of Communications at Howard University.
1995	◆	Received the National Communication Association (NCA) Black Caucus's Distinguished Service Award.
1997	◆	Published "The Study of African American rhetoric" (with Jack Daniel) in *The Rhetoric of Western Thought*.
2002	◆	Published the article, "Manifestations of Afrocentricity on Rap Music" in the *Howard Journal of Communications*.
2003	◆	Received the National Communication Association (NCA) Mentor Award on November 22.

5

Jack L. Daniel

In order to conduct meaningful research on any specific group of black people, or any group of people, one must become aligned with the people being studied in order that one can hear as they hear and see as they see. How can one hear as others hear and see as they see when one perceives  *others within the context of a world view that is antithetical to those one wishes to understand? . . . To discuss Black communication without an understanding of the primary, religious-philosophical assumptions on which it is based would result in the kind of knowledge one would have of Black music without discussing rhythm.*

(Daniel, 1974, p. x)

❖ INTRODUCTION

A cofounder of the National Communication Association's Black Caucus, Jack L. Daniel is known for his proactive and pioneering communication scholarship concerning the oppressed, his liberation-centered critiques of nonprogressive institutionalized norms, and his kind and loving spirit. As the epigraph above so eloquently states, for one's research to be effective in communities, one must become aligned with the people being studied. Throughout his entire life, Daniel has maintained alignment with the Black communities he has studied. In fact, among his contemporaries and his students, he is sometimes known as "The Conductor." During an interview with the first author of this book, he explained the moniker, which is linked to the Underground Railroad. "It was a heavy responsibility, you know, for the conductor to free the slaves. The conductor had to secure the lives of those who entrusted him or her to deliver them to freedom." First and foremost, Daniel sees community uplift as his personal responsibility. When asked what work he would say he is primarily known for, he modestly replied, "My mentoring of young professionals" (J. L. Daniel, personal communication, March 23, 2003).

Although Daniel's responsibility has always been to God, family, and community before all else, he has also been an influential scholar and a mentor to many prominent and up-and-coming intellectuals. When it was unpopular to talk about class-based and racial oppression, Daniel was completing a dissertation on it (Daniel, 1968), a piece of which was published in one of the top-tier speech journals at the time. Furthermore, within the same year of his doctoral graduation, he moved his scholarship to praxis when he cofounded the Black Caucus of the National Communication Association—formerly the Speech Association of America (SAA)—with Molefi Asante, Charles Hurst, Lyndrey Niles, Dorthy Pennington, and others (Daniel, 1995). In 1969, just one year removed from graduate school, Daniel served as guest editor of *The Speech Teacher*, which is now known as *Communication Education*. Two years later, he was guest editor for another themed issue—on Black communication—in *Today's Speech*, now known as *Communication Quarterly*. His approach for both special issues was one that continually questioned the perceptual stance that oppressed groups were innately inferior and that their communicative patterns were reflective of this perceived inadequacy. These two volumes helped to establish his presence as an intellectual in the field of communication.

Recognizing his natural leadership abilities, progressive approach to intellectual life, and overall scholarship, his alma mater, the

University of Pittsburgh, quickly promoted him from assistant professor to associate professor and Black Studies department chair just one year after receiving his doctorate degree. At that time, there were only a few Black Studies programs throughout the nation, and even fewer departments. Along with Nathan Hare and Molefi Asante, Daniel was among only a few scholars who could claim to be a major part of such an achievement from its inception and in the leadership role of department chair. Thereafter, Daniel's work became more firmly centered in African American studies, with particular emphases on orature and on children and educative cultural practices. His work has become mostly rhetorical and critical-interpretive. Daniel may be most well-known for his piece, coauthored with Geneva Smitherman-Donaldson, titled, "How I Got Over: Communication Dynamics in the Black Community" (Daniel & Smitherman-Donaldson, 1976). That essay is considered so monumental that it stands, even today, as a centerpiece of scholarly dialogues concerning Black cultural communicative continuities. Several other important critical works have been published since then. Daniel's more recent research concerning Black parental naming of children gained some media attention, and he and his wife discussed the topic on ABC News's *20/20* television talk show on August 20, 2004. His myriad community-driven research interests and consistent work concerning Black communication have won Daniel a place among prominent scholars in Black communication studies.

In this chapter, we will discuss Daniel's personal background, academic experiences, and contributions to the field of communication. These discussions will be followed by a conclusion and selected references from his body of writings.

❖ BIOGRAPHICAL INFORMATION

Born in the middle of World War II on June 9, 1942, Jack L. Daniel, a native of Johnstown, Pennsylvania, was raised within a family of laborers. His mother, the late Gracie Daniel, was a housewife. His father, the late Russell Daniel Sr., worked on the railroad, in the steel mill, and as a church deacon. Daniel's parents, both of whom were Virginia natives, were not college graduates (his mother had a sixth-grade education, and his father went to Storres Junior College), but they were well-respected and well-known in the surrounding community. Gracie and Russell Sr. raised five children: Russell Jr., Sterlin, Jack, Phyllis, and Stephen. Russell Sr. was a Prince Hall Free and Accepted Mason, Gracie was a member of the Order of Eastern Star, and they reached the highest level in each organization. Daniel understood at an early age that his father was influential in the community, and he developed an early proclivity toward communal action while watching his father mentor others. The Daniel family was far from affluent. In fact, this family of seven lived in public housing for the first 12 years of Daniel's life. While spending six years building a three-bedroom house from the ground up beside his father—who had no formal carpentry training—Daniel and his two older brothers also learned a few lessons about self-reliance and patience. These lessons were fortified year after year as his family grew enough vegetables and fruits during the harvest season to last them throughout the year. In a private interview with the first author of this book, Daniel notes that he never had a store-bought pie until he reached college because his mother always baked pies "from scratch." As with cooked vegetables, he said, "Most of what we ate, we grew, and I thought that is the way you did things" (J. L. Daniel, personal communication, March 23, 2003). Although both of his parents are now deceased, Daniel notices their presence within him, and their values are reflected in his everyday values. He has instilled those same values in his son, Omari, and his daughter, Marijata. Omari is now a secondary educator, poet, and author, and Marijata holds a doctorate in political science from the University of Michigan. Daniel maintains that his grandchildren, Amani, Akili, Deven, and Javon, have also inherited a strong work ethic. To his grandchildren, Daniel is affectionately known as "Papa Two Times." Daniel recalled having a loving and strict household during his childhood:

> Growing up, we obviously were poor, but I never knew it. I never knew it because of the values and child-rearing practices that we got. We were raised as proud people, people who were capable of doing anything. It was always with the caveat that you had to think, use your brain, get a good education, believe in God, trust in God and there was no toleration for foolishness. Foolishness was anything other than worshipping God, getting in your books, and you don't even think about committing a crime. (J. L. Daniel, personal communication, March 23, 2003)

Despite strong family support, Daniel was not a perfect child. He admits to being a problem child who was an A student in schoolwork, but was an F student in conduct because he was a prankster. In contrast, he was also a responsible child. He worked as a newspaper deliverer and "pin boy" at the bowling alley during high school. In his senior year, Daniel was a member of his high school's track and cross-country team, which was ranked number one in the country. Athletic involvement became a primary preoccupation of Daniel—to the extent that it contributed to his failing grades. Even after having taken easier classes to make up for these grades, Daniel's grade point average at the time of his high school graduation was a mere 2.0.

❖ ACADEMIC BACKGROUND AND EXPERIENCE

Upon graduating from high school, Jack L. Daniel was set to enter the military. As a charitable act, however, a White furniture store owner in Johnstown offered to send him and another Black male high school graduate to the University of Pittsburgh at Johnstown for a semester. The White man made the offer because he had heard that both of the boys' fathers were ministers, which assured him that they were of good character. Although the man mistook Daniel's father's role as *deacon* to be equivalent to that of a *reverend*, Daniel did take advantage of this remarkable opportunity.

Without applying to the University of Pittsburgh, Daniel was admitted and was told that he could continue matriculating if he maintained a C average and "kept his nose clean," (J. L. Daniel, personal communication, March 23, 2003), Daniel did so, and excelled in the Air Force ROTC on the trick drill team, spinning a bayonet and rifle. Despite Daniel's enthusiasm for the war in Vietnam and the drill team, he was passed over as a commander because of his race, so he quit the ROTC.

Daniel's sustained study at the University of Pittsburgh eventually led him to earn a scholarship to attend graduate school there in the Department of Communication. His undergraduate degree was in psychology, but Edwin Black—the professor of his communication course—wanted Daniel to attend graduate school in the Department of Communication. Black offered Daniel a fellowship with a stipend.

Still ambivalent about whether he wanted to pursue the military or graduate school, Daniel signed up to join the U.S. Army prior to the Vietnam War. He was to be assigned to a depot in Texas and to hold the rank of a noncommissioned officer, When Daniel was scheduled for departure, however, he refused to go because a beautiful woman pleaded with him to stay and take advantage of the full scholarship to graduate school. Jerlean Evelyn Colley, his wife-to-be, was a college junior, and Daniel would be a first-semester graduate student. Although he was quite excited about being a noncommissioned officer in the military, he followed Jerlean's advice and entered the master's program in the Department of Communication at the University of Pittsburgh, Johnstown. On Christmas day, 1963, Daniel and Jerlean were married.

Daniel became a quick study in this new field of communication and was an exceptional student who found a particular interest in classical rhetoric, research methods, and cross-cultural communication. He studied with Theodore (Ted) Clevenger, who ran a quantitative lab studying general and tonal semantics. Daniel was Clevenger's research assistant and became a statistician specializing in experimental studies. To meet his foreign language requirement for graduate school, Daniel had trained in "high proficiency, scientific Russian." With this talent, Daniel worked with chemistry and physics equations, producing the answers in Russian. He wrote his master's thesis on Blacks' perceptions of White speakers' sincerity, which was one of the earliest studies of culture that examined speaker authenticity and tonal semantics in the field. Later, after entering and matriculating through the coursework of the communication doctoral program, he wrote his dissertation, "Effective and Ineffective Communication on the Parts of Professionals and Non-Professionals When Communicating with Poor People." It marked the beginning of an academic career that would be noted for an emphasis on what Daniel characterizes as "scholarship of the oppressed" (J. L. Daniel, personal communication, March 23, 2003).

By the age of 25, Daniel had been married to Jerlean for four years. He was one year removed from completing his doctorate degree and was an assistant professor at Central Michigan University, although with a meager starting pay of "something like $8500." In retrospect, Daniel laughingly recalled, "I'm thinking, man, I could have been in the military, and they would have covered room and board, and I could have been around the world by now" (J. L. Daniel, personal communication, March 23, 2003). He made the best of that professorship experience, as he has in all his professional positions.

In his entire career, Daniel had only two fiscal year periods away from the University of Pittsburgh. One was from 1967 to 1968, at Central Michigan University as a full-time professor teaching research methods, psychology of speech, and semantics. The other was as an American Council on Education Fellow at Stanford University, from 1973 to 1974. After his period at Central Michigan University, Daniel returned to University of Pittsburgh as an assistant professor. Within only one year, he was promoted and tenured as an associate professor of Communication and Black Studies, as well as becoming the Black Studies Department chair.

During Daniel's transition period to the University of Pittsburgh in 1968, Dr. Martin Luther King, Jr., was assassinated. Daniel remembered,

"Before I could process that, my hair got longer and my suits changed to dashikis, and shoes to combat boots. It was on." (J. L. Daniel, personal communication, March 23, 2003). As the new head of a nascent Black Studies *department*, not *program*, he was already engaged in a struggle for freedom and justice. The unit that Daniel headed was named the Department of Black Community Education, Research & Development. At that time, Black Studies programs were not widely acknowledged as important academic programs. In fact, their tenuous status at many schools as mere certificate programs was a signal of academia's general disregard for Black Studies as a legitimate area of inquiry. In short, despite being underfunded and undervalued, Black Studies programs and departments were important sites of intense activism and hands-on learning. Their curricula were not just comprised of a series of classes on civil rights movements and Black history. They were in the midst of a civil rights movement and they were making history as they fought to expand the rights and privileges of generations of Blacks to come. Daniel was at the helm of this insurrectionary activity within higher educational institutions with Black Studies programs and departments. It was 1969 when he became department chair. Daniel was just 27 years old, and this was only one year after receiving his doctorate degree. Although academic contributions by Black scholars about Black people preceded 1968, the naming and character of *Black Studies* departments were new. This is certainly not to slight either the early Institute of Race Relations at Fisk University established by Charles S. Johnson in 1944 or any of the myriad associations for the study of Black Diasporic peoples established in the early 1900s. The fact is, however, that Black Studies experienced its largest thrust into academia because of changing migration patterns, population shifts, and increased Black enrollment at colleges and universities. Marable (2000) posited:

> In 1950, for example, only seventy-five thousand Negroes were enrolled in American colleges and universities. In 1960 three-fourths of all Black students attended historically black colleges. By 1970 nearly seven hundred thousand African Americans were enrolled, three-fourths of whom were at White colleges. Most of these White institutions were ill-prepared for the eruption of Black student protest they would encounter between 1968 and 1972. (Marable, 2000, p. 7)

Daniel was among the few leaders of Black Studies *departments*. Black Studies programs were increasing rapidly. As Marable (2000) noted, college student protests concerning the absence of a Black Studies curriculum were widespread across the United States—from Washington D.C. to San Francisco. Nathan Hare, who is considered to be the first Black Studies department chair in the United States, had just resigned from Howard University's Department of Black Studies when he was appointed in 1968 to be the nation's first Black Studies chair at San Francisco State University because of the highly publicized student insurgency there. Marable (2000) suggested that the well-organized student protests at San Francisco State offered a template for other student activists seeking curricular reform and the establishment of Black Studies programs and departments within predominately White institutions. Many colleges and universities, especially larger ones, were under pressure to respond. By 1970, Molefi Asante, another recently minted doctor in communication, was been hired as UCLA's Director of the Center for Afro-American Studies. Naturally, Daniel and Asante already knew each other because they were among the very few Blacks within the field of communications who attended the annual SAA conventions.

Daniel had a head start on many of the Black Studies programs in the United States and has since helped to start similar departments at accredited universities such as Central Michigan University, the University of Dayton, and the University of Illinois at Chicago. Whether the protests were at the University of Pittsburgh or somewhere else, Daniel was placed in a precarious position—he was expected to represent the interests of the university while remaining loyal to the civil rights and Black Power movements. For Daniel, this situation was not difficult to navigate because his position was always characterized by his commitment to principle and community.

Due to his diligence and principled leadership, Daniel has had many opportunities, not the least of which was traveling to Tanzania and Nigeria to establish a student exchange program. This experience was followed by his appointment in 1973 as a fellow to the American Council of Education at Stanford University. This was also the year his second child, Omari, was born. Daniel's research and varied administrative positions have taken him around the world to promote and investigate Black communication across the Diaspora, yet he has worked arduously within the communication discipline in general and the National Communication Association in particular.

Cofounding the Black Caucus: One of Daniel's Contributions to the Field of Communication

Daniel's commitment to principled leadership guided his participation in the founding of the Black Caucus of the National Communication

Association, previously called the Speech Association of America (SAA), in 1968. He was joined by Molefi Kete Asante, Cecil Blake, Michael Edwards, Lyndrey A. Niles, Donald H. Smith, Charles G. Hurst, Jr., and Orlando L. Taylor. Daniel also credits Lucia Hawthorne, Melbourne Cummings, Dorthy L. Pennington, and many others for their important contributions to the formative years of the Black Caucus. This group of outspoken scholar-activists would not be ignored. Daniel recounted the details of the Black Caucus's founding in his book, *Changing the Players and the Game: A Personal Account of the Speech Communication Association Black Caucus Origins* (Daniel, 1995). One pivotal moment in the founding of the caucus came during the December 28, 1968, "Open Meeting on Social Relevance" at the Sheraton Hotel in Chicago. This evening colloquium was designed to address issues raised by the ad hoc committee on social relevance of the SAA, a committee that was comprised of a racially diverse mix of 11 liberal communication scholars. With Daniel as chair, the committee prepared "A Manifesto to the Speech Profession," which posed several challenges to leaders and scholars of communication. Each challenge was presented as a question with open queries like this one: "Do the curricula, the textbooks, and the scholarship of the profession do any-thing to increase our understanding of discourse which is not within the White, middle class norm?" Another such challenge asked, "Why is it that more minority group members are not attracted to the speech profession? What have we done to alleviate this problem, and what have we done to encourage dissemination of ideas and opinions of minority group members who are within the profession?" (Daniel, 1995, p. 3). There were eight such challenges, relating to three cate-gories: the inherent bias advocating European paradigms while dis-missing all others within the standard curriculum; the insufficient training of graduate students as future communication scholars who should be able to address socially and contemporarily relevant matters; and the discipline's virtual silence, within all its organs, networks and structures, on social issues pertaining to contemporary society. The manifesto was distributed and discussed before an audience of 200 conference attendees. Daniel began the meeting with an introduction of the committee's concerns. He recalled:

> Suddenly and very deliberately, a short Black male . . . wearing a black turtleneck sweater and dark sunglasses, made his way down the center aisle. . . . Without a single word, he mounted the stage, stridently crossed the platform, and politely but in a non-negotiating fashion took the microphone away from me. . . . Charles Hurst

"ran it down" from A to Z, i.e. he told White people about their personal hang-ups, expounded on racism within the SAA, judiciously used a few words of a profane nature, and conjured up an emotional atmosphere that would not permit the ninety-nine percent White members of the audience to retreat from "involvement" with "social relevance." (Daniel, 1995, pp. 5–6)

This speech was followed by a rousing address by Arthur Smith (i.e., Molefi Asante) akin to that of Hurst. Both speeches were apparently delivered in the best of Black rhetorical form, driven by an evocative, academic call to arms. After this two-hour session, Charles Hurst, the chair of Howard University's Department of Communication, invited Black scholars to meet in his hotel room to strategize about the next steps to be taken. It was there that the founding members of the SAA Black Caucus began to organize. They were fortunate to have scholars such as Orlando Taylor and Gloria Walker to consult because Taylor and Walker had already founded a Black Caucus in the American Speech and Hearing Association. That first unplanned gathering of communication scholars in Chicago led to a series of planned meetings and eventually to discussions of a Black Rhetoric Institute, which was to be run as an "independent Black Caucus" (Daniel, 1995, p. 12). Although the institute never materialized because of lack of available funding and administrative personnel, demand and demonstrations aimed at the SAA leadership persisted. Even still, there were key leaders in SAA who continued to acknowledge and offer some funding for meetings that laid the foundation for the Black Caucus. In 1972, there was a significant six-day "Black Communication Conference" at the University of Pittsburgh, organized by Daniel and funded by the National Endowment for the Humanities and SAA, with Daniel as the principal investigator. There were nine papers, which varied in theme and disciplinary approach, delivered by scholars representing Black Diasporic interests. Those authors were David Baker, Lloyd Brown, Lucia S. Hawthorne, Olive Lewin, Jack Daniel, Imogine Hines, Gerlene Ross, Gloria Walker, Fela Sowande, Arthur Smith, Orlando Taylor, and Ronald Williams. The papers, which expounded on Black music, media, rhetoric, discourse, language development, curriculum, and theory, were assembled and eventually published in a volume (edited by Daniel) titled *Black Communication: Dimensions of Research and Instruction* (Daniel, 1974). Incidentally, the year this anthology was released, the SAA Black Caucus held its first election for the presidency of the unit. Professor Dorthy Pennington and her doctoral student Michael Edwards were elected to chair. *Black Communication* was the first of Daniel's three books published to date. The other two were *Changing the Players and the Game* (Daniel, 1995) and *We Fish: The Journey to Fatherhood* (Daniel & Daniel, 2002).

❖ CONTRIBUTIONS TO COMMUNICATION RESEARCH

Daniel's activistic approach to his research was influenced, in part, by reading Frantz Fanon's *Wretched of the Earth* (1965). He was also influenced by the mentoring he received from ethnomusicologist Fela Sowande and from his colleague, friend, and coauthor Geneva Smitherman-Donaldson. Sowande, an ethnomusicologist trained at the University of London, received an honorary doctorate from the University of Ife in Nigeria and then taught at Howard University and University of Pittsburgh in their Black Studies departments. Daniel had established a collegial relationship with Sowande while serving as his department chair in Black Studies at the University of Pittsburgh. Sowande piqued Daniel's interest in proverb traditions by sending Daniel to Jamaica to study with a few community griots. As departmental colleagues, Daniel and Sowande shared many intellectual exchanges and Daniel recalls enhancing his own understanding of African Diasporic discourses through that relationship. Their intellectual camaraderie also expanded the boundaries of Daniel's research concerning Blacks in the United States. This line of inquiry was strengthened by Daniel's association with Geneva Smitherman-Donaldson, who is indubitably the leading scholar on Ebonics in the United States.

The three areas in which Daniel has left an indelible impact on the field of communications are class-based communication studies, African American language and discourse studies, and research concerning institutionalized racial bias, as described in the following sections.

Class-Based Communication Studies

Much of Daniel's early work was situated around the proposition that Blacks, and certainly Black Studies scholars, could not afford to speak strictly of race and culture without addressing the economic and political conditions of underprivileged Black communities. Foundational scholars such as Carter Godwin Woodson, St. Clair Drake, Horace Mann, Melville Herskovits, and W. E. B. DuBois understood that racism was as much political as economic. Slavery and colonialism were as much political as economic. The civil rights and Black Power movements were as much about the political as the economic.

And now, the history and academic study of Blacks had to include the politics and economics (or political economy) of race, lest the knowledge gained from the struggles for freedom be forfeited. Daniel's decision, during his doctoral program, to investigate how professional and nonprofessional people communicate with poor people was consciously driven by both the political-economic trend in civil rights rhetoric as well as retrospective reflections on his own personal experience. Many major civil rights initiatives and events took place around the time Daniel was completing his dissertation. It was Freedom Summer in 1964, and the Civil Rights Voting Act of 1965 had just passed. Consequently, those who were historically disenfranchised had the right to vote. Thus, they had the democratic privilege of asserting their own opinions and of having those opinions count. Shortly thereafter, the Black Panther Party and Maulana Karenga's organization Us were expanding operations in the West and throughout the nation. In 1968, the Black Power movement was at its height, despite the assassinations of two major civil rights leaders—Malcolm X in 1965 and Martin Luther King, Jr., in 1968. Several political initiatives were at the foundation of Black Power movement activities: educational access, voter registration, community stability and safety, and enhancement of cultural consciousness. All these initiatives emerged from oppressed people asserting their voices.

In his dissertation, Daniel wanted to explore the chasm between oppressed and nonoppressed groups. His communication-based approach considered the way in which the cosmological differences between the two groups prevented social cohesion. In his study, which was later published in truncated form as an article in *Today's Speech,* Daniel wrote that his research "is concerned with revealing some possible communication breakdowns resulting from the poor being alien in an affluent society" (Daniel, 1969a, p. 15). He conducted an ethnography of poor and middle-class people in the Hill District of Pittsburgh, which was then primarily populated by lower-income Blacks. Daniel wanted to know if the indigenous nonprofessional people could communicate more effectively with poor people than the professional middle-class people could. In the article, he presented a review of literature related to class and interaction differences. The purpose of Daniel's study was to examine the perspectives of "nonprofessional," marginalized in-group members and their communication patterns vis-à-vis the dominant, professional, middle-class out-group members' communication patterns. This comparative analysis revealed that if there is a "culture of poverty," it is outwardly manifested via the divergent attitudes between the two groups. These attitudes, according to Daniel, were associated with everything from notions of authority, goal-setting, and religion to delinquency, violence, sex, and money. Daniel explained that the problems that accompanied poverty might not be understood by middle-class professionals who presumed absence or tardiness from school. For example, the poverty might be due to living conditions instead of actual initiative or enthusiasm on the part of the student. The different ranges of experience of these two groups led to different worldviews that affected what they thought about what should happen and when. Even the peer group networks, socially learned behaviors, sources for news and information, and overall standards for communicative effectiveness were distinct, so the criteria for competent communication shifted significantly from one class-based community to the other. The attitudinal and communicative nuances of each class group were accented by Daniel's everyday examples, illustrating how the nonverbal communication of a middle-class professional can intimidate and alienate poor nonprofessionals. For instance, Daniel discussed the encoding and decoding of messages such as the middle class professional's "facial expression of fear and disgust" (Daniel, 1969a, p. 20) when he enters a poor person's home. He concluded by indicating that there was a direct and proportionate relationship between perceived, shared similarities and understanding as well as valuation of others.

This early-career research by Daniel demonstrated another way in which his disciplinary work has been precocious. In 2004, published journals and books centered within the discipline of communication were beginning to comment extensively about issues of class. Although critical-cultural communication scholars have implied class differentials in their work concerning patriarchal hegemony, much of the class-related research has been left to other fields, such as sociology, economics, and labor and industrial relations.

African American Language and Discourse

Although Daniel's earliest work concerned class-based oppression, he is perhaps best known for his groundbreaking work concerning traditional African American oral discourses and their linkage to African carryovers. Two primary areas of research have served as subsets of Daniel's work on oral discourses: communal-oral discourse and the proverb tradition.

Communal-Oral Discourse. Daniel's initial writing on African American rhetoric was in a Black Studies journal called *Black Lines*, published in

1970. This article was followed up years later, in 1976, with a study coauthored with Geneva Smitherman-Donaldson, and published in the *Quarterly Journal of Speech*. The article, titled "How I Got Over: Communication Dynamics in the Black Community" (Daniel & Smitherman-Donaldson, 1976), has been one of the most reprinted and cited of all Daniel's works. During a time when Black communication research was treated as an accessory to "more formidable" mainstream, Eurocentric communication studies, scholars such as Daniel, Molefi Asante, Lucia Hawthorne, Orlando Taylor, Melbourne Cummings, Lyndrey Niles, Dorthy Pennington, Marcia Clinkscales, Charles Hurst, and others were building this most important rubric of communication scholarship from the ground up. Of course, these scholars had to develop and define the conceptual foundations of the field. Although Geneva Smitherman-Donaldson is a sociolinguist and anthropologist by training, language studies were much more well-connected to communication studies than they are today. So it was only natural for Daniel to collaborate with her on a discussion of "the sacred and secular dynamics of the African American communications system . . . which has served to extrapolate, ritualize, and thus preserve the African essence of Afro-American life" (Daniel & Smitherman-Donaldson, 1976, p. 26). With a particular emphasis on the "traditional Black church," Daniel and Smitherman-Donaldson explicated the distinctions between "surface" and "deep" structures of reality as follows:

> Surface structures are objective, empirical, subject to relatively rapid change, constrained by time and space, and non-generative in nature. Deep structures are intangible, subjective, archetypal, not culturally bound, and generative in nature. (Daniel & Smitherman-Donaldson, 1976, pp. 26–27)

In trying to address the range of oratorical patterns within the sacred-secular continuum, Daniel & Smitherman-Donaldson uncovered several now commonly understood aspects of Black discourse: call-and-response, holism, spiritual diunitality, and polyrhythm.

Call-and-response is often witnessed most overtly within church settings, in which there is interaction between the preacher and congregation. The preacher "calls" by saying something similar to "Y'all don't hear me!" or "Can somebody give me an amen?" The congregation's "response" is usually a reply such as "Amen, reverend!" "Preach!" or "Tell the truth!" This call-and-response pattern can also be nonverbal, as exemplified with a handclap that initiates a thunderous applause or a tambourine accompanied by the organ, both "calling for" holy-dancing, "speaking in tongues," and "catching the spirit." In nonchurch encounters, call-and-response might be misunderstood as interruptive depending on the nature of the conversation as well as the interactants involved. It can be considered by out-group members to be interruptive if someone is speaking and the verbal or nonverbal response overlaps with the talk. Nonetheless, in-group members know that the speaker and his or her message are simply being affirmed, which is facilitated via call-and-response.

Holism is another aspect of Black oral discourse that recognizes the connectedness between all activity produced by humans, nature, and the universe. Naturally, holism applies to the link between surface structural differences in customs, language, and discourse and the deep structural similarities among African peoples, such as the reverence for orature. The concept of holism also contributes to the comprehension of harmony between the body, worldview, and communicative events and processes. Consequently, there is interdependence among notions of self, how to construct a sense of self, and God-given spiritual essence.

Spiritual diunitality is another way in which African American discourse is permeated and vitalized. *Diunitality* refers to a "unity throughout" something, so spiritual diunitality is the unity throughout religiospiritual practices and approaches. By referencing John Mbiti's notable work *African Religions and Philosophies* (Mbiti, 1992), the authors elucidated the idea that spirit and matter are not opposite; they are coextensive. In the essay, which emerged from the authors' experiences as members of Baptist churches in Pennsylvania and Tennessee, they claimed that spirituality extends beyond religious, cultural, and temporal boundaries, but remains influenced by and linked to each of them in everyday spiritual discursive practice. This is the same type of balance that also permeates holism and polyrhyhm.

According to Daniel and Smitherman-Donaldson, polyrhythm can be explained as the way in which "the universe moves by the many rhythms that are created by the various, complementary, interdependent forces" (Daniel & Smitherman-Donaldson, 1976, p. 31). Within the church setting, it represents the rhythms present in oratorical delivery, audience response, chronemics, instrumental performance, and spiritual coalescence with God. This dynamic, communally-driven interplay between multiple energies coexisting in the same context is fascinating.

Each of these aspects of oral discourse—call-and-response, holism, spiritual diunitality, and polyrythm—is continued in Daniel's later writings on African American rhetoric.

Proverb Tradition. There's an old proverb from Sierra Leone that says, "Proverbs are the daughters of experience." They are the instructive paraphernalia of everyday life that advise, guide, and direct individuals to be ethical, wise, and cautious citizen-achievers. In three of Daniel's articles on proverbs (Daniel, 1972; Daniel, Smitherman-Donaldson, & Jeremiah, 1987; Daniel & Effinger, 1996) he illuminated these and other functions of proverbs within African, African American, and Caribbean American lives. Daniel, Smitherman-Donaldson, and Jeremiah defined proverbs as "figurative epigrammatic statements that express widely accepted strategies for addressing recurring situations" (Daniel, Smitherman-Donaldson, & Jeremiah, 1987, p. 483). The functions of proverbs, according to Daniel's ethnographic study of proverb usage (Daniel, 1972), are as follows:

- "To store and disseminate the speech community's attitudes, beliefs, values, philosophical assumptions, virtues and vices, and in general much of its worldview" (p. 483)
- To be used by parents to socialize children
- To facilitate and enhance abstract thinking and reasoning
- To serve as rhetorical devices in argument
- To assist in resolving conflict and maintaining harmony
- To advise
- To entertain
- "To reflect ideal behavior and values" (p. 486)
- To reflect history, language and culture
- To introduce moral lessons in a more truncated form than narrative
- To demonstrate eloquence
- To provide insights

As Daniel, Smitherman-Donaldson, and Jeremiah discussed the use and function of proverbs (Daniel, Smitherman-Donaldson, & Jeremiah, 1987), they were careful not to claim African origin for all proverbs used by Africans. They were also conscientious about noting comparisons between different Caribbean and African tribal interpretations, variations, and usages of proverbs. The proverbs discussed in this study were collected from three different locations: Pittsburgh, Detroit, and Antigua. Two hundred of the proverbs emerged from interviews with respondents in Pittsburgh. Incidentally, this list of two hundred proverbs resulted in an earlier self-published monograph, written by Daniel: *The Wisdom of Sixth Mount Zion from the Members of Sixth Mount Zion and Those Who Begot Them* (Daniel, 1979). The categories that evolved from Daniel's cluster analysis were virtues and vices, human nature, sacred and secular commandments, child development, and the nature of reality. The Detroit sample, which contained fewer proverbs (n=80), was part of a larger pilot study on the de-Africanization of Black language. Smitherman-Donaldson led a team of trained researchers in data collection and analysis. Although Daniel's Pittsburgh sample was comprised entirely of church members, Smitherman-Donaldson's sample was constructed from community survey data used by the Center for Black Studies at Wayne State University in Detroit. Her active involvement in recruiting and training interviewers ensured some success in data collection and analysis. The interviews yielded a corpus of 800 proverbs, the most popular of which included "What goes around comes around," You reap what you sow," and "What happens in the dark must come to light." According to Daniel, Smitherman-Donaldson, and Jeremiah, these popular proverbs accented the inevitability of certain outcomes. Another interesting finding was that proverbs were used to teach children about color consciousness and self-esteem, and although churchgoing Black women used proverbs most frequently, they did not necessarily know more proverbs than others did. Also, heuristic discoveries included the fact that fundamentalists and women did not contribute significantly more proverbs than nonfundamentalists or men, contrary to commonly held beliefs based upon prior "proverb use" research (Daniel, Smitherman-Donaldson, & Jeremiah, 1987).

The African Diasporic oral tradition inherent in proverb use among African Americans is indicative of a highly significant literary form that has traversed generations. In their study of "bosom biscuits," Daniel and Effinger explained that "recurring oral nurturing messages" help to develop the "psychological, cognitive, affective, and spiritual selves of African American children so much that adults recall the proverbial advice given to them by their primary caregivers during adolescence (Daniel & Effinger, 1996, p. 186). Daniel and Effinger specifically concentrated on bosom biscuit advice given to African American faculty and administrators early in their lives. Of the 31 participants, they discovered that their maternal caregivers, many having only a high school education or less, gave most of the bosom biscuits. Additionally, the majority of the respondents' primary caregivers came from lower-income backgrounds. As expected, the participants reported that they listened to this advice frequently during childhood, but even more so later in life. The major lessons learned were those concerning ethics, hard work, discipline, altruism, spirituality, education, independence, and achievement (Daniel & Effinger, 1996).

Institutionalized Racial Bias

Child development has been a consistent underlying theme of Daniel's program of research. Whether it is learning through proverbs or via institutionalized constructions of race, Daniel has been concerned with the effects that formal and informal learning has on children. Similar to the way in which the Daniel & Effinger (1996) study explored primary caregivers' guidance of their children, Daniel and Daniel's (1999) essay concerning "the hot stove" as a metaphor for racism was particularly insightful as a way to examine the kinds of effects that lifelong parental advisement has had on children's self-esteem, resiliency, and adaptability. This study was especially unique in the field of communication because adaptive and protective factors associated with racism were rarely discussed in the literature. Daniel and Daniel shared a series of personal and vicariously learned anecdotes related to racism directed at Black children, and note that many African American primary caregivers have come to rely on the transmission of "survival messages" composed of narratives and proverbs as key strategies for preparing their children for the future prospect of racism directed solely at them. Without denying the complexity of parenting, as well as children's message receipt and meaning-making, Daniel and Daniel clearly offered sound considerations for parents faced with the responsibility of protecting African American children's identity development (Daniel & Daniel, 1999).

Part and parcel of the discussion of identity development is naming. Sociolinguists and communication scholars have long maintained that the act of naming is one of the most important privileges and facets of being human. It is not only a creative activity but also an empowering and defining one. In their article, "Preschool Children's Selection Of Race-Related Personal Names," Daniel and Daniel contended that names could hold certain stereotypical perceptions and presumptions regarding destiny, intelligence, age, attractiveness, ethnicity, religion, gender, and activity (Daniel & Daniel, 1998). They reminded readers that one of the most powerful and damaging aspects of slavery was the required change to slave names. By taking away their given names, slavemasters stripped away both the slaves' sense of entitlement to self-definition and a claim to a distinct familial lineage and cultural heritage. This disintegration of children's linkage to a larger cultural collective posed a severe identity complex and initiated a cycle of "de-Africanization" as Daniel, Smitherman-Donaldson, and Jeremiah (1987) called it. This was evident in the early doll studies conducted by Kenneth and Mamie Clark and also in Daniel and Daniel's study (1998), which was a spin-off of the Clarks's

study of 1939. Instead of using dolls as a stimulus for researcher-child interaction about friendship selection and personality attributions, Daniel and Daniel used personal names. The sample was drawn from White and Black children who lived in Pennsylvania between 1990 and 1993 and were participants in a Pennsylvania Head Start Program. Interestingly, Daniel and Daniel chose to omit any skin color information to see whether children would still use personal names only as a basis for racial stereotyping. To ascertain whether stereotyping occurs at such an early age, the researchers introduced the children to two games: "Guess who?" and "Who looks like you?" This symbolic play presented the children with scenarios in which they had to figure out who did positive or negative things. In the study, 102 Black and 80 White 4- and 5-year-old participants were asked this question: "Who looks like you?" The results indicated that through this symbolic play, 70 percent of the children selected common White personal names. These names came from the Commonwealth of Pennsylvania Department of Health, Division of Health Statistics and Research's 1990, 1991, 1992, and 1993 listings of the most frequently given White names. The Black names used in the study were also gathered from this database's listing of the most frequently given Black names. Although Black and White respondents tended to associate more negative traits and behaviors with the Black names, there was a significantly greater propensity to do so among the White child participants. So, young children as young as 4 years old were already developing racial stereotype associations with personal names. Naturally, this stereotyping schemata often continues into adulthood (Daniel & Daniel, 1998).

In an August 20, 2004, interview broadcast on the ABC News program *20/20*, Daniel and his wife explained that those subscribing to negative social constructions of race have facilitated stereotyping people because of their names, but concluded that it is not necessarily a reason to avoid Black-sounding names for Black children. In fact, the couple indicated that they rejected White-sounding names for their own children, Omari and Marijata, because they did not want to allow the "assimilation process [to] dissolve who we were as a people" (ABCNews.com, p. 2).

The assimilation process is also a primary intermediating factor in formal learning processes among children. The curricular bias within academia was another subject critiqued by Daniel. He began writing about this in 1971, shortly after beginning his career in the professoriate. Immediately, he found that the predominate educational resources and literature at his disposal were Eurocentric. Of course, this was problematic for two reasons: It was the only kind of curricula offered

to students and it was dismissive of all non-Eurocentric approaches to communication studies. As a result, Daniel decided to write fervently and frequently about this topic, beginning with mainstream communication journals such as *Today's Speech, Speech Teacher,* and the *Journal of Communication.* Likewise, he exposed this conundrum in interdisciplinary Black Studies journals such as *Black Lines* and *Black Scholar* and as part of communication textbooks. This was redoubled by his efforts within the Speech Communication Association as he helped to lay the foundation for the emergence of the Black Caucus, whose primary mission was curricular and disciplinary reform.

❖ CONCLUSION

Throughout Jack L. Daniel's entire career, he has been a champion for radical progressive change. He has tirelessly fought for cultural inclusiveness and distinction. He has taught, mentored, and led communication scholars. His research has influenced generations of scholars—and does so today. In his latest book, *We Fish: The Journey to Fatherhood* (Daniel & Daniel, 2002), he and his son Omari developed a work of "creative nonfiction" that surpasses while integrating the genres of nonfiction and creative writing. They did so while sharing their autobiographical narratives about family, manhood, fatherhood, culture, and intergenerational learning. This book, with its unbridled depiction of their lives, was complemented by recollections of fishing, their principal father-son bonding activity. Through poetry, letters, and prose, the authors revealed the deeper multifaceted meanings of everyday life as someone's child, brother, husband, uncle, and relative, but also as Black men living in a country that regularly dismisses and pathologizes Black males. The book is designed to innovatively address these concerns "outside the confines of sociopolitical texts" (Daniel & Daniel, 2002, p. 2), and they do so with forceful accuracy, compelling narrative, and powerful imagery.

We Fish: The Journey to Fatherhood is an excellent example of why Daniel is considered a pioneer in communication research. He was not the founder of the field of African American communication, but that his originality, his commitment to positive social change, and his approaches to communication inquiry have significantly affected the development of communication studies on class, African American oral discourse, and institutionalized racial biases. As a pioneer of communication research, Daniel rightfully has been nicknamed "The Conductor" because of his undying dedication to community uplift.

❖ REFERENCES

ABCNews.com. (August 20, 2004). The name game: Can a Black sounding name hurt your career prospects? Retrieved August 25, 2004, from abc-news.go.com/sections/2020/Business/Black_Names_040820.html.

Daniel, J. E., & Daniel, J. L. (1998). Preschool children's selection of race-related personal names. *Journal of Black Studies, 28*(4), 471–490.

Daniel, J. L. (1968). *Effective and ineffective communication on the parts of professionals and nonprofessionals when communicating with poor people.* Unpublished doctoral dissertation, University of Pittsburgh, Pittsburgh.

Daniel, J. L. (1969a). The poor, aliens in an affluent society: Cross-cultural communication. *Today's Speech, 18*(1), 15–21.

Daniel, J. L. (1974). (Ed.). *Black communication: Dimensions of research and instruction.* Annandale, VA: Speech Communication Association.

Daniel, J. L. (1979). *The wisdom of sixth Mount Zion from the members of sixth Mount Zion and those who begot them.* Pittsburgh, PA: Author.

Daniel, J. L. (1995). *Changing the players and the game: A personal account of the Speech Communication Association Black Caucus origins.* Annandale, VA: Speech Communication Association.

Daniel, J. L., & Daniel, J. E. (1999). African American childrearing: The context of a hot stove. In T. J. Socha & R. C. Diggs (Eds.), *Communication, race and family: Exploring communication in Black, White, and biracial families* (pp. 25–44). Mahwah, NJ: Lawrence Erlbaum.

Daniel, J. L., & Daniel, O. C. (2002). *We fish: The journey to fatherhood.* Pittsburgh, PA: University of Pittsburgh Press.

Daniel, J. L., & Effinger, M. (1996). Bosom biscuits: A study of African American intergenerational communication. *Journal of Black Studies, 27*(2), 183–195.

Daniel. J. L., & Smitherman-Donaldson, G. (1976). How I got over: Communication dynamics in the Black community. *Quarterly Journal of Speech, 62*(1), 26–39.

Daniel. J. L., Smitherman-Donaldson, G., & Jeremiah, M. (1987). Makin' a way outa no way: The proverb tradition in the Black experience. *Journal of Black Studies, 17*(4), 482–508.

Fanon, F. (1965). *The wretched of the earth.* New York: Grove Press.

Marable, M. (2000). Introduction: Black studies and the racial mountain. In M. Marable (Ed.), *Dispatches from the ebony tower: Intellectuals confront the African American experience* (pp. 1-28). New York: Columbia University Press.

Mbiti, J. (1992). *African religions and philosophies.* Portsmouth, NH: Heinemann.

Further Reading

Daniel. J. L. (1969b). Black folks and speech education. *Speech Teacher, 19*(2), 123–129.

Daniel. J. L. (March 1969). The facilitation of White-Black communication. *Journal of Communication, 20*(2), 134–141.

Daniel. J. L. (Spring 1971). (Guest Ed.). *Today's Speech*, 1–73.

Daniel. J. L. (1972). Towards an ethnography of Afro-American proverbial usage. *Black Lines*, 2(4), 3–12.

Daniel. J. L. (1981). Black culture (English) in perspective. In G. Smitherman (Ed.), *Black English and the education of Black children and youth* (pp. 289–301). Detroit: Wayne State University Press.

Daniel. J. L. (1983). Black children: Counteracting bias in early childhood. *Interracial Books for Children Bulletin*, 14(7/8), 8.

Daniel. J. L., Daniel, J. E., Poag, L. & Smitherman-Donaldson, G. (1987). The nurturing roles of Black church women. *The Griot*, 6(3), 33–43.

Jack L. Daniel

Photo courtesy of Jack L. Daniel

Early 1940s	Born in Johnstown, Pennsylvania.
1963	Received bachelor's degree in psychology from the University of Pittsburgh.
1965	Received master's degree in communication from the University of Pittsburgh.
1967	Became assistant professor, Central Michigan University.
1968	Received doctorate in communications from the University of Pittsburgh. Wrote dissertation on "Effective and Ineffective Communication on the Parts of Professionals and Nonprofessionals When Communicating with Poor People." Became assistant professor of Communication, University of Pittsburgh.
1969	Was guest editor of *The Speech Teacher*: "Black Folks and Speech Education." Published "Communication Breakdowns between Middle Class and Poor People," in *Today's Speech*. Later edited a special issue of *Today's Speech* based solely on black communication in 1971. Served as consultant for implementation of Black Studies at the University of Dayton, Ohio. Became chair and associate professor, Department of Black Studies, University of Pittsburgh (from 1969 to 1973).
1970	Served as member of board of directors of the *Journal of Black Studies* at UCLA (from 1970 to 1972).

1972	Received Faculty of Arts and Sciences Research Grant for studying "Afro-American Proverbial Usage at the University of Pittsburgh."
	Served as member of board of directors of the American Red Cross, Pittsburgh, Pennsylvania.
1973	American Council on Education Fellow, Stanford University.
1974	Edited *Black Communication: Dimensions of Research and Instruction.*
1974	Became associate dean, College of Arts and Sciences and associate professor, University of Pittsburgh (1974 through 1978).
1976	Published *How I Got Over: Communication Dynamics in the Black Community* with Geneva Smitherman.
1977	Became secretary, National Communication Association Black Caucus.
1980	Served as member of the board of directors of INROADS/Pittsburgh, Inc.
1984	Became associate professor of Communication, University of Pittsburgh (1984 to present).
1986	Studied at the Institute for Educational Management, Harvard University.
1988	Became vice president and then president, National Communication Association Black Caucus (1988 to 1989).
1990	Published "How I Got Over and Continue to Do So In Our Mothers' Churches" with Geneva Smitherman-Donaldson.
1992	Became vice provost of Academic Affairs, University of Pittsburgh (1992 to present).
1995	National Communication Association held the "Spotlight Program on the Contributions of Jack L. Daniel."
	Published *Changing the Players and the Game: A Personal Account of the Speech Communication Association Black Caucus Origins.*
1997	Received the National Communication Association's "Presidential Award for Contribution to the Black Caucus."
	Became interim dean, College of General Studies, University of Pittsburgh (1977 to 1979).
2000	Published *We Fish* with Omari Daniel.
2001	Became vice provost and interim dean of student affairs, University of Pittsburgh (2001 to present).

6

Oscar H. Gandy, Jr.

Production for the market is a defining aspect of capitalist relations in the production of culture. ... Understanding the nature of the process of commoditization is central to our perspective on the changing importance of race and race relations to the supply of media materials with racial content.  *Commodification represents a shift in the locus of power over production decisions. Prior to commodification, goods were produced on the basis of their potential for meeting individual and social needs. As commodities, the decision about whether or not to produce a particular good is based upon whether or not it can produce a profit in the marketplace.*

(Gandy, 1998, pp. 99–100)

❖ INTRODUCTION

Oscar H. Gandy, the Herbert I. Schiller Term Professor in the Annenberg School for Communication at University of Pennsylvania, is a leading communication scholar in the United States. Gandy specializes in the intersections of race, media responsibility, information technology, political economy, and surveillance. In the mid-1970s, when computing technology was in its infancy stage of development in the United States, Gandy was completing a dissertation on the confluence of technology-driven instructional/informational systems as governmental commodities and the pervasive impact of public and industrial economic capital. His primary concern, as implied by the opening quote, was with how government subsidies used for the promotion of online instruction were actually part of a political strategy to enhance big business and produce a capitalist-driven instructional economy. After Sputnik, the development of information technology for educational purposes was seen by the United States as an advantage that would strategically position the United States favorably with respect to its competitor, the Soviet Union.

By examining the use of power in this way Gandy could situate his critical-theoretic writings very early in his career, critiquing structured systems of information technology and public policy. Although poststructuralism has come to carry many meanings, it can be argued that Gandy's work falls on the cusp of the domains of Marxist critique and very early communication-related poststructuralist studies as it pertains to the way in which politically fragmented institutionalized structures such as media industries seek to govern and constrain societies. Although Marxists believe that the state monitors and controls the people via structured practices, poststructuralists do not agree that surveillance is the sole province of the state. In fact, they would argue that everyone participates in surveillance—and that it is a principal influence on the social construction of identities. Gandy applied a Marxist perspective in his early writings, and much of that perspective continued later, but he has developed a broader perspective on who constitutes a media audience and how media privacy is maintained. Applying his background in sociology, economics, and communication behavior, Gandy published his first two books: *Government and Media: An Annotated Bibliography* (1975) and *Beyond Agenda Setting: Information Subsidies and Public Policy* (1982), which has become one of his most frequently cited and foundational works. As his career has progressed, many of his writings remain nuanced and well-received.

While in college at University of New Mexico for two years, Gandy's interest in critically assessing institutional structures was being shaped by his participation in and association with a number of left-wing organizations as well as his exposure to the ideas of radical scholars such as Howard Meier. Meier, a unionist and mine organizer-turned-sociologist, was one of Gandy's professors and for whom Gandy worked as a research assistant. While at University of New Mexico, Gandy protested and demonstrated against governmental structures that disenfranchised or discriminated against marginalized groups. After having studied or taken classes with a slew of radical scholars—from Emile McAnany to Martin Carnoy and Hank Levin—Gandy was armed with a radical consciousness and a will to fight for peace and justice. Over the years, these internal driving forces have carried over into much of his work concerning topics from racial segmentation and discrimination in information technology studies to studies of conflicts between corporate and consumer interests with respect to media privacy and surveillance.

Gandy has been a writer, producer, and director of public access television programs as well as a prolific scholar and active leader in the field of communication. Given his many contributions, it is easy to speak effusively about his research. In this chapter, we will broaden our discussion to include his personal background, academic experiences, contributions to the field of communication, and a list of selected references from his body of writings.

❖ BIOGRAPHICAL INFORMATION

On August 24, 1944, Oscar H. Gandy was born in Amityville, New York to Rita and Oscar Gandy, Sr. Unfortunately, he did not get to know his parents well because his mother was hospitalized for much of his life, and his father chose not to support his wife and children. Gandy lamented, "He escaped to Canada shortly after finding out that his wife was ill" (O. Gandy, personal communication, May 15, 2004). As Gandy's mother's health declined and eventually led to her dying of cancer, his father was absent without leave. A Korean War veteran, Oscar Gandy, Sr. worked for awhile in the aerospace industry—on the assembly line at Grumman Aircraft in Long Island, in particular—so he had enough experience to become an inspector in a manufacturing plant at Canadian Airlines. He took the job in Canada and left his family. Gandy's aunt, Clifford Fitz, reared him and his sister, Sheila. Gandy described her as "a marvelous woman, an intellectual without a whole lot of book learning, but she made sure we had everything we ever needed and quite a bit of what we wanted as well" (O. Gandy, personal communication, May 15, 2004).

Gandy's aunt Clifford was educated at Tuskegee Institute, an historically Black college in Tuskegee, Alabama, which was founded by Booker T. Washington and developed to enhance the condition of Blacks by training them in industrial education. With that paradigmatic model, she was trained in interior decorating and upholstery refurbishment. Although it is unclear whether Clifford ever finished college, with her training she worked as a freelance interior designer, usually for White people who needed her services in their homes. When she was not doing that, Clifford worked as a domestic, cooking and cleaning in White people's homes. Although she "never really had too many pennies to rub together" (O. Gandy, personal communication, May 15, 2004), she knew she had to work very hard to financially support Gandy and Sheila. Yet she was never heard to complain and she clearly wanted to ensure that the two children had the best education and exposure to the arts that she could afford—by paying tuition to send them to private Catholic schools for their entire elementary and secondary education.

Gandy's aunt Clifford died while he was still in high school, and she was unable to see Gandy graduate with his associate of arts degree from Nassau Community College. After she passed, Gandy's grandmother, Maggie Williams, became a parental figure for Gandy and his sister. Because Gandy was 23 years old, Maggie was not necessarily a legal guardian for both of them, but still provided a place to call home. Maggie (who worked at Sperry Gyroscope Corporation as a line cook) was very proud that upon his graduation from Nassau Community College, Gandy was hired by Sperry as an engineering clerk. He recalled recognizing that this was clearly part of the company's sympathetic program of diversity hiring, but he noticed that when his grandmother would be working on the steam tables and "look up to see me getting lunch in the cafeteria where she worked, she was very proud" (O. Gandy, personal communication, May 15, 2004).

❖ ACADEMIC BACKGROUND AND EXPERIENCE

Gandy's aunt Clifford insisted that he and his sister go to Catholic schools, so they attended parochial schools for 12 years. Gandy and Sheila went to grade school at Our Lady of Loretto, a three-mile walk from their home. Gandy received his secondary education at Chaminade High School (both schools are in the Nassau County, New York area). Gandy remarked in a personal interview with the first author of this book:

When I was at Chaminade, I was not a good student. I was just a bad kid, always misbehaving. It eventually got me kicked out, but after my aunt straightened me out, she begged them to accept me back. I had already had these plans that I would go to Canada to live with my father, but then I was accepted back into the school so that never happened. (O. Gandy, personal communication, May 15, 2004)

Gandy graduated from Chaminade High School, but not without a personal struggle. He gained weight and ballooned to 260 pounds. Without much guidance, Gandy then decided to enroll at Nassau Community College. It was a tumultuous time for the nation during his first year because President John Fitzgerald Kennedy had just been assassinated. The national tone was intense, and the civil rights movement was well under way. For Gandy, however, this tumult did not necessarily affect his consciousness in any noticeable way until some time later. In 1964, Gandy graduated with an associate of arts degree and began working at Sperry Gyroscope Corporation as an engineering clerk. He cynically described himself as "the spook who sat by the door" (O. Gandy, personal communication, May 15, 2004) because that was actually where his desk was located—at the front door to the engineering section. Because it seemed to Gandy that he was the only African American working in that area, Sperry was an isolated place for him, and he worked there for only a year before leaving New York.

Gandy decided that he wanted to be more independent, so he applied to two schools: the University of California at Berkeley and the University of New Mexico (UNM). He chose to attend the University of New Mexico and enrolled as a sociology major. Of course, he already had a two-year degree, so he needed only two more years to receive a bachelor's degree. The two years at the University of New Mexico, from 1965 to 1967, represented a crucial time in Gandy's life. He noted, "During those two years, much of my formative development took place—politically, socially, culturally, and intellectually" (O. Gandy, personal communication, May 15, 2004). Gandy elected to commute rather than live in the dormitory, so he moved to an adobe apartment, which had a muddy exterior and a dusty interior. Although the apartment was a bit messy at times, its rent was only $28 per month, and it was seen as a unique place to live—not to mention that Gandy appreciated his landlord and the neighbors. As Gandy remembered, "The multicultural mix of people in New Mexico at that time was tremendous. It was an awesome place to be. We would go out to the Pueblos' reservation and would be allowed to watch ceremonial dances and rituals with Kachinas, which were ceremonial figures on stilts that were like shadow figures. It was truly fascinating" (Oscar H. Gandy, personal communication, May 15, 2004).

Gandy's ideological transformation occurred during this period as well. He was associated with both the Du Bois Club and the Students for a Democratic Society (SDS). The Du Bois club was a far left-wing group that was rooted in activist community involvement, and the SDS was a New Left group that was part of the peace movement. Gandy was most involved with the SDS, although had close ties to the Du Bois Club. He developed a very strong identification with the radical left and the antiwar movement, and he became a sponge for ideas related to radical revolution. During Gandy's matriculation at UNM, he became a research assistant for Harold Meier, who was a unionist who became an organizer for mine workers before transitioning careers to become a professor. Meier was very interested in examining whether people were able to move across class lines through education. Gandy's job as research assistant was to do cross-tabulations on Meier's data. Gandy used a cumbersome, noisy, and error-ridden research apparatus known as a Frieden calculator to do data entry processing. Fortunately, remote data entry processing was also becoming more available, so Gandy learned how to use that instead. He also used punch cards, which needed to be taken to a lab for processing. Gandy's work was a valuable resource for Professor Meier, and Gandy was treated as a core-searcher. It was especially exciting to be working with a noted sociologist doing survey-based research, manipulating data, and helping to interpret results about social mobility among generations. Besides working with Meier, Gandy also expanded his knowledge about learning psychology and social movement research. This was a also a time of personal experimentation for Gandy. He demonstrated and protested against the establishment and developed a sense of who he was. Gandy also developed an interest in motorcycle riding during this time, so he owned two motorcycles and joined a group of cyclists who called themselves the "Motorcycle Timing Association." They would time balloons to be released during speeches as a way to protest, and involve themselves in other protest and demonstration activities. As he explains, "it was a coming-of-age time of my life" (O. Gandy, personal communication, May 15, 2004).

After graduating with a sociology degree from UNM, Gandy applied to University of Pennsylvania and was admitted into its Social Work program. He and Nikki Giovanni were in the Social Work master's degree program at the same time and they both left the program before completing their degrees. Gandy briefly had a subspecialty in community organization before realizing that the program was not what he needed. He realized it while doing his practicum at a West Philadelphia community organization with a White supervisor who seemed incompetent. Gandy decided that the situation, coupled with his discomfort in the program, was enough to make the experience not worthwhile for him. So he left Philadelphia to go to Oakland, California, where a gay friend of his from UNM's Du Bois Club was involved in the Black Panther Party. He stayed in the basement of his friend's house, selling encyclopedias to pay his way. Briefly after he arrived in Oakland, a female friend of his named Judith invited him to return home and offered her apartment as a place to stay for a while, but Gandy noted, "As the story goes, I came back and never left" (O. Gandy, personal communication, May 15, 2004). The two of them met at an antiwar mobilization dance organized to raise money to charter a bus to go to a series of demonstrations against the war. He accepted her invitation and moved back to Philadelphia in 1968. Within a year, Gandy and Judith found themselves at Woodstock in upstate New York to enjoy the music, the mud, and the madness of the time. Although they were initially were just friends, they found themselves very attracted to one another and were married within two years after Gandy's return to the area.

Other events were also taking place in Gandy's life. As fate would have it, noted communication scholar and progenitor of cultivation theory, George Gerbner, discovered Gandy and invited him to reapply to the University of Pennsylvania, this time in the Walter H. Annenberg School for Communication's master's degree program. Gandy was honored, immediately accepted the invitation to apply, and was admitted in 1968. A year later, in 1969, Gandy became a writer and producer for a community affairs program, targeted at the African American community, which he named *Right On!*. The program was sponsored by WCAU-TV, a CBS affiliate. The title and content of the program was perhaps more incendiary Gandy initially imagined. He knew it would spark some attention because "right on!" was the phrase the Black Panther Party coined. Despite the good things the Panthers did for communities—such as food and clothing drives—the media attempted to destroy their credibility by referring to them as civilly disobedient troublemakers and violent organizers. Although no network television affiliates dependent on corporate advertising dollars wanted to be associated with that kind of organization, *Right On!* survived for two years, mainly because Gandy had a very supportive director of community programming, Inez Gottlieb. It also succeeded because the content did what it was supposed to do—address community concerns. Even after a special consumer-education documentary program called

"Check It Out" was aired, which featured University of Pennsylvania student Olu Hassan Ali doing critical interpretations of consumptive politics, Gottlieb's undying support was there. Gottlieb, a friend of Ruby Dee and Ossie Davis, supported both Gandy and the host of *Right On!*, Bill Adams. Gandy recalled that Adams always ended his show with the phrase, "Be black, stay black and keep moving. Right on!" After two years writing for and producing the show, Gandy chose to concentrate solely on his research and graduate studies. He was never really interested in the corporate aspects of television; his involvement was driven by his interest in community organization, part of the social work background he had cultivated at the University of Pennsylvania. Gandy finished his coursework, wrote his thesis, graduated with his master of arts degree in communication behavior, and began considering his next steps.

George Gerbner, considered by Gandy to be the only mentor he has ever had, knew that Gandy would be looking to continue his work in media after earning his master's degree. Grebner recommended Gandy to his friend, Herbert I. Schiller, at the University of California at San Diego (UCSD). Herb Schiller was looking for someone to teach television production, build a studio, and supervise students in the studio. He knew that Gandy was ideal for the job, so he made an offer. Gandy accepted and embarked on one of the most valuable and important opportunities of his career. Schiller had just written *Superstate: Readings in the Military-Industrial Complex* (1970) and was working on his next book, *The Mind Managers* (1973), to be released three years later. Both these monographs were important texts concerning the political and economic effects of state apparatus.

Schiller was developing a college called the Lumumba-Zapata College within UCSD (Maxwell, 2003). The college was named after Patrice Lumumba, the first prime minister of the democratic Republic of the Congo, and Emiliano Zapata, the Mexican revolutionary. Schiller's leading role in establishing this college came as an invitation from the students and administration after student protests for a more conscious university effort to critically address the fragmentation of justice and the state of political unrest within its curriculum and elsewhere. Until his death in 2000, Schiller was a radical, left-wing political economist interested in the corporatization of ideas and ideals, which constricted information flows and freedom of expression. The college underwent several name transformations: Lumumba-Zapata College, Third College (because it was the third college of the university and it implicitly referenced third world people), and Marshall College, to honor Thurgood Marshall. Although the college was designed to address the concerns of marginalized peoples and was to be populated by African American, Hispanic American, Native American, and progressive White students, the racial climate at the time became so overwhelming that it severely counteracted the mission of the college.

UCSD was a great place to be for the radical left in the early 1970s, especially with scholars such as Herb Schiller and noted media responsibility and public culture researcher Mike Real. Gandy arrived in 1971 and was there for two years before entering Stanford University's doctoral program in Public Affairs Communication. At Stanford, Gandy was thoroughly trained in a very different orientation to the study of education—the economics of education. His training came from several Marxist professors, such as John (Jack) Gurley, who was a finance professor who wrote a book called *Challengers to Capitalism: Marx, Lenin, , Stalin and Mao* (Gurley, 1998), which became an important tool for Gandy when discussing radical economic perspectives. During his doctoral program, Gandy's cognate in economics became critical to his intellectual development. Gandy learned economics of development, economics of health, economics of technology, economics of education, and so forth. He was immersed in examining institutions from various economic standpoints. One major influence on his work was Emile McAnany, now Walter E. Schmidt Professor of Communication at Santa Clara University. McAnany's research on the role of information in media development, particularly cultural industries and global audience consumption, was instrumental in helping Gandy to conceptualize how audiences receive information and how media structure information, as well as how communication development functions most successfully. During this time, he also honed his multimethodological orientation by learning quantitative, qualitative, and critical methods and analytic techniques.

Gandy developed his TrEE model around this time, for which he is most well-known in many academic circles. The acronym TrEE stood for Transformation, Effectiveness, and Efficiency. In a conference paper that later became the impetus for his work in Tanzania, he explained that successful initiatives pertaining to African development are dependent upon not only the presence of various imports such as technology, food, and other resources but also upon how effective and efficient the imports are and their transformative capacity. Consider, for example, the tsunami disaster of December 2004. Nearly 300,000 people in Somalia, Sri Lanka, Thailand, and other countries were killed by the sudden rush of tsunami waves caused by an earthquake in Sumatra that shifted two very large tectonic plates that control the sea floor of India and most of Southeast Asia. With the massive destruction that left thousands of survivors homeless and without basic resources, these developing countries are still trying to recover. With Gandy's model in operation, relief efforts have to consider not just the number of resources being flown in from various humanitarian agencies but also how effective those resources are in recuperating communities and how efficiently the recovery process is running. In other words, as one set of communities is getting relief, are there newly arising issues that are springing up when another set is being been resolved? Also, progress has to be measured by considering the area's economic stability. For the relief measures to restore the country, they must have transformative capacity, which is evidenced by a variety of factors including restabilization of housing and real estate, employment, health care, education, and so on. It is only when the effectiveness, efficiency, and transformative capacity are aligned that a relief and development model can be said to be successful. Although seemingly quite complex, it was designed as a simple and instructive model, and has become one of which Gandy is very proud.

While completing his doctoral coursework, Gandy took classes from two very well-known scholars who influenced his work: Martin Carnoy, professor of education and economics, and Hank Levin, another radical political economist professor. They shaped Gandy's dissertation and facilitated perspectives on "education production functions," the idea that if a school can be metaphorically understood as a factory, we need to not only understand and assess the products but also the inputs and outputs if we are to properly comprehend and evaluate school systems. This is a line of research that has evolved to the extant resurgence of what is now understood as human capital theory. Gandy's dissertation was thus a pastiche of concepts explored in various classes such as Marxist political economy as well as economics of education and technology all angled to examine "Instructional technology and the reselling of the Pentagon" (O. Gandy, personal communication, May 15, 2004), a manuscript that adopted much of Herbert Schiller's political and theoretical positions. In this manuscript, Gandy criticized a capitalist subsidy for education, for introducing technology into schools—what Gandy called the capitalization of education. He believed that if the promoters of education technologies were to be successful, they would need to have a cadre of educators who were technologists and supporting monopoly firms that would capture the industry. In this case, the industry was that of defense contractors. The idea was to reveal how capitalism worked while initiating a political strategy concerning information technology. So, if capital could be understood as a catalyst for change within big government structures, it could use its influence to provide an economic subsidy for the process of managing information technology demand. Of course, it turned out that it did not change teaching because teachers still maintained power and authority.

Before graduating from Stanford in 1976 with a doctorate in Public Affairs Communication, Gandy and Judith adopted a baby girl and named her Imani. When Imani was almost two years old, Gandy graduated from Stanford, traveled to India and Tanzania, and then returned to a post-doctoral fellowship at the Annenberg School. While at Annenberg, he received two job offers: from the University of Illinois at Urbana-Champaign and from Howard University. He decided to go to Howard University, and he claimed:

> [Howard University] was the best thing that happened to me, intellectually and in terms of developing my racial identity. I had been the only Black kid throughout my high school years and the only Black kid in my graduating class at Stanford. And now I was teaching at an all Black school. . . . I learned a lot about myself and about how Africans and African Americans relate to one another and approach education. (O. Gandy, personal communication, May 15, 2004)

He had colleagues and colleagues with spouses who had socialist orientations, and Gandy was married to the daughter of Jewish communists. So, he found many commonalities in terms of perspective and worldview across the university.

At Howard University, Gandy was hired to teach television production, but he preferred doing research on media rather than media production. After earning tenure and having taught production for about eight years, he was able to delve into a more prominent research role as director of Howard's newly forming Center for Communications Research. In 1987, he was appointed to the faculty at the University of Pennsylvania's Annenberg School for Communication. Gandy is still there, and is now serving as Herbert I. Schiller Professor of Communication.

❖ CONTRIBUTIONS TO COMMUNICATION RESEARCH

Oscar H. Gandy has developed several lines of research throughout his career, as indicated by the dates noted in parentheses next to each theme he has addressed in his publications. Yet, these lines of research are not to be understood exclusively because much of his research overlaps with other lines. We have simply provided several themes to capture some of the complexities of his work in several areas of mass media studies. There are four rubrics noted: (1) Information Technology and Educational Subsidy; (2) Race, Discrimination, Segmentation, Media Framing and Media Consumption; (3) Privacy and Surveillance; and (4) Media Development.

Information Technology, Educational
Subsidy, and Media Framing (1975–2003)

Gandy's work on information technology and education subsidy arose out of his training related to Marxism and political economy studies. The tasks of Marxist critique and political economics are to expose the production, distribution, and "sale" of technologies, bureaucracies, and social relations to ultimately overturn the social order toward greater human good. In uncovering the complexities of bureaucratic practices, Gandy also expounded upon the nature of market structures and capitalist-driven economies. In *Beyond Agenda Setting: Information Subsidies and Public Policy* (Gandy, 1982) and in several articles concerning information subsidies in health, Gandy deconstructed how media education is laced with political intentions. Using an information theory approach, Gandy also analyzed survey data he received from George Gerbner about media headlines in nursing-related news stories. For Gerbner, this was useless data, but Gandy discovered a gold mine. As he sifted through the data, he found that the headlines were often quite different from the news story. He became intrigued with what this meant with respect to which headlines get selected for different audience segments. Gandy explained:

I pursued the idea that it had something to do with the nature of the market. It had something to do with the nature of the audience and the headline writers and the editors' perception of the audience that would explain the headline. I argued that it was the extent to which the people in those markets were dependent upon the healthcare system. That would explain whether or not the newspaper would publish what I characterized as the "scare" headline—"Doctors Cause Death," and this, lo and behold, explained a lot of variance across those markets, in the newspapers that I had, on the basis of the expenditures that were being made in those markets. These expenditures were being made for prescription and non-prescription drugs. Essentially, there were market factors that could explain content. (O. Gandy, personal communication, May 15, 2004)

Gandy (1980a; 1981) published two studies related to health information and subsidized news, in which he argued that news story content and headlines were not innocently constructed. Instead, they were framed for certain audiences. This same logic continued for studies of race-related news stories.

Race, Discrimination, Segmentation and Media Consumption (1979–2003)

The study of race, discrimination, market segmentation, and media consumption is one of the most significant areas of Gandy's research. He has written most frequently on this topic, and his capstone writing on this theme came with the release of *Communication and Race: A Structural Perspective* (1998). The impetus for Gandy's exploration of media consumption practices emanated from his early work with the nursing study described earlier. In those works, he concerned himself with market factors that could explain media content. For example, if the target media audience were composed of elderly people reliant on prescription drugs, producers of media content would attempt to reflect the concerns of that audience via pertinent headlines and themes. Likewise, Gandy found that racial segmentation occurred in media markets in which there was a high concentration of certain races. So, racial composition led to race-related news stories and stories framed to appeal to or agitate readers of that race-related market segment (Davis & Gandy, 1999; Gandy, Kopp, Hands, Frazer, & Phillips, 1997).

Although many scholars have discussed minority representations in the news (Dixon & Linz, 2000; Entman, 1992; Entman & Rojecki, 2000), Gandy heuristically studied the use of a discrimination frame based on the proportion of minorities in a given market of several newspapers. He discovered that the press tended to promote structural practices that reinforced stereotypes of minorities (Gandy et al, 1997; Goshorn & Gandy, 1995; Dates & Gandy, 1985). Because of the latent discrimination inherent in such practices, such bias virtually went unnoticed. Gandy recognized that these practices are not the result of consumer demand; they are instead the result of a larger mainstream institutional agenda to suppress minority voices, lives, and perspectives—leaving them on the margins and as perennial targets for discrimination. These divisive structures are enwrapped in audience production functions. In trying to make sense of programming decisions, Gandy extended Hank Levin and Martin Carnoy's idea of "education production functions" to include "audience production functions," which are the result of seeing media audiences as products of a system that has its own market inputs and outputs that influence how it will function (Gandy, 1979; Gandy & Signorielli, 1981).

Media use is also intricately connected to press coverage. Gandy posited:

> Depending on the ways in which the problem of inequality is framed, then, press coverage may lead citizens toward, or away from, support of particular public policies. Although the response of individuals to media constructions seems also to vary in response to social similarities and differences in their background and social circumstance, the influence of media is substantial. (Gandy, et al, 1997, p. 160)

If Blacks, for example, are framed in news stories as violent criminals, poverty-stricken, uneducated, and morally incapacitated, that is the way some audience members will begin to perceive Blacks because they will sense that they have enough evidence from the media to justify such a posture. The impact on social perceptions is especially adverse when the media framing begins to place the responsibility of structured disadvantage on minorities because audiences are manipulated into believing that minority victims of social problems are entirely or primarily at fault. Media facilitates these ideas via frames.

In their study of 29 newspapers and more than 6,000 individual stories about cross-racial social, economic, and health disparities, as well as general inequalities and discriminatory practices, Gandy et al (1997) noted that four of the most frequent frames were as follows: (1) the relatively high probability of Black loss or disease, (2) the lower probability of Black success, (3) the greater probability of White success, and (4) the lower probability of White loss or disease. Gandy and his associates found that newspapers published in places in which there is considerable Black political power and/or educational attainment tended to have significantly fewer news stories about Black loss. In other words, the frames were less stereotypical. If constraints can be defined as "the ability to predict agreement, acceptance, or rejection of an idea based on other variables" (Davis & Gandy, 1999, p. 371), then certainly the journalistic constraints are lessened in regions in which minority racial compositions are high and there is an exceptional amount of privilege enjoyed by minorities. The implications are clear: Communities in which Blacks enjoy more political clout and resources are less likely to accept discrimination as a reason for low success, so they are not inundated as much with negative references and journalistic constraints on news framing. In other situations, in which the city is larger and the political clout is minimal, this practice of negative framing continues, although it absolves any responsibility of government and policymakers and leaves a deleterious strain on human relations.

Gandy has explored media programming, media use, and press constraints related to African Americans. His research has yielded penetrating results that have revealed patterns of consumption, ideological orientations, media framing, and media evaluation. His work boldly criticized media for its discriminatory practices and deceptive regimes of truth. In his examination of racially coded media content, he uncovered structural tendencies that promote negative racial representations. Additionally, he found that media exposure is, in the first place, an individual choice that is determined by a variety of factors related to personal background. Contrary to media's stereotypical biases, however, the effects of media can lead to an enhanced racial group identity and media orientation (Barber & Gandy, 1990; Davis & Gandy, 1999; Gandy & Baron, 1998; Gandy, Matabane, & Omachonu, 1987).

Privacy and Surveillance (1986–2003)

Although media reliance and uses vary significantly, media privacy is always a concern. The word *surveillance* has always had a negative connotation in the United States. Gandy (1989c) asserted that modern surveillance consists of software that senses information about the environment around it. This software is then used to determine the attendance of people and how active they are being. Still called "the new technology," computer technology allows for unknown, unbiased sources to process all types of information and to track Web site visitation patterns. Also, post-September 11, surveillance is also being used to determine whether an individual has the possibility to commit a crime rather than to see if they have actually already committed a crime. The problem is that it creates stereotypes of individuals who commit crimes. Many people of specific age, race, and sex are being searched because of past observations. Furthermore, more and more businesses are now using surveillance as a way to monitor the productivity of workers. Gandy suggested that the United States is the largest supporter and consumer of surveillance. The Internal Revenue Service even uses surveillance to obtain information about money spending and annual income.

The threats to privacy are also present in simple household surveys. From 1978 to 1984, it was found that a majority of citizens felt that polling individuals was helpful and helped businesses make products better for the consumer. In 1983, however, another poll found that the majority of individuals were concerned about their privacy, especially in the credit industry. Gandy pointed out that the government also found many ways to get around the privacy laws that were created in the United States. Although many individuals hate getting junk mail and sales calls, they never asked to be "taken off the list." In 2004, legislation was approved that allowed consumers to call a government number to be "taken off the list" that businesses use to generate phone calls to consumers asking for their opinions. Privacy is one of the most critical aspects of new information technology.

Gandy's landmark book, *The Panoptic Sort: A Political Economy of Personal Information* (1993a), systematically examined the nature of surveillance within media industries by adopting the metaphor of the Panopticon. According to Foucault (1980), the Panopticon was a nineteenth century prison structure that allowed "prisoners" to see without being seen, and the "prisoners" were not entirely imprisoned by the state. This is the way Foucualt envisioned the nature of social and ideological discipline. Rather than being disciplined solely by the state, people disciplined themselves via surveillance. Gandy explained that this is also the way media industries operate; they develop certain frames, involuted by stereotypes and social constructions, which are efficiently maintained by social systems so that people use these frames to develop daily impressions about others while also coming to "discipline" themselves. The machinations of this discursive disciplining process automatically call into question whether people can independently construct their worldviews or whether these constructions are inherited and recycled through multiple discourses. Likewise, as Gandy's work facilitated discovery of the origins of these discourses, he also examined how stereotypical impulses are sustained by the media, and how minority audiences are compelled to use media despite the potentially damaging effects.

In 1993, Gandy found that although attitudes toward privacy as a public policy concern were increasing, little research had been done that examined these attitudes in isolation. Instead, a spate of studies had been completed that included privacy issues as a question on a survey, and many of these surveys were produced by corporations. In his book, *African Americans and Privacy* (1993b), Gandy analyzed the use of media by Blacks. His results indicated that Blacks were increasingly wary of any threats to maintaining privacy despite their exclusion from demographic marketing surveys in which their privacy would be at greater risk if they chose to participate. He intuited:

> African Americans appear to be concerned about privacy because the loss of control over personal information means greater susceptibility to discriminatory exclusion from employment, insurance, and credit. African Americans continue to be mistrustful of power, but they are apparently no more distrustful of government than other citizens. (Grady, 1993b, p. 193).

As Gandy explained in several studies concerning the competing tensions of introducing greater personal privacy at the expense of greater institutional surveillance (1989a; 1989b; 1989c; 1990a; 1990b; 1993a), the risks may severely outweigh the benefits for minorities. As marginalized group members seek to keep up with the demand for greater technological access, they have had to be even more aware of technological invasiveness. The advantages appear to be too great to ignore, but there are aspects of these innovations that raise many privacy concerns, as Gandy illustrated in his studies of audience tracking and caller ID technologies. Truly, capitalism has complicated interracial relationships and has inspired the inequitable distribution of resources to minorities. Likewise, capitalism has encouraged minorities to take a look at risks and to be ever-cautious of new ways big business and government seek to institute nuanced discriminatory and segmentation practices and policies that further promote social division. The most frightening revelation of Gandy's work is that technologies, like the politics that drive them, are amoral (Gandy & Baron, 1998). It is not that they are immoral, but that they have little to no regard for morality, so the ethical principles that should govern mainstream technological practices are instead devoid of them, unless somehow enforced as a result of consumer demand. Privacy and surveillance are not inherently negative aspects of technology; it is how they are enacted and secured within a market-driven economy that becomes problematic.

Media Development (1983–1992)

So far, we have discussed Gandy's research related to technological innovations in the United States. The concerns of new media and technology in the United States (a super power) are quite different from those of developing nations. In another line of research, Gandy explained practical ways to evaluate and develop media technology in third world nations. Through this part of his program of research,

Gandy encouraged the steady development of media infrastructures in third world nations (Gandy, Espinosa, & Ordover, 1983). During his tenure at Howard University, from 1977 to 1987, his work on communication and media development expanded. He traveled frequently to countries throughout Europe and Africa to examine media concerns. Prior to being appointed to the faculty at Howard University, Gandy begun working on a model for media development, which he was able to critique, expand, and apply most often while at Howard. Within this chapter, we will limit our discussion of his media development work to that paradigm.

As mentioned in the introduction to this chapter, Gandy developed his TrEE model in the early 1970s, representing Transformation, Effectiveness, and Efficiency (usually discussed in reverse order). In a conference paper that later became the impetus for his work in Tanzania, he explained that successful initiatives pertaining to African development are dependent upon not only the presence of various imports such as technology, food, and other resources but also upon how effective and efficient the imports are and their transformative capacity.

As Gandy explored the needs and assessments related to developing media in third world countries, he discovered that much of his economics and sociology background was especially useful. The principal questions were as follows: How does a country begin to develop, distribute, and use new media? What economic factors are involved in this venture? How do politics influence the development of media? How will the consumers access this new technology? What are the costs and benefits for using a new technology as opposed to keeping or enhancing the old technology? These were all questions answered in Gandy's TrEE model.

Gandy (1992a) asserted that effectiveness is about whether the new media works in a manner that is the least cumbersome and most facilitative among all technological approaches. Efficiency is cost-related. This is the most pertinent factor to consider as a third world nation considers whether to adopt new media. If a single unit is 10 times the cost of another type of unit, then deciding which is most efficient is based on outputs and money saved rather than just on monies spent. Transformation is the final aspect of the TrEE model. The primary concern of transformation is whether the institutionalization of new media will significantly enhance the nation's ability to get things done. Gandy proposed six criteria for evaluating transformative capacity: *capital import dependence* (whether the new media will require a high capital/labor ration); *labor import dependence* (whether imported labor will result in an unwanted shift of labor costs, worker habits, or salary benefits); *sectoral balances* (whether any sectors of the nation, like that of agriculture or industry, will be adversely effected by the shift to new media); *ethnic/regional balance* (whether the new media will advantage one segment of population over another); *labor force utilization* (whether there will be an imbalance in labor force because of a call for a new kind required skill); and *prestige* (whether at the advent of this new media, it will become a symbol of prestige). These six criteria, with the last one being admittedly much less significant than the others, were developed to ascertain the transformative capacity of media development. The whole TrEE model has been used in several of Gandy's other studies of media development as an evaluation model.

❖ CONCLUSION

Oscar H. Gandy has written extensively about the strategic division of communities via mass-mediated practices as well as media responsibility and regulation. He has continually argued that information technology is an important resource driven by market structures and belabored by limited structural constraints, public policies, and bureaucratic agendas. Audiences are at risk, particularly Black audiences, and public opinion polls verify this. As long as there are few media owners, there will be adverse media framing and resultant negative public opinions. Gandy's research has demonstrated that when audiences are cognizant of mediated social control and structural threats to privacy, their cognitive structures and interpretive assessments exemplify that awareness when using media. Indeed, the real racial divide in public opinion about technology is about cultural worldview and the way in which culture allows for different ways of processing information, rather than simply interracial relations in a vacuum (Gandy, 2002). Gandy argued that media influences racial and social perceptions and discourses in ways consumers are just now beginning to understand. Through his research, Gandy has shown readers how media industries function to primarily insulate their own interests without exposing either their profit-driven strategies or the risks of this kind of advancement to consumers. Gandy noticed:

We have seen the ways in which the images of people of color have changed in patterns that reflect changes in the estimates of the economic value of racially and ethnically homogenous audiences.

These shifts in evaluation have been influenced by shifts in population that have been influenced in quite complex ways by shifts in global political economy. (Gandy, 1998, p. 235)

The commoditization of minority audiences will perhaps always be a facet of capitalist media that sees people as commodities within segmented markets. As these commodities increase in value, however, so also will the voices of the people—resulting in a different kind of media framing compelled by a different set of market interests. Gandy has demonstrated this as well.

Oscar H. Gandy has been one of our most important thinkers in the field of media communication. He has adopted an interdisciplinary approach to the study of media and public opinion as well as race and surveillance. Like so many others in this volume, he has been a champion of African American inclusion as well as audience empowerment and he continues to define and lead the intellectual discourses concerning the intersections of race, media responsibility, information technology, political economy, and surveillance.

❖ REFERENCES

Dates, J. L., & Gandy, O. (1985). How ideological constraints affected coverage of the Jesse Jackson campaign. *Journalism Quarterly, 62*(3), 595–600.

Davis, J., & Gandy, O. (1999). Racial identity and media orientation: Exploring the nature of constraint. *Journal of Black Studies, 29*(3), 367–397.

Dixon, T., & Linz, D. (2000). Overrepresentation and underrepresentation of African Americans and Latinos as lawbreakers on television news. *Journal of Communication, 50*(2), 131–154.

Entman, R. M. (1992). Blacks in the news: Television, modern racism and cultural change. *Journalism Quarterly, 69*(2), 341–361.

Entman, R. M., & Rojecki, A. (2000). *The black image in the white mind: Media and race in America*. Chicago: University of Chicago Press.

Foucault, M. (1980). *Power/knowledge: Selected interviews and other writings, 1972–1977*. New York: Pantheon.

Gandy, O. (1979). Audience production functions: A new look at the economics of broadcasting. *Media Asia*, 170–179.

Gandy, O. (1980a). Information in health: Subsidized news. *Media, Culture and Society 2*(2), 103–115.

Gandy, O. (1981). The economics of image building: The information subsidy in health. In E. McAnany, J. Schnitman, & N. Janus (Eds.), *Communication and social structure* (pp. 204–239). Westport, CT: Praeger Publishers.

Gandy, O. (1982). *Beyond agenda setting: Information subsidies and public policy*. Norwood, NJ: Ablex Publishers.

Gandy, O. (1989a). The surveillance society: Information technology and bureaucratic social control. In M. Siefert, G. Gerbner, & J. Fisher (Eds), *The information gap: how computers and other new communication technologies affect the social distribution of power* (pp. 61–76). New York: Oxford University Press.

Gandy, O. (1989b). Information privacy and the crisis of control. In M. Raboy & P. Bruck (Eds.), *Communication for and against democracy* (pp. 59–73). Montreal: Black Rose Books.

Gandy, O. (1989c). The surveillance society: Information technology and bureaucratic social control. *Journal of Communication, 39*(3), 61–76.

Gandy, O. (1990a). Tracking the audience: Personal information, privacy and the current crisis in capitalism. In J. Downing, A. Mohammadi, & A. Sreberny-Mohammadi (Eds.), *Questioning the media* (pp. 166–179). Newbury Park, CA: Sage.

Gandy, O. (1990b). Caller identification: The two-edged sword. In D. Wedemeyer & M. Lofstrom (Eds.), *Pacific telecommunications: Weaving the technological and social fabric* (pp. 207–214). Honolulu: Pacific Telecommunications Council.

Gandy, O. (1992a). Media planning for development: Transformational criteria for the selection of information technology. In M. Cummings, L. Niles, & O. Taylor (Eds.), *Handbook on communications and development in Africa and the African Diaspora* (pp. 196–205). Needham Heights, MA: Ginn Press.

Gandy, O. (1993a). *The panoptic sort: A political economy of personal information.* Boulder, CO: Westview Press.

Gandy, O. (1993b). African Americans and privacy: Understanding the Black perspective in the merging policy debate. *Journal of Black Studies, 24*(2), 178–195.

Gandy, O. (1998). *Communication and race: A structural perspective.* New York: Edward Arnold and Oxford University Press.

Gandy, O. (2002). The real digital divide: Citizens v. consumers. In L. Leivrow & S. Livingstone (Eds.), *The handbook of new media* (pp. 448–460). Thousand Oaks, CA: Sage.

Gandy, O., & Baron, J. (1998). Inequality: It's all in the way you look at it. *Communications Research, 25,* 505–527.

Gandy, O., Espinosa, P., & Ordover, J. (1983). (Eds). *Proceedings from the tenth annual Telecommunications Policy Research Conference.* Norwood, NJ: Ablex Publishers.

Gandy, O., Kopp, K., Hands, T., Frazer, K., & Phillips, D. (1997). Race and risk: Factors affecting the framing of stories about inequality, discrimination and just plain bad luck. *Public Opinion Quarterly, 61*(1), 158–182.

Gandy, O., Matabane, P., & Omachonu, J. (1987). Media use, reliance and active participation: Exploring student awareness of the South African Conflict. *Communication Research, 14*(6), 644–663.

Gandy, O., Rivers, W., Miller, S., and Rivers, G. (1975). *Government and media: An annotated bibliography.* Stanford, CA: Institute for Communications Research.

Gandy, O., & Signorielli, N. (1981). Audience production functions: A Technical approach to programming. *Journalism Quarterly, 58*(2), 232–240.

Goshorn, K., & Gandy, O. (1995). Race, risk and responsibility: Editorial constraint in the framing of inequality. *Journal of Communication, 45*(2), 133–151.

Gurley, J. (1988). *Challengers to capitalism: Marx, Lenin, Stalin and Mao.* New York: Addison-Wesley.

Maxwell, R. (2003). *Herbert Schiller (Critical Media Studies).* New York: Rowman & Littlefield.

Schiller, H. I. (1970). *Superstate: Readings in the military-industrial complex.* Urbana: University of Illinois Press.

Schiller, H. I. (1973). *The mind managers.* Boston: Beacon Press, 1973.

Further Reading

Barber, J. T., & Gandy, O. (1990). Press portrayals of Black and White U.S. representatives. *Howard Journal of Communications, 2*(2), 213–225.

Gandy, O. (1980b). Market power and cultural imperialism. *Current Research in Peace and Violence 3*(1), 47–58.

Gandy, O. (1986). (Ed.). *Communications: A key to economic and political change.* Selected proceedings from the 15th annual Communications Conference of the Center for Communications Research, Howard University, Washington, DC.

Gandy, O. (1992b). Fear of flying: Developing nations and the coming information wars. In M. Cummings, L. Niles, & O. Taylor (Eds.), *Handbook on communications and development in Africa and the African Diaspora* (pp. 214–222). Needham Heights, MA: Ginn Press.

Gandy, O. (1996). Coming to terms with the panoptic sort. In D. Lyons & E. Zuriek (Eds.), *New technology, surveillance and social control* (pp. 132–155). Minneapolis: University of Minnesota Press.

Gandy, O. (2001). Racial identity, media use, and the social construction of risk among African Americans. *Journal of Black Studies, 31,* 600–618.

Oscar H. Gandy, Jr.

Photo courtesy of Oscar H. Gandy, Jr.

1942	Born in Amityville, New York.
1965	Received associate's degree from Nassau Community College.
1967	Received bachelor's degree in Sociology from University of New Mexico.
1969	Wrote and produced *Right On!*, WCAU-TV public affairs television series (1969–1971).
1970	Received master's degree in Communication Behavior from University of Pennsylvania.
	Became member, Writer's Guild of America.
1971	Lectured at The Third College, University of San Diego.
1973	Ford Foundation Fellow, National Fellowships Fund, Stanford University (1973–1976).
1975	Published *Government and Media: An Annotated Bibliography*.
1976	Received doctorate in Public Affairs Communication from Stanford University.
	Served as Postdoctoral Fellow, Annenberg School of Communication, University of Pennsylvania (1976–1977).
1977	Became assistant professor and coordinator of Broadcast Production Department of Radio, Television, and Film, Howard University (1977–1980).
1982	Published *Beyond Agenda Setting: Information Subsidies and Public Policy*.

1985	◆	Served as acting director, Proposed Center for Communications Research, Howard University, School of Communications (1985–1986).
1986	◆	Became director, Center for Communications Research, Howard University School of Communications.
1987	◆	Received grant for project on telecommunications and privacy (1987–1990).
		Served as associate Professor, Annenberg School for Communication, University of Pennsylvania.
1991	◆	Became professor, Annenberg School for Communication, University of Pennsylvania (1991–Present).
1993	◆	Served as Fellow at the Freedom Forum Media Studies Center of Columbia University to study "Statistical Reality: The Role of the Press in the Communication of Risk".
		Published *The Panoptic Sort: A Political Economy of Personal Information*.
1998	◆	Published *Communication and Race. A Structural Perspective*.
		Received the Dallas Smythe Award from the Union for Democratic Communication.
		Became Information and Society Term chair (Herbert I. Schiller Professor), University of Pennsylvania (1998–Present).
2000	◆	Received the Wayne Danielson Award, University of Texas at Austin.
		Received the Year 2000 Presidential Award from the Association for Education in Journalism and Mass Communication.
2001	◆	Named the LeBoff Distinguished Visiting Scholar by New York University.

7

Stuart Hall

A "raw" historical event cannot, in that form, be transmitted by, say, a television newscast. Events can only be signified within the aural-visual forms of the televisual discourse. In the moment when a historical event passes under the sign of discourse, it is subject to the entire complex formal "rules" by  *which language signifies. To put it paradoxically, the event must become a "story" before it can become a communicative event. In that moment the formal sub-rules of discourse are "in dominance," without, of course, subordinating out of existence the historical event so signified, the social relations in which the rules are set to work or the social and political consequences of the event having been signified in this way.*

(Hall, 1980, p. 129)

❖ INTRODUCTION

Currently chair of London's International Institute of Visual Arts, Stuart Hall is known by many as "the father of critical cultural studies." He is a husband, father, musician, and public intellectual. In the early 1990s, Hall hosted a BBC series on the Caribbean, *Redemption Song*, and an easy listening show—Radio 4's *Desert Island Discs*. Hall gained some notoriety for his BBC 2 Open Door program, "It Ain't Half Racist, Mum," which aired in 1979. As a preeminent figure of the cultural studies movement, his work spans more than four decades of intellectual thought and political discourse. Following the legacy of Raymond Williams and Richard Hoggart, Hall is responsible for the burgeoning scholarship in critical media studies that has influenced the work of Sut Jhally, Issac Julien, Herman Gray, Henry Giroux, Paul Gilroy, Lawrence Grossberg, and Angela McRobbie— to name a few. The latter three are his protégés and produced an edited book, *Without guarantees: In honour of Stuart Hall* (Gilroy, Grossberg, & McRobbie, 2000), which honored Hall's Marxist theoretical approach to the study of cultural identities and media texts. The preface of the book includes the following acknowledgment of his vast influence:

> These writings are firstly and most importantly a gift. Their testimony to Stuart Hall's influence, and the esteem in which he is held by the contributors, affirm our profound appreciation for his work, our respect for his wisdom, his creativity, his language and, above all, his lengthy record of serious scholarly intervention in various interconnected fields. Though it may be indiscreet to admit it, the pieces collected here demonstrate how his imaginative pursuit of political ends by other than obviously political means has inspired and motivated us. (Gilroy, Grossberg, & McRobbie, 2000, p. ix)

From his modest boyhood roots in colonial Jamaica, Hall has interrogated systems of political oppression through his writings in a way with which all people can identify. His work creates an active space for political and ideological struggle as well as social transformation.

The author of more than 200 published book chapters and journal articles, Hall has positioned himself as the pioneering voice for a middle theoretical position between Raymond Williams's culturalist and Louis Althussers's structuralist approach to the concepts of ideology and hegemony. His theoretical framework diverges from the three general perspectives of Marxists who study ideology and hegemony: (1) political economists, who view the production and consumption of cultural artifacts as determined by the economic forces of the culture;

(2) culturalists, who argue that culture is developed (but not determined) out of the joint "social consciousness" of people engaged in everyday practices and cultural patterns; and (3) structuralists, who contend that the "unconscious connections" between everyday experience and dominant cultural codes constitute culture, whereby lived experience is simply the "effect" of cultural production. Hall has used these concepts to develop a "hybrid" form of Marxist theory. He rejects political economism as a means to uncover the features of cultural production because of its limited focus on "the most generic aspects of the commodity form" (Hall, 1986a, p. 43). His work embraces culturalism and structuralism, yet he advances a perspective of "limited structuralism," in which theoretical and conceptual development *aid* in the understanding of everyday cultural practices. In sum, Hall critiques structuralists as being too preoccupied with conceptualization, which prioritizes the role of theory to explain lived experience. Along the same lines, he promotes a broader view of the culturalist perspective, which he believes does not focus enough on theory development. He argues that culturalist analyses focus too heavily on experience and/or historical agency. Thus, Hall's work on Marxist theory and social justice posits that neither structure nor experience completely determines ideology. Instead, dominant ideological formations such as race, class, and gender are constantly challenged by subordinate ideologies in a "cultural interplay" of discourse. To Hall, this interplay is part of the process of cultural production, along with consumerism, social relations, and the institutionalization of ideological dominance. This conceptualization is indicative of his leftist politics.

Over his career, Hall has edited several journals such as *Universities and Left Review* and *New Left Review* (which incidentally later became the same journal), and lectured before numerous academic constituencies. His ideas about the relationships between consumers of media, media texts, and their means of production have been a tremendous influence on the British cultural studies, American cultural studies, and postmodernist movements of the 1970s, 1980s, and 1990s. While Hall's abundant scholarship has been both critiqued (Slater, 2001; Wood, 1998), and revered (Giroux, 2000; Wise, 2003), the aim of this chapter is to highlight his early beginnings in Jamaica, chronicle his political and scholarly travels, and discuss his profound contributions to communication research.

❖ BIOGRAPHICAL INFORMATION

Stuart Hall, a jazz pianist and renowned scholar, was born in Kingston, Jamaica in 1932 into a lower-middle-class colonial Jamaican family. He had at least one brother named George. Hall's ambitious, hard-working father worked for the United Fruit Company for most of his life. Hall recalled that he "was the first Jamaican to be promoted in every job he had; before him, those jobs were occupied by people sent down from the head office in America" (Chen, 2003, p. 484). Although both of Hall's parents grew up in middle-class families, their experiences were quite different from one another. Hall's father belonged to an ethnically mixed (African, East Indian, Portuguese, and Jewish), "colored" lower-middle-class family. He owned a small country drugstore outside of Kingston. Hall realized early in his life that he did not want to go into business like his father. Hall's lack of ambition to follow in his father's footsteps led to tensions between the two, and his relationship with his mother was also tense. Hall described her as "an overwhelmingly dominant person," and recalled that their relationship was both "close and antagonistic" (Chen, 2003, p. 485). His mother was a "fair colored" Black woman who had been adopted by her biracial aunt. She grew up with two male cousins who were educated in England and became a doctor and a lawyer. Thus, Hall's mother enjoyed many of the luxuries of middle-class life that his father did not have. Hall summarized the impact of these differences on the family dynamics of his early life as follows:

So what was played out in my family, culturally, from the very beginning, was the conflict between the local and the imperial in the colonized context. Both these class factions were opposed to the majority culture of poor Jamaican black people: highly race and color conscious, and identifying with the colonizers. (Chen, 2003, pp. 484–485)

Thus, Hall grew up in a family in which his dark skin marked him for exclusion and ridicule. It was clear to him that not all people of African descent were the same. Like others in this volume, Hall's life was influenced by racial politics. Unlike the American segregationist criteria of the "one drop" rule, which identified *any* person with African ancestry in the United States (despite the hue of their skin) as simply "Negro," its form and expression were different for him because English colonialism also distinguished *between black people*. This intraracial caste system influenced his life from the very beginning:

I was the blackest member of my family. The story in my family, which was always told as a joke, was that when I was born, my sister, who was much fairer than I, looked into the crib and she said "Where did you get this coolie baby from?" Now "coolie" is the abusive word in Jamaica for a poor East Indian, who was considered the lowest of the low. So she wouldn't say "Where did you get this black baby from?" since it was unthinkable that she could have a black brother. But she *did* notice that I was a different color from her. This is very common in colored middle-class Jamaican families, because they are the product of mixed liaisons between African slaves and European slave-masters, and the children then come out in varying shades. (Chen, 2003, p. 485)

Feeling like the outcast of his family, Hall remembers being encouraged to socialize with light-skinned Blacks because many of his dark-skinned friends were not accepted into his family home. He resolved to disregard the rejection from his family in an effort to find his own place in the complex racial strata discovered in his youth. Hall recalled:

They always encouraged me to mix with more middle-class, more high color, friends and I didn't. Instead, I withdrew emotionally from my family and met my friends elsewhere. My adolescence was spent continuously negotiating these cultural spaces." (Chen, 2003, p. 485)

Hall's sister was also emotionally affected by the ideologies of their upbringing. He recalled a particularly tense situation involving her choice in a dating partner:

When I was seventeen, my sister had a major nervous breakdown. She began a relationship with a young student doctor who had come to Jamaica from Barbados. He was middle-class, but black and my parents wouldn't allow it. There was a tremendous family row and she, in effect, retreated from the situation into a breakdown. I was suddenly aware of the contradiction of a colonial culture, of how one lives out the color-class-colonial dependency experience and of how it could destroy you, subjectively. (Chen, 2003, p. 488)

Hall's sister was given electric shock treatment, from which she never recovered. Thus, Hall had to somehow come to terms with the fact that his family valued a system of oppression that positioned him as invisible and insignificant when compared with other members of the extremely color-conscious society. The significance of these early experiences was clear to Hall and readers of his work. His work on signified identities, the argument that identity is embodied and enacted in everyday social relations, is intimately linked to the search for belonging and acceptance that characterized his youth. Interestingly, Hall recalled:

> My family would never have—in a thousand words—ever thought of itself as Black; the word would not have entered its vocabulary. And you have to know the colonial Caribbean to know how utterly unthinkable it would have been for this middle-class family to think about anything like that. ("A conversation with Stuart Hall," 1999)

In the mid-1960s, Hall returned home and had a conversation with his mother, who remarked that she hoped Americans did not think he was Black and that native Jamaicans did not mistake him for an immigrant. Hall was told soon after by someone else that he *had* transformed a bit, that he *had* essentially been socialized enough to behave a bit differently from native Jamaicans who remained in Jamaica. In that instance, he began to question his cultural identity and wonder whether he had become someone different from who he was before he left Jamaica for Britain. All at once, these moments led to, as Hall explained, "the first time that I ever thought of myself as Black" ("A conversation with Stuart Hall," 1999). In 1964, Hall married a long-time friend, Catherine Barrett—a woman who was 13 years his junior. They have two children: Rebecca, who has a doctorate in English and is interested in mulattoes in fiction literature, and Jess, who works as a cameraman.

From that time forward, rather than dismissing the influence of English colonialism and American slavery in his life, he regarded it as part of his "personal history:"

> My own formation and identity was very much constructed out of a kind of refusal of the dominant personal and cultural models which were held up for me. I didn't want to beg my way like my father into acceptance by the American or English expatriate business community, and I couldn't identify with that old plantation world, with its roots in slavery, but which my mother spoke of as a "golden age." (Chen, 2003, p. 485)

Hall's resistance to the color caste system of mid-twentieth century Jamaica mirrored the concerns of his generation. Jamaican Blacks who fought and spoke out in support of the country's independence rallied together. Led by Michael Manley, a popular political leader of the time, newly emerging Jamaican Rastafarian groups also lobbied for a political voice and were partially responsible for Jamaica's independence in 1962. The formation of local resistance groups and political parties was meaningful to Hall. Through them, he saw strength and power unlike he had ever seen before. He recalled that "Bright kids like me and my friends, of varying colors and social positions, were nevertheless caught up in that movement, and that's what we identified with" (Chen, 2003, p. 486). The energy of socialist politics awakened Hall's cultural, political, and communal consciousness. It caused him to reflect on the global as a seedling of the local that had been magnified. Hall came to understand how social transformation and public consciousness have to evolve from a sense of local identity. This inspiration sparked the numerous writings, lectures, and social critiques that made Hall one of the most prolific critical cultural scholars of the past 50 years.

❖ ACADEMIC BACKGROUND AND EXPERIENCE

In his youth, Stuart Hall attended one of a series of small primary schools for boys that were modeled after the English public school system. He described his early education as "very classical" (Chen, 2003, p. 486). Hall studied Latin, English colonial history, European history, and English literature. Yet his political interests encouraged him to ask questions outside of the "narrowly academic, British-oriented" instruction he received (Chen, 2003, p. 488). He wanted to learn more about contemporary world issues in courses on Caribbean history, the Cold War, and American politics. Resolved to leave the depressing conditions of Black Jamaican life, Hall saw social activism and higher education as two viable ways to take charge of his future and give other Caribbean nationalists a voice. In 1951, Hall left Jamaica after high school to continue his education because there were no local universities in Jamaica until Northern Caribbean University (formerly West Indies College) achieved senior college status in 1959.

Hall's early intellectual influences were his teachers, who challenged him to explore his passions and to seek knowledge on subjects that his formal training would not provide. Although no single teacher seemed to have affected his life more than others, he reported that collectively they "gave me a strong sense of self confidence, of academic achievement" (Chen, 2003, p. 487). He learned more about American politics, the Russian revolution, and the Cold War—areas of study that he was not familiar with. Hall was strongly encouraged to read about the ideas of Marxism and was particularly drawn to ideas espoused in *The Communist Manifesto* (Marx, 1964). This work addressed the questions of poverty, colonialism, and the problem of economic development in Jamaica that Hall had been asking throughout his entire life. Unlike many of his university colleagues, Hall saw the answers to these questions in political, rather than economic, discourses. He recalled:

A lot of my young friends, who went to university at the same time I did, studied economics. Economics was supposed to be the answer to the poverty which countries like Jamaica experienced, as a consequence of imperialism and colonialism. So I was interested in the economic question from a colonial standpoint. (Chen, 2003, p. 488)

Hall saw the problems of Jamaica and other newly emancipated post-colonial countries as embedded in political constructions of class and privilege. Ironically, he would take these ideas with him to Oxford University as a Rhodes Scholar—a scholarship named after Cecil Rhodes, a "paragon" of colonialism (Gandesha, 2000, p. 22).

Hall described his academic course as "a journey" that began with his move to England. He recollected the day of his arrival in the following words:

My mother brought me, in my felt hat, in my overcoat, with my steamer trunk. She brought me, as she thought "home" on the banana boat, and delivered me to Oxford. She gave me to the astonished college scout and said, "There is my son, his trunks, his belongings. Look after him." She delivered me, signed and sealed, to where she thought a son of hers had always belonged—Oxford. (Chen, 2003, p. 489)

In England, Hall was free to explore socialist politics and to meet other independent leftists who shared his politics. He found an open marketplace for his seemingly rebellious ideas and enjoyed the opportunities that England offered him. Although Hall was never a member of the Communist party, many of his close friends were. He was so enamored with his experiences in England that by 1957, he knew that he would never return to live in Jamaica. The dualism of Hall's position against British colonialism and his desire to live and learn in England was a necessary cultural dichotomy for Hall. He recalled:

In spite of my anti-colonial politics, it had always been my aspiration to study in England. I always wanted to study there. It took quite a while to come to terms with Britain, especially with

Oxford, because Oxford is the pinnacle of Englishness, it's the hub, the motor, that creates Englishness. (Chen, 2003, p. 492)

Hall saw himself at the center of cultural repression and rigidity in England, yet he was able to speak out against it from this place. Although his mother was not particularly pleased with his politics, she agreed that Hall was where he belonged. Until the death of his parents, Hall found it continually difficult to face the Jamaica he knew as a child and was delighted to see the changes taking place there after its independence:

I felt easier in relation to Jamaica, once they [my parents] were dead, because before that, when I went back, I had to negotiate Jamaica through them. Once my parents were dead, it was easier to make a new relationship to the new Jamaica that emerged in the 1970's. This Jamaica was not where I had grown up. For one thing, it had become, culturally, a black society, a post-slave, post-colonial society, whereas I had lived there at the end of the colonial era. So I could negotiate it as a "familiar stranger." (Chen, 2003, p. 490)

Hall likened his experiences of negotiating Jamaican and British cultures to the experiences of many natives of the Caribbean who traverse multiple cultural spaces, never feeling completely assimilated into any of them.

After completing his studies at Oxford, Hall decided to remain in England and to pursue a master of arts degree from Morton College. During this time, he became increasingly committed to anti-Stalinism and anti-imperialism. Along with others who identified themselves as neither communist nor imperialist, Hall formed the Socialist Society— "a place for meetings of the independent minds of the left" (Chen, 2003, p. 492). The group quickly became the political conscience of the left, causing the Oxford branch of the Communist party to fold. He described this shift as a significant one in the history of British cultural studies: "We had the moral capital to criticize *both* the Hungarian invasion and the British invasion [of Germany]. That is the moment—the political space—of the birth of the first British New Left" (Chen, 2003, p. 493). The new movement attracted intellectuals, students, trade unions, tenant associations, and others who wanted involvement in the new political voice they saw brewing. Hall was heavily involved in the journalistic outlets of the group. He served as an editor of the *The New Reasoner* and *The New Left Review*, along with E. P. Thompson,

Raymond Williams, and other well-known leftists of the time. Led by the intellectuals, 26 *New Left Review* clubs formed in and around London between 1956 and 1962.

In 1961, Hall left the *Review* to teach at Chelsea College in London. He was appointed as a lecturer there to teach film and mass media studies at a time when no one else was teaching film anywhere. His work with the New Left also afforded him an opportunity to teach cultural studies courses. In 1964, he coauthored *The Popular Arts* with Paddy Whannel (Whannel & Hall, 1964) which launched his career in British cultural studies. Because of his profound and well-received writings, Hall was invited by Richard Hoggart to the University of Birmingham and the Centre for Contemporary Cultural Studies (CCCS). Hoggart had just founded the Centre in 1964 and was eager to develop its research initiatives, ideologically diverse habitat, and reputation. Hall and other colleagues in sociology, history, and literature followed the path of Hoggart and Williams and began laying the foundation for the field of cultural studies (Gandesha, 2000, p. 23). When Hoggart left to occupy a position at UNESCO, Hall became director of the Centre in 1968. The *critical paradigm,* which explored the inextricable link between power and media, emerged in the early 1970s out of the work of the Centre. Around this time, both the CCCS and the Leicester Centre for Mass Communication Research became quite well-known as major organizations generating leading cultural studies research. Although both embraced Marxist ideology, their approaches were a bit different. The CCCS produced research primarily related to cultural processes, whereas the Leicester Centre focused predominantly on economic processes and therefore could be characterized as classically Marxist. The CCCS group would explain media as socially transforming, capitalist-driven, modernist vehicles that inform about culture and its processes through symbols and visual representations. However, the Leicester Centre researchers would view the "culture industries" as intentionally amoral—not immoral, because an economically driven vehicle has no regard for morality, except as it helps to achieve profitable ends. These industries concentrate on expanding the consumer base, which leads to profit, rather than being preoccupied with how audiences understand culture. In this way, audiences were seen as merely commodities or symbols of exchange within volatile markets, yet they were the primary means of stabilizing the industry's economy. Out of this philosophical base and under the leadership of scholars such as Graham Murdoch and Peter Golding, the Leicester group developed the political economy approach. This distinction between CCCS and the Leicester Centre became increasingly clear among CCCS researchers.

As persons mainly from working class and colonial backgrounds, they maintained that although the media were clearly driven by capitalism, they also served important functions as an industry to shape public consciousness. During his tenure in Birmingham, Hall produced some of his most groundbreaking work. During his first year there, in 1964, he married his long-time sweetheart, Catherine Barrett—a White English social historian and feminist. Things were coming together successfully in his personal and professional life.

In the 1970s, Hall found himself growing weary of the constant fight to keep the Centre open. Because of his role as the "father" of British cultural studies, there was a general perception that he was obliged to stand as the leading figure to defend the separate political agendas of Black graduate students, feminists, and working-class Whites. This was one among many struggles that led Hall to the decision to leave the Centre in 1979—a particularly difficult but necessary decision. He reflected on the circumstances surrounding this decision in the following statement:

> In the early days of the Centre, we were like the "alternative university." There was little separation between staff and students. What I saw emerging was that separation between generations, between statuses—students and teachers—and I didn't want that. I preferred to be in a more traditional setting, if I had to take on the responsibility of being the teacher. I couldn't live part of the time being their teacher, and being their father, being hated for being their father, and being set up as if I was an anti-feminist man. It was an impossible politics to live. (Chen, 2003, p. 500)

His desire to leave also challenged Hall to anticipate the next step in his career. While under his direction, the Centre became a hotbed for the best and brightest intellectual constituency. During Hall's tenure, he noticed that the Centre no longer served its original function, which was to incorporate socialist politics into academic discussions of culture, society, and transformation. According to Hall, its popularity and success also resulted in it becoming "the pinnacle of a very selective education system" (Chen, 2003, p. 501). He did not desire an appointment with a traditional sociology department. Rather, he embraced the challenge of teaching cultural studies to nonacademic audiences. He wanted to be in a setting in which a cultural studies curriculum was made accessible to all interested persons despite their academic standing. The Open University, an unconventional interdisciplinary institution committed to challenging the selectivity of higher education, seemed like the perfect place to continue the *New Left* legacy. Hall remained there until his retirement in 1997. He continues to write and lecture about Marxism, media discourses, and Diasporic cultural identity.

❖ CONTRIBUTIONS TO COMMUNICATION RESEARCH

Although Stuart Hall's work has been published and reprinted in the journals of several disciplines, he was trained in English. Although he later became a professor of sociology, he was never a formal student in that department, so not one of his degrees is in that discipline.

Early in his career, in the late 1950s, Hall became editor of the very first New Left journal, *Universities and Left Review*. When this publication linked with the *New Reasoner* to become the *New Left Review,* it also became an important sociopolitical journal for cultural studies *and* for Hall, as it was the place where he would publish many of his earliest writings. He was the editor in a London office, above a Soho coffeehouse he co-owned and operated to help finance the journal. He did all this while working as a substitute teacher in a secondary modern school, an educational environ designed for kids who do not test well on the elementary school diagnostic exam that all British children take at age 11.

His work in media and film studies began in the 1960s, yet his work had not been published in mainstream communication books and journals until the 1980s. This was especially interesting as Hall trained communication scholars such as Lawrence Grossberg in the late 1960s and beyond. Grossberg was sent by political economist James Carey, a colleague of Richard Hoggart, to study with Hall at the CCCS in 1968. Despite Grossberg's affinity for Deleuze and Guattari, which was of much less interest to Hall, we mention Grossberg to say that Hall's significant influence on communication research in the United States was present even before the 1980s. The following sections will review his contributions to communication studies in two areas of the field: intercultural and interracial communication and media communication.

Intercultural and Interracial
Communication/Cultural Theory

Stuart Hall wrote approximately 15 articles and book chapters on race and ethnic identity formation and negotiation during the 1980s and 1990s. His approach to the topic of race and ethnic identity has been predominately theoretical. Heavily influenced by Gramscian ideology, Hall explored the way studies of race, ethnicity, and racism could be traced back to Marxist ideas of hegemony, power, and class struggle. In his article, "Gramsci's Relevance for the Study of Race and Ethnicity," Hall (1986a) uncovered how Gramsci's nonacademic critique of the conditions of 1870s Italy could be applied to concrete academic discussions of race, power, and sociopolitical relationships. By introducing the contributions of Marxist thought to the practice of identity negotiation and group formation from British cultural studies, he was able to provide theoretical support for those interested in the newly emerging discourse in intercultural and interracial communication. That year, in the same journal (the *Journal of Communication Inquiry*), Hall published "The Problem of Ideology: Marxism without Guarantees" (1986b). He argued that despite the potential of Marxism to explain and describe the struggles of "subaltern classes," there was still much work to do to provide a theoretical framework that could stand up to social scientific scrutiny. For Hall, the answers to the questions of racism and racist ideologies were to be found within the spate of epistemological concerns about the realities of everyday experiences with racism and methodological concerns about how to access the multiple ways in which these experiences are interpreted by racists and targets of racism. In another theoretical turn, Hall's piece in the book *Black Popular Culture* (1992b) described how contemporary discussions of Black popular culture essentialize what it means to *be* Black in popular culture. He commended the work of Cornel West and bell hooks for articulating the need for increased consciousness about African American experiences in the Unites States. At the same time, he cautioned American cultural critics not to overly invest in notions of the "collective" Black experience. He contended that popular culture has provided a space in which racial differences can be articulated and challenged. However, the desire to emphasize the idea of difference within this space can encourage false notions of an "authentic" Blackness. He wrote:

> The essentializing moment is weak because it naturalizes and dehistoricizes difference, mistaking what is historical and cultural for what is natural, biological, and genetic. The moment the signifier "black" is torn from its historical, cultural and political embedding and lodged in a biologically constituted racial category, we valorize, by invasion, the very ground of the racism we are trying to deconstruct. In addition, as always happens when we naturalize historical categories (think about gender and sexuality), we fix that signifier outside of history, outside of change, outside of

political intervention. And once it is fixed, we are tempted to use "black" as sufficient in itself to guarantee the progressive character of the politics we fight under the banner—as if we don't have any other politics to argue about except whether something's black or not. (Hall, 1992b, p. 27)

This critical statement is the philosophy that undergirds Hall's thinking. Hall maintains that ideology is unavoidably linked to language and representation. So what we signify or symbolize is practically as real as the thing itself if it represents how we approach the world. In other words, Blackness has competing definitions that only become real when manufactured ideologies are translated into a community's universe of discourse and then consumed by the local citizens of that community. This is a potent web of signs, signifiers, and signification.

This complex mode of deconstructing culture by unraveling learned and often imposed ideologically imbued meanings is the hallmark of critical cultural studies. It is because of this sophisticated approach that renowned scholars such as Lawrence Grossberg, Henry Giroux, Paul Gilroy, Gayatri Spivak, Paulo Freire, and others have developed lines of inquiry parallel to Hall's approach. Any reader of their works can recognize the synergistic influence of Hall's concerns in the shape of their careful discussions of racial/ethnic identity and communication processes. His concerns about how cultures, particularly Black cultures, are represented in popular discourse are infused in his writings about media texts.

Media Communication/Reception Theory

Hall's scholarship on race and mediated imagery began in the 1970s, when many academics took up the challenge of critiquing media institutions as sites of ideological struggle between the "powerful" controllers of the medium and the "powerless" consumers of it. Hall's position on this issue was unique because it was both academic and activist in scope. For instance, during an interview in 1971, Hall shared the following remarks to a "visibly shocked" BBC television audience: "There is something radically wrong with the way black immigrants—West Indians, Asians, and Africans—are handled by and presented on the mass media" (Chronicle World, 2003). Hall was clearly indicting British media. His emotional reaction that year was attributable to his awareness that images of Blacks in media had become increasingly disparaging and, in his opinion, disrespectful. Hall was the new director of the CCCS at the time and saw his opportunity to promote change and awareness through it. In 1980, he published the groundbreaking piece, "Encoding/Decoding," in which he argued that mass media are a means for the "haves" to gain willing support for dominant ideologies from the "have-nots." He further argued that this support functions to reinforce the importance of those ideologies—and thus maintain the status quo. Hall contended that in the process of describing "events," media institutions *encode* dominate ideologies into their "stories." However, these stories are decoded by members of media audiences in one of three ways: (1) They can adopt the *dominant* code; that is, members have the option of simply accepting the stories of mass media as encoded, without challenging them. (2) They can apply a *negotiable* code, in which audience members may acknowledge the dominant ideologies provided, yet they may do so from their own subject position. (3) They can substitute the dominant code for an *oppositional* code, which rejects the dominant ideologies and promotes critical analysis of the "stories" told by mass media. Although exclusively theoretical, Hall's writing on audience reception theory was the first of its kind to consider the idea that consumers of mass media decode its messages from within their own social situations and cultural spaces. His work implies that encoded readings are not necessarily adopted by readers/listeners/watchers by default. Five years later, Hall's work was formally introduced to the field of communication with his article, "Signification, Representation, Ideology: Althusser and the post-Structuralist Debates" (Hall, 1985), which appeared in the then-new journal *Critical Studies in Mass Communication* (now called *Critical Studies in Media Communication*). Hall had just begun work with Grossberg on articulation theory. This conceptual approach emerged from Hall's reading of Althusser, who claimed that articulation is the interface between power, culture, discourse, production, and consumption. Althusser was mostly concerned with ideology and state apparatus and took up a position that dominant practices cause individuals to hold an ideology that functions only as an imaginary escape from people's actual lived conditions.

This grappling with the nature, scope, and definition of articulation helped Hall to understand encoding and decoding better because articulation is simultaneously a critical elaboration and disentanglement of concrete and hypothesized lived experiences. It is a way of both making meaning and turning meaning on its head to see whether the inverse interpretation makes sense. When Hall discusses articulation, he generally uses the words "articulation with." For example, he might say that a text is *articulated with* hegemony or *articulated with* mass media to suggest that discourse can be intermingled, interjected, or interpolated with something else to produce many meanings. In that way, the text asserts or expresses its positionality as much as it intersperses it. Likewise, Hall tries to make clear, through his articulation theory, that one can articulate (i.e., express) a political position without being fixed in that position, but no matter how ephemeral, the fact that one took up a position at all is an important act of articulation. Articulation, by its very nature, is elusive and fluid. It is not static for long because it is always questioning itself, and yet it is what we do naturally without even thinking about it as articulation theory. This is why identities represent intersecting realities that sometimes appear as contradictory impulses.

In "Signification, Representation, Ideology: Althusser and the post-Structuralist Debates" (1985), Hall argued that no meanings are "fixed." In fact, they are created by complex sets of social and political discourses, forming what he called an "ideological field." Thus, media outlets and institutions *contribute* to ideological fields of race and gender constructions; they do not control them. Additionally, he suggested that the problem of representing Blacks in media in a more enduring light lies in the sociohistorical problem of White social domination. He described these fields as the result of social tensions that have roots in capitalism and forced labor—namely, the African slave trade. He wrote: "This signifying chain was clearly inaugurated at a specific historical moment—the moment of slavery" (Hall, 1985, p. 110). According to Hall, then, the role of media is twofold. It serves as a site for signifying practices of subordination and marginalization yet it might also be a site of intense ideological struggle.

Hall's work in media communication encourages media agencies to challenge themselves and cultural studies scholars to push forward in their explorations of theory and praxis as they promote cultural shifts from right to left. His contributions to communication theory and his political work are vastly different from almost all the other pioneers in this book. Hall's work stands in contrast to that of the African American scholars in this book, in part because he has a different cultural standpoint—one that is an indigenous third world perspective. That does not make him better or worse, but it does suggest something different about how he comes to the conversation about culture and Black identity. Hall is featured here for many reasons. Besides the obvious fact that he is a pioneer in cultural and communication studies, he is also ideologically different. He is very cautious about what culture means. He does not hold fast to one theoretical approach, cultural standpoint, or methodological orientation. He believes wholeheartedly in multiplicity of identifications and a fractured Blackness. He is a citizen of British society and culture, which means he comes to the conversation of Blackness with a different set of nationalist politics that traditionally emphasizes variations within Blackness and a tentativeness of connections between Black Diasporas. This has heavily influenced his social activism, intellectual perspective, and personal politics. Communication and cultural studies are enriched because of his courageous, unique, and insightful approach to culture.

❖ CONCLUSION

Over his impressive career, Stuart Hall has written at length about the need for academic scholarship to reach out to nonacademics and to promote social change. His fearless activism in both scholarly and lay circles is nothing less than laudable. His international and interdisciplinary reputation precedes him wherever listeners are fortunate enough to hear him speak. Hall is not only an internationally renowned public intellectual but he is also proficient in Russian, perhaps as a result of his anti-Stalinist, post-graduate school days. Though he never joined the Communist party, he clearly stood for leftist politics and was the founding editor of the *New Left Review*. Although retirement has distanced Hall from large intellectual circles, we are still privileged in that his commitment to academic activism has not waned. He continues to write and lecture about Diasporic identities and calls for American and British cultural studies scholars to expand the breadth of their methodologies to social scientists and nonacademic audiences. It is our hope that young scholars will heed his call and carry on his legacy.

❖ REFERENCES

Chen, K. H. (2003). The formation of a Diasporic intellectual: An interview with Stuart Hall. In D. Morley & K. H. Chen (Eds.), *Stuart Hall: Critical dialogues in cultural studies* (pp. 484–502). New York: Routledge.

Chronicle World. (2003). Retrieved January 12, 2004 from http://www.chronicle world.org/

A conversation with Stuart Hall. (1999). *Journal of the International Institute, 7*(1). Retrieved January 15, 2004 from http://www.umich.edu/~iinet/journal/v017n01/Hall.htm

Gandesha, S. (2000). Stuart Hall. *Canadian Dimension, 34*(3), 22–24.

Gilroy, P., Grossberg, L., & McRobbie, A. (2000). *Without guarantees: In honour of Stuart Hall.* London: Verso.

Giroux, H. A. (2000). Public pedagogy as cultural politics: Stuart Hall and the "crisis" of culture. *Cultural Studies, 14*(2), 341–360.

Hall, S. (1972). *Situating Marx: Evaluations and departures.* New York: Human Context Books.

Hall, S. (1980). Encoding/decoding. In S. Hall, D. Hobson, A. Lowe, & P. Willis (Eds.), *Culture, media, language: Working papers in cultural studies (1972–1979)* (pp. 1–17). London: Hutchinson.

Hall, S. (1985). Signification, representation, ideology: Althusser and the post-structuralist debates. *Critical Studies in Mass Communication, 2*(2), 91–114.

Hall, S. (1986a). Gramsci's relevance for the study of race and ethnicity. *Journal of Communication Inquiry, 10*(2), 5–27.

Hall, S. (1986b). The problem of ideology: Marxism without guarantees. *Journal of Communication Inquiry, 10*(2), 28–43.

Hall, S. (1988). *The hard road to renewal.* New York: Verso.

Hall, S. (1992b). What is this "black" in black popular culture? In D. Morley & K. H. Chen (Eds.), *Stuart Hall: Critical dialogues in cultural studies* (pp. 465–475). New York: Routledge.

Hall, S. (1995). *Resistance through rituals.* New York: Routledge.

Hall, S. (1997). (Ed.). *Cultural representations and signifying practices.* Thousand Oaks, CA: Sage.

Hall, S., & Gieben, B. (1992). *The formation of modernity.* New York: Blackwell.

Marx, K. (1964). *The communist manifesto.* New York: Monthly Review Press.

Slater, A. (2001). [Review of the book *Visual culture: A reader*]. *Disability and Society, 16*(1), 175–178.

Whannel, P., & Hall, S. (1964). *The popular arts.* London: Hutchinson.

Wise, J. M. (2003). Reading Hall reading Marx. *Cultural Studies, 17*(2), 105–112.

Wood, B. (1998). Stuart Hall's cultural studies and the problem of hegemony. *British Journal of Sociology, 49*(3), 399–414.

Further Reading

Hall, S. (1990). Cultural identity and Diaspora. In J. Rutherford (Ed.), *Identity: community, culture, difference* (pp. 41–57). London: Lawrence & Wishart.

Hall, S. (1992a). Cultural studies and its theoretical legacies. In L. Grossberg, C. Nelson, & P. Treichler (Eds.), *Cultural studies* (pp. 277–294). New York: Routledge.

Hall, S. (1994). Cultural studies: Two paradigms. In R. Davis & R. Schleafer (Eds.), *Contemporary literary criticism: Literary and cultural studies* (pp. 337–352). London: Longman.

Hall, S. (1999). Thinking the Diaspora: Home-thoughts from abroad. *Small Axe, 6,* 1–18.

Hall, S. (2003). Marx's notes on method: A "reading" of the "1857 introduction to the *Grundrisse.*" *Cultural Studies, 17*(2), 113–149.

Hall, S., Critcher, C., Jefferson, T., Clarke, J., & Robert, B. (1978). *Policing the crisis: Mugging, the state, and law and order.* London: Macmillan.

Hall, S., & du Gay, P. (1996). *Questions of cultural identity.* Thousand Oaks, CA: Sage.

Martin, J., & Hall, S. (1997). Cultural revolutions. *New Statesman, 126*(4363), 24–27.

Stuart Hall

Photo courtesy of Stuart Hall

1932 ◆ Born in Kingston, Jamaica.

1950s ◆ Moved to Bristol, where he attended Oxford University as a Rhodes Scholar.

Received a master's degree from Merton College.

Joined E.P. Thompson, Raymond Williams, and others to launch two radical socialist journals: *The New Reasoner* and the *New Left Review*.

1961 ◆ Began to teach film and mass media studies at Chelsea College in London.

1964 ◆ Coauthored *The Popular Arts* (with Paddy Whannel).

Invited by Richard Hoggart to the University of Birmingham and the Centre for Contemporary Cultural Studies (CCCS).

1968 ◆ Became director of the Centre for Contemporary Cultural Studies (CCCS).

1972 ◆ Published *Situating Marx: Evaluations and Departures*.

1973 ◆ Published *Encoding and Decoding in the Television Discourse*.

1978 ◆ Published *Policing the Crisis*.

1979 ◆ Left the CCCS to teach at the Open University, an unconventional, interdisciplinary institution committed to challenging the selectivity of higher education. Was professor of sociology from 1979 until his retirement in 1997.

1980 ◆ Published the groundbreaking piece *Encoding/Decoding*.

1985 ◆ Formally introduced to the field of communication with his article "Signification, representation, ideology: Althusser and the post-structuralist debates" in *Critical Studies in Mass Communication* (now called *Critical Studies in Media Communication*).

1986 ◆ Published "Gramsci's relevance for the study of race and ethnicity."

Published "The problem of ideology: Marxism without guarantees."

1988 ◆ Published *The Hard Road to Renewal*.

1989 ◆ Published *Resistance Through Rituals*.

1992 ◆ Published *The Formation of Modernity*.

1996 ◆ Published *Questions of Cultural Identity* (with Paul du Gay).

1997 ◆ Published *Cultural Representations and Signifying Practices*.

Retired from Open University.

8

Marsha Houston

(aka Marsha Houston Stanback)

Research on the Black English Vernacular (BEV) has so often focused on male interaction networks that scholars have tended to regard Black men as the more proficient users of dialect structure, and to consider vernacular speech events to be the exclusive  *province of men. In short, neither contemporary research on language and gender nor that on Black communication coherently describes Black women's communicative experiences.*

(Houston Stanback, 1985, p. 177)

❖ INTRODUCTION

Marsha Houston is one of the most outspoken contemporary writers on African American women's communication patterns and has been a champion of social justice. Houston's work earned her the privilege of being the first to hold the Nancy Reeves Dreux Chair in Women's Studies at Tulane University. Houston has received numerous other honors, including two Distinguished Book Awards and the 2002 Southern States Communication Association Outreach Award. In 1964, she was one of the first seven African American undergraduate women students to enroll at Emory College (the undergraduate school of liberal arts and sciences) of Emory University and she graduated with high honors. Houston's intellectual tenacity and zeal are evident in her writings about gender, race and ethnicity, and sociolinguistic behavior. Throughout her academic career, she has taught courses on the topics of language and gender, communication of prejudice, African American womanhood, and interracial and intercultural communication, to name a few. While occupying the position of chair of Communication Studies at the University of Alabama at Birmingham, Houston served on countless editorial boards and as a member of numerous community outreach organizations.

Houston has made many significant contributions to the academy. She is a founding member of both the Feminist and Women's Studies and African American Communication and Culture Division of the National Communication Association (NCA), and has served as chair of each unit. She also played a vital role in the organization and development of two academic conferences that resulted in significant contributions to African American communication scholarship. In 1988, The Power of the Spoken Word: The Oratory of Dr. Martin Luther King, Jr. Conference was sponsored by Atlanta's Martin Luther King, Jr. Center for Nonviolent Social Change and the Educational Policies Board of the Speech Communication Association (now the National Communication Association), on which she was the first African American woman to serve. The conference resulted in the first collection of communication scholarship on King's work: *Martin Luther King Jr. and the Sermonic Power of Discourse* (Lucaites & Calloway Thomas, 1993). Two years later, she planned the Eighth National Conference on Research in Gender and Communication with the theme *Difficult Dialogues: Gateways and Barriers to Women's Communication Across Cultures* which aimed to "move studies of communication and gender in African American communities from marginal discussion to goal oriented agendas with significant social impact" (Marsha Houston, personal communication, June 12, 2001). Both conferences provided a rare space for scholarship focused on the fortification of African American community consciousness.

In addition to her work in the discipline, classroom, and community, Houston has mentored many African American woman scholars, who often feel isolated in the academy. She freely shares with young scholars, who search for their place in a predominately White and male field of study, her philosophy about the importance of looking beyond environmental obstacles. In theory and practice, Houston embodies the African American adage of "lifting as we climb." In a personal interview with Houston, she reflected on her goal to contribute to the lives of other African American women scholars:

> I think for perhaps the past five years, a part of what I have been attempting to do is to do what I can to make a space for younger scholars, especially Black women who are doing feminist work, to find a space and to have access to the field. I'm not so much interested now in producing a lot of work, what I'm interested in is making sure that whatever power I have is used to help others make a space for themselves. (Marsha Houston, personal communication, June 12, 2001)

Indeed, Houston's efforts have helped to empower an entire generation of young African American women scholars to approach the study of communication from their own subject positions. Her commitment to the profession and to the lives of women was acknowledged in 1994 with the Francine Merritt Award for Distinguished Service to Women in the Communication Discipline.

Houston has served as guest lecturer and consultant at several colleges and universities throughout the United States. She continues to serve as an example of the benefits of unyielding determination and concern for community.

❖ BIOGRAPHICAL INFORMATION

Marsha Houston was born on November 29, 1945 in Greensboro, North Carolina as the youngest of three daughters. Her mother, Lillian Tyson Houston from Winston-Salem, North Carolina, and father, Roosevelt Houston of Greensboro, divorced early in her life. Houston's immediate family consisted of her mother, eldest sister Josephine Coward, brother-in-law Jather Coward, and niece Janice Coward. Like most of the pioneers in this volume, she grew up in the segregated south of the 1950s and 1960s. The dual influences of the developing civil rights and women's rights movements were extremely influential in shaping Houston's social and political views. She learned early in her childhood about the intricacies of personal relationships and became intrigued by them.

Houston was particularly fascinated by African American relational strategies such as her mother and sisters negotiating what she called the "double-shift" (Houston, 2000a, p. 23) of being homemakers and workers. During most of her formative years, Houston's mother worked as a lab technician for a microfilm company, her sister Josephine was an educator, and her sister Gloria (Ogelsby) was a recreation specialist. Early observations of these significant women in her life taught Houston how (and why) to be attentive to career, home, and family in a way that symbolized how critical each of these areas of life were to African American women's identities. This vision provided her with a sense of how domestic responsibilities, career challenges, and relational maintenance complement each other to constitute a full life. These women also taught her the value of being assertive, which is probably no surprise to those who know Houston well. She noted, "We're all pretty feisty," (Marsha Houston, personal communication, June 12, 2001), a temperament that goes back to her great-great-grandmother, an ex-slave known as "Mama Candace" and other women in her mother's family.

Houston also learned the value of education early in her life. Her hometown had two historically Black colleges: Bennett College and North Carolina Agricultural & Technical (A&T) State University. Through proximity, she came to know several college professors and children of college professors during her formative years. In fact, Houston recalled that her best friend's mother was a French professor. By the time she began her high school career, she was certain that life as a college professor would provide her fulfillment, freedom to express her ideas, and the ability to perform for the benefit of others. Considering herself "a ham" in her youth, the idea of performing in front of a class offered much more appeal than struggling to become an actor because African Americans then had few theatrical options other than denigrating roles as servants or social deviants (Marsha Houston, personal communication, June 12, 2001).

Her early role models ranged from successful Black people whose experiences were reported in popular magazines such as *Jet* and *Ebony* to people in her community who were successful in their careers. Most significantly, she reported that her mother and sisters served as key role models in her life. Her sisters, who were already college students at the time of Houston's birth, showed her that Black women could manage marriages, families, and careers. Houston's outspoken personality, fondness for performing, and commitment to expressing her values and beliefs made her a natural in the classroom (Marsha Houston, personal communication, June 12, 2001).

❖ ACADEMIC BACKGROUND AND EXPERIENCE

Marsha Houston recalled taking great interest in her education and described herself as having been a good student. She was selected for both the National Junior and Senior Honor Societies in her formative educational years. In addition to her interest in academics, she fondly remembered summer opportunities to participate in children's theatre at Bennett College and that she became "hooked" on drama when she was 7 years old. During each of her years at James B. Dudley High School, Houston had leading roles in "Dudley Thespian" drama club plays, and won recognition in statewide drama competitions. A lover of both the written and spoken word, Houston also won recognition for her poetry from North Carolina A&T State University. She graduated from Dudley as cosalutatorian of her class in 1964 and was awarded a Rockefeller Scholarship to Emory University in Atlanta, Georgia. At Emory, Houston found several opportunities to foster her love for performance.

During her time at Emory, Houston participated in Theater Emory and the university's prestigious Barkeley Forum Debaters. As an English major, she was selected for the English Department's rigorous Honors Program and was tapped for the Women's Honor Organization (WHO), the highest honor a woman could receive at Emory during the time of her enrollment. She served as WHO president during the 1967–68 academic year. Houston was also a founding member of the Emory Black Student Alliance (BSA). In the spring of Houston's senior year, Dr. Martin Luther King, Jr., was assassinated. Houston and other members of the Emory BSA responded to the depth of the tremendous national loss by mounting a readers' theatre production of Langston Hughes's *Montage of a Dream Deferred* to raise the first funds for Martin Luther King, Jr., scholarships for minority students at Emory. She earned her bachelor's degree in English with high honors in 1968 and received a University Fellowship from the University of North Carolina at Chapel Hill to pursue an advanced degree in dramatic art.

At UNC, Houston's areas of concentration were theatre history and literature with a cognate in speech communication. A readers' theatre production that she wrote and directed as an assignment for a class taught by Professor Martha Nell Hardy provided the first opportunity for UNC's first Black freshman dramatic arts majors to perform. When she began her thesis, *The Federal Theatre's Black Units: A Study of their Social Relevance*, in the spring of 1969, her intention was to complete her master's degree and then obtain a doctorate in theatre. But she met and fell in love with Howard Stanback, then a fiery student activist at Wake Forest University. She dropped out of graduate school to marry him in August 1969, and went to work while he completed a master's degree in social work at Case Western Reserve University. In 1972, after the birth of their first son, Zuri Akili, Houston returned to UNC and completed her master's degree.

Houston then began a more than 30-year career as an educator, serving as a faculty member at five colleges and universities and as the chair of two communications departments. She saw a career in education as a viable way to achieve balance between work and family in a way that other careers did not offer. So even before earning her doctorate, Houston began her academic career in 1972 as an English and speech instructor at Clark College (now Clark Atlanta University) in Atlanta, Georgia. During four years on the Clark faculty, her intellectual interests shifted from theatre to speech communication.

In 1976, when Houston's husband took a post in the School of Social Work at the University of Connecticut, the family moved to Hartford, and Houston began looking for a doctoral program in speech communication. She enrolled at the University of Massachusetts at Amherst in 1978 as a part-time student, and eventually obtained University and Danforth Foundation Fellowships that enabled her to become a full-time student. Her initial academic interests included foci in media studies, African American language studies, and communication styles. She was critical of communication literature that, she suggests, did not reflect her experiences. She has never assumed that Black voices should be the only voices available to interested scholars. Yet, her concern was that if Black people did not tell their own stories, in their own words, someone else might tell them "in a way that we can't support" (Marsha Houston, personal communication, June 12, 2001). After a graduate interpersonal communication seminar cotaught by esteemed scholars Vernon Cronen and W. Barnett Pearce, Houston decided to concentrate in interpersonal communication and rhetoric. When it came time to write her dissertation, she was able to assemble what she called a "dream team" of progressive women scholars as her committee. Houston's chair was Fern Johnson, a pioneer in feminist language and communication studies, and her members were Jane Blankenship, a noted rhetorician, and Charlena Seymour, a pioneering Black woman scholar in Communication Disorders who eventually became the first Black women provost at the University of Massachusetts at Amherst. Her dissertation, *Code-Switching in Black Women's Speech* (1983) was nominated for an NCA dissertation award.

During her doctoral studies, Houston developed valuable mentoring relationships with members of the Speech Communication Association's Black Caucus, then a newly developing academic circle. She recalled that the first Black communication scholar she ever saw presenting a paper on Black women was Dorthy Pennington. Pennington's presentation at an International Communication Association conference was included in a panel about communication and women of color. She recalled, "To hear Dorthy talk about communication, race, and gender was very liberating for me" (Marsha Houston, personal communication, June 12, 2001). Houston's exposure to the idea of studying the communication patterns of Black women spawned the directions of her career future.

Houston's experiences were not without both personal and intellectual challenges. She was divorced while pursuing her doctoral degree, and struggled to "re-negotiate the world as a single parent" to her 10-year-old son, Zuri (Marsha Houston, personal communication, June 12, 2001). She also struggled in her efforts to bring together her interest in the "intersections of gender, race, and class in a way that was meaningful to me, and in a way that would be acceptable to the major outlets in the field" (Marsha Houston, personal communication, June 12, 2001). Finding acceptance for her work was difficult, yet through several invitations to contribute to book projects and special volumes of journals, Houston was able to locate an audience for her work. She especially credited feminist communication scholars Cheris Kramarae and Lana Rakow for their inclusion of her scholarship in their collections early in her career. Some resistance to her work came from feminist scholars themselves, who were unable to see the significance of her focus on African American women's issues. She also perceived some resistance to her ideas from African American male scholars, who sometimes rejected her arguments about gender equality in African American romantic relationships. Despite these adversities, Houston's resolve to include African American women's issues in these discussions kept her from giving up. Her steadfast determination proved to open many doors for other scholars, who realized the significance of studying communicative behavior at the intersections of race and gender.

❖ CONTRIBUTIONS TO COMMUNICATION RESEARCH

Much of Marsha Houston's work focuses on the ways that communicators negotiate perceptions of difference among themselves. Such perceptions guide human action and choice-making. Her academic background in English, dramatic art, and communication studies encouraged her to ask questions about how everyday linguistic uses are influenced by gender and racial/ethnic ideologies. For Houston, these uses constitute the enactment of cultural standpoints. When her scholarship was first introduced to the field, few other writers articulated the need to analyze gender and communication in the Black community. Before Patricia Hill Collins' *Black Feminist Thought* (1990), Houston postulated that the experiences of Black women are unique, thus challenging the perspective that all women have a common experience with oppression. She has additionally challenged White feminist and interpersonal scholars for their "slow acknowledgment of the scholarly importance of Black women's issues and experiences" (Marsha Houston, personal communication, June 12, 2001). She reflects on this challenge proudly, saying, "I think that I've opened up these conversations. I've raised some questions, stepped on a few toes, and made some arguments at a time when no one else was arguing them in print" (Marsha Houston, personal communication, June 12, 2001). Although she considers herself a feminist scholar, Houston's body of work encompasses two major genres: intercultural/interracial communication and communication and Black feminist theory.

Intercultural/Interracial Communication

Like many interracial and intercultural communication scholars, Houston began her scholarly career examining the structures and ideologies that create superior/subordinate social relationships between people of different racial/ethnic groups. Her first article was an essay with W. Barnett Pearce titled "Talking to 'The Man': Some Communication Strategies Used by Members of 'Subordinate' Social Groups," which was published in *The Quarterly Journal of Speech* (Houston & Pearce, 1981). In the article, Houston and Pearce analyzed four recurring communication patterns that are common between members of social groups who perceive their relationship as asymmetrical. They specifically argued that the functions and uses of passing, tomming, shucking, and dissembling communication strategies are directly related to distinct perspectives of intergroup relations. Thus, they posited the idea that communicators who perceived themselves as socially "inferior" to their counterparts carefully assess (1) expectations of the "superior" communicator, (2) their ability to avoid compliance with the expectations, and (3) the importance of the superior's expectations before acting. The authors used the coordinated management of meaning theory to argue that:

> [T]he behaviors of tomming, shucking, and dissembling are identical—that is, in all three cases, the lower-statused person behaves just as the higher statused person expects a social inferior to act. These forms of communication function differently, though: tomming and dissembling are consistent with an other-cultural perspective; and shucking with a co-cultural perspective. Further, shucking and passing are very different behaviorally, but both are consistent with a co-cultural perspective. Finally, tomming is honest, while all the others involve a kind of deception which we describe as "concatenated coherence." (Houston & Pearce, 1981, p. 24)

The authors argued for a "transcultural theory" of communication exchange that illuminates the cultural context of communicative action and provides theoretical and discursive space for understanding human communication in its various (and coexisting) forms. Prior to this essay, other Black writers such as Asante [Smith] (1973), Baugh (1983), Daniel and Smitherman-Donaldson (1976), and Garner (1983) investigated the functions of Black linguistic performance for Black communities. Yet, this article extended the extant disciplinary vocabulary for discussing top-down interpersonal relations.

Moreover, Houston's first review essay, "White talk Black talk: Inter-racial friendship and communication amongst adolescents," published in *Southern Journal of Communication* (Houston Stanback, 1988a), offered significant commentary about the need for communication scholars to acknowledge the heterogeneity of interracial communication encounters in their work. After the communication discipline took notice of the works of Asante, Cummings, Daniel, Pennington, Smitherman-Donaldson, Taylor, and others, Houston thought it was important for writers to be cautious about characterizing the attitudes and behaviors of Blacks in essentialist terms. She argues that analyses of interracial communication must recognize the multiple perspectives that exist within Black and White communities. She wrote:

> An examination of interracial communication ought to reveal the perspectives of both racial groups in order to clarify the nature of communication between them . . . While it is essential to contrast

Black and White perspectives, it is equally important not to misrepresent each group as homogeneous in attitudes and behaviors. (Houston Stanback, 1988a, p. 209)

Houston's cultural consciousness and cautious approach to interracial studies were heavily influenced by her desire for all marginalized people to be given a voice. Even with these extant multiple voices, if only a single voice on interracial communication was heard, it would undoubtedly illuminate some perspectives while leaving other ways of knowing and performing culture silent. One of her goals within her research published in the 1980s was to create spaces where multiple cultural perspectives could be heard and thereby validated in the communication literature.

Houston considers her greatest achievement in this area of research to be the "widely used and much imitated" anthology, *Our Voices: Essays in Culture, Ethnicity, and Communication* which she coedited with Alberto Gonzalez and Victoria Chen (Gonzalez, Houston, & Chen, 2004). First published in 1994, this work received the 1995 outstanding book award from the NCA International and Intercultural Communication Division. *Our Voices* broke new ground in intercultural scholarship as the first anthology to include work written exclusively by scholars of color and as a work that foregrounded dynamic, lived cultural experiences rather than static, universalized theories of lived reality.

Communication and Black Feminist Theory

Realizing the power of language in shaping Black Americans' social and political relationships early in her life, Houston was interested in exploring the stories told about Black women's communication. She saw the need to add to the body of work produced by notable feminist communication scholars such as Cheris Kramarae, Karlyn Kohrs Campbell, Fern Johnson, Anita Taylor, Sonja & Karyn Foss, and Julia Wood by identifying the ways in which traditional feminist theories tended to exclude the perspectives of Black women. Although her experience in the analysis of sociolinguistic behavior helped her to articulate how uses of language function to shape women's lives, her work stands firm in the idea that women's lives are not shaped in the same ways. She recognized that additional dialogues were needed in the literature about how Black women's everyday communication behaviors are influenced by the "double jeopardy" of racial and gendered oppression (Beale, 1970, p. 93). Having personally observed the numerous social roles that many Black women take on simultaneously, it was clear to Houston that such independence and resolve were directly related to the communicative patterns of Black women in their everyday lives. In the book chapter titled: *Language and Black Women's Place: Evidence from the Black Middle Class*, she wrote:

> Adequate explanations of Black women's speech demand the realization that Black women are both Black *and* female speakers. In other words, adequate explanations of Black women's speech must be grounded in clear conceptions of Black cultural definitions of women's roles and women's speech. (Houston Stanback, 1985, p. 179)

Thus, extension of popular feminist paradigms required clear articulation of the experiences of Black women as different from those of White women.

In 1988, Houston published the article: *What Makes Scholarship About Black Women and Communication Feminist Communication Scholarship?* in *Women's Studies in Communication* (Houston Stanback, 1988b). She argued that feminist theory places sexism at the helm of female oppression without acknowledging the numerous ways in which women find themselves oppressed in the world. To use a "linear" term such as *sexism* to describe the extended history of women's silenced voices in social, political, and scholarly circles erases how systems of oppression *intersect* in the lives of women. One consequence of viewing feminist theory in this way is the continued marginalization of non-White women's voices in explanations of how social ideologies limit women's expressiveness and social mobility:

> Feminist theory is essential to feminist scholarship because it provides the explanatory frame that accounts for women's place in the social order and the central experiences of women. To consider either racism or sexism as the more powerful oppressive force in African-American women's lives is to misperceive their experience. Thus feminist scholarship should use an inclusive and systematic form of feminist theory to account for all the oppressive forces that define African-American women's place in the social order. (Houston Stanback, 1988b, p. 28)

Houston contended that to understand Black women's communication it is important to understand Black women's roles in both domestic and public spheres. This duality of experience marks the core distinction between the language behavior of Black women and White women, who have been historically relegated to the domestic sphere.

Since her initial efforts to expand the scope of Black feminist theory, Houston has introduced key dialogues on African American women's communicative behavior to the field of communication. Her works included her chapter in *Our Voices* titled "When Black Women Talk with White Women: Why Dialogues Are Difficult" (Gonzalez, Houston, & Chen, 2004); "Writing for My Life: Intercultural Methodology and the Study of African American Women" (Houston, 2000b); "Multiple Perspectives: African American Women Conceive Their Talk" (Houston, 2000a); the award-winning anthology, coedited with Olga Davis, *Centering Ourselves: African American Feminist and Womanist Studies of Discourse* (Houston & Davis, 2002); and a chapter, coauthored with Karla Scott, of the Sage *Handbook of Gender & Communication*, titled *Negotiating Boundaries: The Language of Black Women's Intercultural Encounters* (Houston & Scott, in press).

Houston's goal to help create a space for other Black feminist scholars is realized in numerous works. She is frequently cited by scholars within and outside of the field of communication, including Patricia Hill Collins' *Black Feminist Thought* (Collins, 2000) and Jones and Shorter-Gooden's *Shifting: The Double Lives of Black Women in America* (Jones & Shorter-Gooden, 2003). Houston has been a mentor and friend to numerous leading Black womanist and feminist communication scholars, including Brenda J. Allen, Olga Davis, Janice Hamlet, Tina Harris, Katherine Hendrix, Joni Jones, and Karla Scott. Their works convey similar ideas about the intersections of race, gender, and sexual oppression and their influences in the lives of women. Finally, Houston's current book series with Hampton Press on African American communication and culture is a testament to her continued efforts to mentor young scholars and a provide a scholarly space for articulating the experiences of African Americans.

❖ CONCLUSION

Marsha Houston, a pioneer in communication research, has endured the adversities of post-segregationist racial attitudes, a dissolved marriage, single motherhood, and resistance to her scholarship and ideas. Nonetheless, as a leader, she exemplifies the strength of character and determination that is needed to drive any academic discipline forward. As a scholar, she has helped to open the doors for scholarly discussions about African American women's experiences. As a teacher and mentor, she continues to lend a hand (and ear) to young scholars looking for advice and direction. Her contributions to the field of communication and the lives of others will stand as a testament to all others who truly aspire to effect change.

❖ REFERENCES

Asante, M. K. [Arthur Smith] (1973). *Transracial communication*. Englewood Cliffs, NJ: Prentice Hall.

Baugh, J. (1983). *Black street speech: Its history, structure and survival*. Austin: University of Texas Press.

Beale, F. (1970). Double jeopardy: To be black and female. In T. Cade (Ed.), *The black woman* (p. 93). New York: Signet.

Collins, P. H. (2000). *Black feminist thought* (2nd ed.). New York: Routledge.

Daniel. J. L., & Smitherman-Donaldson, G. (1976). How I got over: Communication dynamics in the Black community. *Quarterly Journal of Speech, 62*(1), 26–39.

Garner, T. (1983). Playing the dozens: Folklore as strategies for living. *Quarterly Journal of Speech, 69*(1), 47–57.

Gonzalez, A., Houston, M., & Chen, V. (2004). *Our voices: Essays in culture, ethnicity, and communication* (4th ed.). Los Angeles: Roxbury.

Houston, M., & Davis, O. I. (2002). *Centering ourselves: African American feminist and womanist studies of discourse*. Cresskill, NJ: Hampton Press.

Houston Stanback, M. (1983). *Code-switching in Black women's speech*. Unpublished doctoral dissertation, University of Massachusetts, Amherst.

Houston Stanback, M. (1985). Language and Black women's place: Evidence from the Black middle class. In P. Treichler, C. Kramerae, & B. Stafford (Eds.), *For alma mater: Theory and practice in feminist scholarship* (pp. 177–193). Urbana: University of Illinois Press.

Houston Stanback, M. (1988a). [Review of White talk, Black talk: Inter-racial friendship and communication amongst adolescents.] *Southern Speech Communication Journal, 53*(2), 208–210.

Houston Stanback, M. (1988b). What makes scholarship about Black women and communication feminist communication scholarship? *Women's Studies in Communication, 11*(1), 28–32.

Houston Stanback, M., & Pearce, W. B. (1981). Talking to "The Man": Some communication strategies used by members of "subordinate" social groups. *Quarterly Journal of Speech, 67*(1), 21–30.

Jones, C., & Shorter-Gooden, K. (2003). *Shifting: The double lives of Black women*. New York: Harper Collins.

Lucaites, J., & Calloway Thomas, C. (1993). *Martin Luther King Jr. and the sermonic power of discourse*. Tuscaloosa, AL: University of Alabama Press.

Further Reading

Chen, V., Gonzalez, A., & Houston, M. (2000). *Communication strategies for making effective connections: An intercultural toolkit: Intercultural communication, communication & diversity, community building, interpersonal skills.* Baltimore: Annie E. Casey Foundation.

Houston, M. (1992). The politics of difference: Race, class, and women's communication. In L. Rakow (Ed.), *Women making meaning: New feminist directions in communication.* New York: Routledge.

Houston, M. (1993). The "Dog Theory" and beyond: African American women's communication about male-female relationships. In J. W. Ward (Ed.), *African American communications: A reader in traditional and contemporary studies* (pp. 39–47). Dubuque, IA: Kendall Hunt.

Houston, M. (1995). Women and the language of race and ethnicity. *Women and Language, 18*(1), 1–2.

Houston, M. (2000a). Multiple perspectives: African American women conceive their talk. *Women and Language, 23*(1), 11–17.

Houston, M. (2000b). Writing for my life: Intercultural communication methodology and the study of African American women. In J. N. Martin & O. I. Davis, (Eds.), *Ethnicity and methodology. Special issue of the International Journal of Intercultural Relations, 24,* 673–686.

Houston, M. (2002a). Seeking difference: African Americans in interpersonal research, 1970–2001. *Howard Journal of Communications, 13,* 25–43.

Houston, M., & Scott, K. (in press). Negotiating boundaries: The language of Black women's intercultural encounters. In J. Wood & B. Dow, (Eds.), *Handbook of gender and communication.* Thousand Oaks: Sage.

Houston Stanback, M. (1989). Feminist theory and Black women's talk. *Howard Journal of Communications, 1,* 187–194.

Marsha Houston

Photo courtesy of Marsha Houston

1950s — Born in Greensborough, North Carolina.

1968 — Received bachelor's degree in English from Emory College of Emory University.

1972 — Taught at Clark College in Atlanta, Georgia (1972–1976).

1973 — Received a master's degree in dramatic art with a concentration in theatre history and literature from the University of North Carolina at Chapel Hill.

1977 — Taught at Western New England College in Springfield, Massachusetts (1977–1980).

1980 — Presented "Dissembling, Passing, Shucking, and Tomming: A Theoretical Analysis of Some Forms of Intercultural Communication" to the International Communication Association in Acapulco, Mexico.

1981 — Coauthored (with W. Barnett Pearce), "Talking to 'The Man': Some Communication Strategies Used by Members of 'Subordinate' Social Groups" in the *Quarterly Journal of Speech*.

1982 — Became assistant professor at the University of Southern Mississippi.

Served as newsletter editor and secretary for the Black Caucus of the National Communication Association (1982–1984).

1985 — Became associate professor of English and Sociology and director of the Communication Studies Program at Spelman College.

Published "Language and Black Women's Place: Evidence from the Black Middle Class" in *For Alma Mater: Theory and Practice in Feminist Scholarship*.

1986 ◆ Served as member of the Educational Policies Board of the National Communication Association (1986–1989).

1987 ◆ Became chair of the Department of Communication at Georgia State University.

Served as member of the Search Committee for Executive Director (NCA) (1987–1988).

1988 ◆ Published "What Makes Scholarship About Black Women and Communication Feminist Communication Scholarship?" in *Women's Studies in Communication*.

Served as southern states representative to Legislative Council (NCA) (1988–1990).

Served as reader for Bostrom Young Scholars award (Southern States Communication Association).

Served as member/chair of the Resolutions Committee (Southern States Communication Association) (1988–1991).

Planned and organized The Power of the Spoken Word: The Oratory of Dr. Martin Luther King, Jr., a national scholarly conference cosponsored by the SCA Educational Policies Board and the Martin Luther King, Jr., Center for Nonviolent Social Change, Atlanta, Georgia.

1990 ◆ Became associate professor of Communication and Women's Studies at Tulane University.

Served as vice-chair and convention program planner, Feminist and Women's Studies Division (NCA) (1990–1991).

Planned and organized Difficult Dialogues: Gateways and Barriers to Women's Communication Across Cultures, Eighth National Conference on Research in Gender and Communication; jointly sponsored by Georgia State University, Spelman College, Emory University, Dekalb College, and Agnes Scott College, Atlanta, Georgia.

1991 ◆ Published "Difficult Dialogues: Report on the Eighth Annual Conference on Research in Gender and Communication" in *Women and Language*.

Served as chair, Feminist and Women Studies Division (NCA) (1991–1992).

1992 ◆ Published "The Politics of Difference: Race, Class, and Women's Communication" in *Women Making Meaning: New Feminist Directions in Communication*.

1993 ◆ Published "The 'Dog Theory' and Beyond: African American Women's Communication About Male-Female Relationships" in *African American Communications: A Reader in Traditional and Contemporary Studies*.

Served as member/chair of Time and Place Committee (SSCA) (1993–1995).

1994   Published *Our Voices: Essays in Culture, Ethnicity, and Communication* with Alberto Gonzalez and Victoria Chen.

Became first holder of the Nancy Reeves Dreux Chair in Women's Studies, Tulane University.

Won Francine Merritt award for Distinguished Service to Women in the Speech Communication Association and the Discipline.

1995   Won Distinguished Book award, SCA International & Intercultural Communication Division for *Our Voices: Essays in Culture, Ethnicity, and Communication.*

Served as chair, Francine Merritt Award Committee for the Women's Caucus (NCA).

1996   Served on the Awards Committee (NCA).

1998   Served as program planner, NCA Seminar Series.

Served as vice-chair and convention program planner/chair, African American Communication and Culture Division (AACC) (NCA).

1999   Served as immediate past chair and representative to Legislative Council AACC Division (NCA).

Became professor and chair of Communication Studies at the University of Alabama.

2000   Published "Multiple Perspectives: African American Women Conceive Their Talk" in *Women and Language.*

2001   Served as chair, Ad Hoc Committee on Black Caucus/AACC Division Endowment (NCA).

2002   Edited *Centering Ourselves: African American Feminist and Womanist Studies of Discourse* with Olga Idriss Davis.

Published "Seeking Difference: African Americans in Interpersonal Research, 1970–2001," in the *Howard Journal of Communications.*

Received Distinguished Book Award from the NCA African American Communication and Culture Division.

Received the Outreach Award from the Southern States Communication Association.

2004   Received Delta Sigma Rho/Tau Kappa Alpha National Honorary Society's Outstanding Alumna award.

9

Joni L. Jones /
Iya Omi Osun Olomo

Performance work in the academy subverts the mind/body split even while it appears to exist on the physical end of that inappropriate binary, because performance is at once physical and intellectual, visceral and cerebral.

(Jones, 1997, p. 58)

❖ INTRODUCTION

Joni Lee Jones is a distinguished writer, performance ethnographer, performer, videographer, and theatre director. Many consider Jones, a doctor of educational theatre, to be one of the most outstanding contributors to the practice of performance ethnography of the decade. Her performance and production efforts address several significant social issues, including racism and sexism in the academy and the "wounds that exist between African-American men and women" (Jones, 1993, p. 236). Because of her cathartic approach to African and African American theatre, Jones's work is widely recognized in several disciplines: theatre, dance, Africana studies, and communication.

As the preceding quote suggests, in addition to the therapeutic potential that Jones's work offers, Jones also provides a means to view performance as scholarship. In 2002, Jones was awarded the National Communication Association's Leslie Irene Coger Award for Distinguished Performance. One member of the award-nominating committee wrote that her work "seemingly merges with other forms of scholarship to become argument, critique, conversation, embodied theory and cere-mony" (NCA Distinguished Scholar Award Recipients, 2002). In her efforts to advance the development of a distinctively African American dramaturgy, Jones has taught many in the academy about the value of "living the life of one's work" and of the "interconnectedness of schol-arship, performance and production" (J. L. Jones, personal communi-cation, March 24, 2004).

Jones, who is associate director of the Center for African American Studies at the University of Texas at Austin, has received numerous awards, including a Fulbright for performance studies in Nigeria. Moreover, Jones taught at Obafemi Awolowo University and contributed "Theatre for Social Change" workshops for the Forum on Governance and Democracy in Ile-Ife, Osun State in Nigeria. She has also directed multiple theatrical productions in Washington, D.C., Texas, and Massachusetts. Jones is an accomplished performing artist and scholar who is perhaps most noted in the theatre community for two critical works: *sista-docta* and *Shakin' the Mess Outta Misery.* Her work has appeared in several presti-gious and noted publication outlets such as *The Drama Review, Theatre Insight, Text and Performance Quarterly,* and *Black Theatre News.*

❖ BIOGRAPHICAL INFORMATION

Born on the south side of Chicago in 1955, Joni L. Jones was influenced by the changing political and social climate of the civil rights movement of the 1960s and 1970s, as have most of the pioneers in this volume. Her mother, Dorothy Mae Brown Jones, and father, William Edward Jones, were natives of Louisiana and Texas, respectively. Jones grew up in a family structure that she described as "aware of itself as a Black middle class family" (J. L. Jones, personal communication, March 24, 2004). She had three older sisters: Regina Elaine Patrick, A. LaVerne Love, and Willetta Doreen Wordlaw. Although governmental politics was not a primary topic of conversation in her family, Jones recalled feeling a real sense of the transformative power of the civil rights movement across state borders, cultural ideologies, and religious factions, all happening primarily through actively engaged Black voices being heard and Black bodies being seen protesting for social justice. Jones learned at an early age how the political struggles of these years shaped the everyday realities of her family life. The postsegregationist social milieu defined her adolescence. Jones suggested that the "swirl of energy" that accompanied the civil rights movement was awe-inspiring" (J. L. Jones, personal communication, March 24, 2004). Her sisters were also quite conscious of the importance of the movement. In fact, LaVerne was a founding member of the Chicago branch of the National Black Feminist Organization. Although Jones was significantly younger than her sister, she recalled that LaVerne's activism was empowering for her and others in the surrounding Chicago communities.

Jones's family left metropolitan Chicago and moved to Markham, Illinois, a predominately Black suburban subdivision, when Jones was 5 years old. In Markham, Black families resided on one side of the main thoroughfare, whereas White families lived on the other. However, Jones attended integrated schools with the other Black, White, and Latino children of the community. Jones was proud to have that educational opportunity, although she was aware of the presence of racism still dormant in the minds of her White peers and their families.

During her youth, Jones's father worked as a machinist and was very active in the Urban League and the automobile manufacturers' union. Later in his life, he worked for the Social Security Administration until his death. Jones vividly recalled how the transition from blue-collar to white-collar work seemed to "make his spirit happier" (J. L. Jones, personal communication, March 24, 2004). Jones's father died in 1968, when she was 13 years old. The loss of her father changed both the structure of Jones's family and the way in which she envisioned female strength, power, and perseverance.

Although both of Jones's parents worked, her mother's role shifted significantly after Jones's father's death. As the primary wage earner of the now all-female family, Jones's mother struggled to meet the challenges of everyday family life. She worked several jobs during Jones's adolescent years. Jones recalled the enormous sense of empowerment and pride she felt in seeing her mother successfully maintain the family home and still be able to send Jones and her sister, Willetta, to college. It was the goal of both parents that all their children receive a college education. Although Jones's mother never attended college, she had various forms of professional training and experience, including work as a cashier at E. J. Korvetts and Spiegel department stores, as an employee of the U.S. Postal Service, and as a mental health technician by the time of her retirement.

Jones described her relationship with her older sisters as "crucial" to her development into womanhood, her artistry, and her scholarship. She recalled that her relationships with them helped her to understand what to expect from her life. Observing her sisters' lives unfold taught her a great deal about "relationships with men, what sisterhood might mean and what the role of education was" (J. L. Jones, personal communication, March 24, 2004). It was in seeing such strength and perseverance from her mother and sisters that Jones was motivated to pursue a line of scholarship in which the importance of lived experience and deconstructed everyday realities was paramount.

❖ ACADEMIC BACKGROUND AND EXPERIENCE

Education was valued highly in Joni L. Jones's family. Her father attended Prairie View A&M University, and her mother graduated from du Sable High School in Chicago. She recalled having the impression that "school was just something you did and you did well; it just wasn't even an option to do anything else" (J. L. Jones, personal communication, March 24, 2004). So, attending college was an expectation for Jones and her sisters instead of a choice. She recalled an early childhood ritual of delivering her report card to her parents for their review. Jones specifically remembered the "moment of holding my breath" while awaiting her father's approval of her academic performance. Naturally, she was always relieved when he did approve, and this was one of the motivating factors toward succeeding in each of her lifelong educational endeavors.

Jones recalled having a "deep and abiding relationship" with some of her teachers. She speaks of them fondly in stating that she "really cared about them, and truly believed that they cared about me." As previously noted, Jones's early educational years took place during a time of racially charged social politics. Thus, she recalls the tension of trying to navigate through and understand the nature of her relationships with teachers during this time of social transformation.

One of her most vivid memories during this time occurred during a heavy snow day in Chicago. Students of her school district were released from school early due to the inclement weather, but she and other students in her class were asked to clean the snow off their teachers' cars before they left for home. At first thought, Jones recalled perceiving this activity as fun until she reinterpreted the image of her teacher looking through one of the school windows at the group of Black students cleaning her car. She described the image as one that was especially striking because she also recalled feeling somewhat unequal in this experience because the group of students cleaning the cars walked home from school that day (as they did every day) in the snow, whereas the teachers who were having their cars cleaned drove home without offering rides to the students. She described this experience, this microinequity, as an "instance of quiet racism," and believed it to be one of the defining moments of her youth. Microinequities are, as one organization puts it, "those small slights which in themselves are not important and often seem funny in retrospect, but have the cumulative impact of drops of water on a rock" (Joint Math Meetings, 1994). The experience taught Jones that being Black in America meant having less power and privilege than Whites had. The direct message of this experience was that she could *clean* her White teachers' car, but could not *ride* in it (J. L. Jones, personal communication, March 24, 2004).

Reflecting on her relationships with former teachers, Jones now interprets the concern they showed for her development as almost "paternalistic" and "condescending." Yet, she also acknowledged how significant these relationships were for her self-esteem and confidence—realizing the importance of teacher immediacy and attention on student development. Despite the complexity of these relationships, she stated, "I had some teachers who made me feel exceptional." Jones believes that these teachers made a tremendous difference in her life (J. L. Jones, personal communication, March 24, 2004).

Jones graduated from high school in 1973. She described herself in high school as a "good student," and recalled studying very hard and being well-liked during this time in her academic life. She grew very fond of literature, language, and the practice of studying texts. After high school, Jones attended MacMurray College in Jacksonville, Illinois, a small private institution affiliated with the United Methodist Church. The choice to attend MacMurray was a valuable one because the transition from high school to college was relatively smooth. In 1977, Jones graduated summa cum laude with a bachelor's degree in speech and theatre. She recalled that the most difficult task at college was navigating her way through a predominately White academic institution. Jones has fond memories of her undergraduate education: "I got the best education *ever* at MacMurray (J. L. Jones, personal communication, March 24, 2004).

Jones's transition to graduate school was more challenging. Upon the advice and encouragement of her undergraduate mentor, Dr. Phillip Decker, Jones attended Northwestern University for her graduate program in performance studies. She entered graduate school with a strong interest in Black aesthetics and sought to explore the landscape of Black artistic production and its implications for politics and the spirit. Jones described her experiences with instructors during this time as "sharply different from what I had experienced ever before." She said that her relationships with them were "distant" and "critical." Her most profound memory of the year she spent there is of the perception of superiority others had toward her. After graduating in 1978, Jones recalled leaving Northwestern feeling confused and disheartened from the experience. She remembered the experience vividly and suggested, "My master's program did a lot to undermine my feelings of competence and success" (J. L. Jones, personal communication, March 24, 2004).

Reflecting on Northwestern, Jones concluded that her time there was difficult primarily because "the style of thinking, which had served me very well in the past" was not valued in the new educational environment. She noted, "I didn't ask the same kinds of questions, didn't approach literature in the same way—I just didn't seem to feel like I belonged there" (J. L. Jones, personal communication, March 24, 2004). Jones struggled externally in relationships with others and internally in terms of self-doubt. She often felt that her self-perception of intellectual inferiority placed her outside of the norm in academia. She also felt isolated and alone when outside of the academic environment.

Jones overcame the emotional impact of her early graduate school experiences by seeking mentorship from other African American scholars in the field. She recalled desperately needing understanding people with whom she could share her experiences and feelings. She acknowledged Marsha Houston, D. Soyinyi Madison, and Dwight Conquergood as key people in her intellectual and professional development. Houston served as Jones's informal mentor and was always willing to listen and advise her during difficult times as an assistant professor. Madison and Conquergoods's work motivated Jones to continue blending activism with scholarship. She described them as people who "live the life of their work, they don't merely report on it from a distance" (J. L. Jones, personal communication,

March 24, 2004). The support she received from them and others helped Jones push forward with her life and career.

Jones took an appointment at the University of Maryland in 1978. She taught courses in oral interpretation, group discussion, interpersonal communication, and several others. After four years in College Park, Maryland, she accepted a position at the College of William & Mary, where she successfully established and developed the Black Thespian Society. Jones remained in this appointment until 1983, when she accepted an appointment at Howard University to teach courses in oral interpretation, speech and debate, and persuasion. She also began working on her doctoral degree while teaching at Howard. In fact, she described the Howard campus environment as "extremely important" in prompting her to continue her studies because she was on a campus where discussions of Africa and the African Diaspora were "just a natural part of everyday talk" (J. L. Jones, personal communication, March 24, 2004). Howard functioned to validate and confirm Jones's interests in a way that she had never known. The collective intellectual environment and acceptance of Afrocentric ideas helped her shape a career path that was central to her identity and academic interests. Describing the environment at Howard, she said, "What's in the air; what is permissible in the environment goes a long way towards shaping what our intellectual pursuits are" (J. L. Jones, personal communication, March 24, 2004). The atmosphere there provided the motivation and support Jones needed to complete her degree in educational theatre at New York University in 1993. Jones is currently an associate professor of performance studies at the University of Texas (UT) at Austin. She also serves as associate director for the Center for African and African American Studies. Much of her work with the center is designed to create a venue for the UT and Austin communities to explore African and African Diasporic philosophies and engage in scholarship that "deepens our understanding of race, gender, class, sexuality, and nationhood" (J. L. Jones, personal communication, March 24, 2004).

Jones's appointment at the University of Texas at Austin began as a joint position in the departments of theatre and dance and communication studies. As an assistant professor, Jones found it very difficult to establish her performance work and teaching in theatre history as suitable for tenure in both departments. At the same time, the communication department became more empirically oriented. This was a particularly challenging time for Jones because she struggled to establish herself as an artist-scholar in a department that no longer recognized the value of her work, so her position was subsequently changed to a full-time appointment in theatre and dance. Yet through it all,

Jones refused to be invalidated by the academy—she continued to perform and create. She argued that all of life is performance, and that the performance of identity was a necessary and critical area of significant study (J. L. Jones, personal communication, March 24, 2004).

Jones described her pedagogical approach as "emergent pedagogy" in that she seeks to shape her teaching style to the content of the classes she teaches. She enjoys the collaborative and reflexive qualities of this approach and its potential to increase student learning opportunities. Jones' commitment to new ways of thinking about scholarship, learning, activism, and instruction influences her performance work in innovative and thought-provoking ways. For Jones, life experiences are far too valuable to underestimate their influence on personal, professional, and social life. This belief greatly influences her approach to all things.

❖ CONTRIBUTIONS TO COMMUNICATION RESEARCH

Joni Lee Jones has conceived, directed, and performed more than 20 creative works over her career. These works include *Searching for Osun* (2000), *sista-docta* (1994), *Broken Circles: A Journey through Africa and the Self* (1994), and *Wild Women and Rolling Stones* (1992). Jones's stellar performance work has been honored by the National Communication Association, U.S. Department of Education, Austin Chronicle of Theatre Critics, Outstanding Young Women of America, and Washington Theatre Festival. Her passion for performance and African-based theatre has also resulted in numerous guest performer invitations. In 1997, Jones received a prestigious Fulbright Fellowship to teach and study at Obafemi Awolowo University in Nigeria, where she conducted Theatre for Social Change workshops for the Forum on Governance and Democracy in Ile-Ife.

Jones's written scholarship has been particularly significant to the growing body of knowledge in performance ethnography. It was Victor Turner, one of Jones's major influences, who maintained that people's performances reveal their inner selves, sort of tattling on the interpreting artists. Performance ethnography offers remarkable illustrative potential because it is concerned with not only how the artist lives life and interprets individual and collective experiences but also how life itself is culturally constructed and imbued with meanings awaiting interpretation and action. To be clear, however, performance ethnographers place a premium value on "local knowledge"; that is, knowledge that is specific to the individuals living in the context of a local cultural community and behaving in accordance with their own cultural interpretations of everyday social rituals, norms, roles, functions, events, and activities. Of course, a major distinguishing characteristic of performance ethnography versus other types of ethnography is that the observations of the field researcher are then interpreted *and* performed. One of the heuristic qualities and principal challenges of performance ethnographers is the preservation of that experience through performance. What for some might seem to be a fleeting moment in a string of normal, everyday enacted discourses can be considered by the performance ethnographer to be an important episode deserving of critical attention. This point is probably best explained by Richard Schechner's statement that performance is a "restored" or "twice-behaved behavior" (Schnecher, 1990, p. 36). At its best, performance is a redundant activity that captures the subtle authentic nuances of already-lived experience via a performed interpretation. Naturally, the danger in restorative performance is that even if done carefully, it can leave an oppressed community even more vulnerable by trying to sanitize experience or by disrupting, misinterpreting, or displacing subjectivity and voice. In other words, the performance ethnographer has to be ever mindful of the politics of representation, of not re-creating the self in the process of performative articulation of someone else's lived experience (de Certeau, 2002). This superimposition, which can be dangerous and debilitating, can occur with even the slightest restorative act, which is why the performance ethonographer's role is so critical. She must be self-reflexive, respectful, meticulous, ethical, and observant of cultural intricacies and narrative intertextualities while also being cognizant of her character and relationship to the audience. Jones's pioneering performance and ethnographic communication research strongly embrace Victor Turner's conceptualization of performance as an act of liminality or existing on the borders of a culture's inside/outside (Turner, 1986). Furthermore, her work vividly illustrates a clear understanding that a given culture's inside/outside is not a binary configuration. There is a seamless web of significance between each that represents the fluidity and sometimes contradictory impulses of everyday life.

Loosely described as "a cross between journalism, theatre, and anthropology" (Swanson, 1999, p. 1), performance ethnography envisions all humans as actors of public life. It prioritizes the ways in which humans construct and participate in cultural expression to understand the "social dramas" of everyday life. Under this paradigm, the ethnographer seeks to understand how cultural performances (i.e., rituals, festivals, and so on) serve as forms of public address. This understanding is achieved through intense field study, which is later transformed into a performance of the experience that can be shared with others. In *The*

Anthropology of Performance, Victor Turner described the value of studying cultural performance as follows:

> [C]ultural performances are not simple reflectors or expressions of culture or even of changing culture but may themselves be active agencies of change, representing the eye by which culture sees itself and the drawing board on which creative actors sketch out what they believe to be more apt or interesting "designs for living." (Turner, 1986, p. 24)

Turner's critique of textual positivism as a primary means of studying communication resonated with Jones in a way that few others had. The work of scholars such as Dwight Conquergood, Richard Schechner, and D. Soyini Madison offered Jones the validation and intellectual home she searched for throughout her graduate school career.

Although very invested in the scholarly tenets of the performance paradigm, Jones described herself as an "artist-scholar" because the term acknowledges the interconnectedness of scholarship, production, and performance (J. L. Jones, personal communication, March 24, 2004). Her personal philosophy frames her researcher identity; therefore, she does not subscribe to a standard empirical model of research that objectively detaches the researcher and cleanses her interpretations. Instead, her holistic approach acknowledges the intertextuality of life. She also considers herself an activist in the sense that her work often calls for some form of social change and transformation. Jones's article "Improvisation as a Performance Strategy for African-based Theatre" (Jones, 1993) discussed studying the Egungun, Apidan, and Ogunde theatrical performances of the Yoruba to incorporate characteristics of them into two Yoruba-based performances that were enacted by university students. In her observations of the Yoruba, Jones identified several common characteristics of Yoruba performance. Of them, she argued that improvisation offers the most resonance with and transformative potential for African American life, thus she "fashioned a dramaturgical/performance paradigm that relied heavily on improvisation" (Jones, 1993, p. 233). The performances were geared toward "healing the wounds that exist between African-American men and women" (Jones, 1993, p. 236). The function of healing in these productions was paramount, as Jones noted in the following excerpt:

> Performance as healing is an essential feature of the African-based productions with which I have worked: the healing is the way in which such performances achieve efficacy . . . by offering

[participants] an opportunity to actively explore their own solutions to social problems, performance can begin to heal the wounds of a community by allowing all present to physically participate in the examination of those wounds. (Jones, 1993, p. 235)

With the goal of community healing in mind, Jones is optimistic about the power of performance to yield social transformation. Evidence in this case does not follow the conventions of empirical paradigms; instead, she noted:

Even without empirical evidence demonstrating that healing occurred, I am encouraged by the fact that at the end of one performance two police officers on duty stopped to see what was going on in the gym, and they stayed to eat and play drums while everyone danced. . . . The freedom that is at the heart of improvisation gives space for this communal interaction, and it is this interaction that is a step toward healing community wounds. (Jones, 1993, p. 59)

Thus, personal transformation via performance is the hallmark of Jones's contributions to communication research.

Although her study of improvisation has received widespread acknowledgement across academic disciplines, Jones believes that her work *sista-docta* has been most noted throughout her career. *sista-docta* offers a challenging critique of the academy's treatment of diversity, equal opportunity and inclusion. She presented this critique in auto-ethnographic form, allowing herself to use her own experiences as an African American woman professor at predominately White institutions to share the common struggles of African American women professors with her listening audience. The performance, which was recalled and also critiqued by Jones in her essay chronicling the experience of performing *sista-docta* for different audiences (Jones, 1997), resists the ideologies of White male dominance, Black female eroticism, and the invisibility of blackness and whiteness as defining social constructs:

By being oblivious to the politics of their own whiteness and White consciousness, White faculty remain unable to see blackness, to experience black as a sociopolitical identity construct interwoven around and through a White identity construct. sista-docta can confront the White-centered assumptions upon which the academy is based, insisting that White faculty acknowledge their contribution to the White sensibility of the academy. (Jones, 1997, p. 60)

Although the tone of the performance is subversive in its intentions to make observers uncomfortable at times, its transformative power comes from Jones's ability to strongly compel members of the audience to reflect on their participation in and perhaps enabling of the oppressive ideologies that characterize academic life. Jones confronts these ideologies through autobiographical performance to promote the kind of healing needed to enhance opportunities and access for more women and scholars of color in the academy. *sista-docta* takes a bold step in her call for social transformation.

Jones has made remarkable strides in the field of communication. She has been an artist, director, producer, author, teacher, activist, and mentor. Her work spans continents, disciplines, and perspectives. Even as she espouses transformational politics through her work, she has undergone her own transformation, which is signified by her newly assumed Yoruba name: Iya Omi Osun Olomo. Through her contributions to communication studies, we see her honest and penetrating critiques of debilitating social practices and her interpretive performances restored for the sake of reflection and transformation. These contributions have been and continue to be inspiring to all who know her work.

❖ CONCLUSION

Joni Lee Jones (aka Iya Omi Osun Olomo) was the 2002 recipient of the National Communication Association's Leslie Irene Coger Award for Distinguished Performance. As demonstrated throughout this chapter, Jones is a dynamic scholar, activist, and promoter of radical progressive social transformation. In addition to challenging systems of racism and sexism in the academy, Jones's work challenges "the academy's predilection for print scholarship" (Jones, 1997, p. 51). Given what she perceives as a "devaluing" of performance scholarship in academic departments, Jones also sees her work as a way to show members of the academy "how the qualitative provides some missing pieces in the research puzzle; pieces that empirical data does not always expose" (J. L. Jones, personal communication, March 24, 2004). Jones argues that performance work has a valuable place in the process of knowledge generation, yet continues to be ill-considered as a form of scholarship because it resists the biases of logical positivism:

Performance is a form of embodied knowledge and theorizing that challenges the academy's print bias. While intellectual rigor has long been measured in terms of linguistic acuity and print productivity that reinforces the dominant culture's deep meanings, performance is suspect because of its ephemeral, emotional, and physical nature. (Jones, 1997, p. 53)

Jones offers a distinct voice for performance scholars who find their intellectual pursuits diminished by "the linguistic and textualist bias of speech communication [that] has blinded many scholars to the preeminently rhetorical nature of cultural performance—ritual, ceremony, celebration, festival, parade, pageant, feast and so forth" (Conquergood, 1991, p. 188). In this way, Jones's work challenges us all to reflect on the ways in which we envision scholarship and to include the efforts of those whose work exists outside of that vision. Her critiques of self, community, and society remind us that scholarship is truly for transformation. This goal remains at the forefront of Jones's efforts, and we expect that her contributions to the academy will continue to influence its future directions.

❖ REFERENCES

Conquergood, D. (1991). Rethinking ethnography: Towards a critical cultural politics. *Communication Monographs, 58*(2), 179–194.

de Certeau, M. (2002). *The practice of everyday life.* Berkeley: University of California Press.

Jones, J. (1993). Improvisation as a performance strategy for African-based theatre. *Text and Performance Quarterly, 13*(2), 233–251.

Jones, J. (1997). sista-docta: Performance as critique of the academy. *Drama Review, 41*(2), 51–67.

Joint Math Meetings. (1994). *Micro-inequity skits.* Retrieved September 14, 2004, from http://www.maa.org/features/skits_intro.html.

NCA Distinguished Scholar Award Recipients. (2002). Retrieved September 14, 2004, from http://www.natcom.org/awards/coger/2002.

Schechner, R. (1990). *Between theater and anthropology.* Philadelphia: University of Pennsylvania Press.

Swanson, C. D. (1999). Joni L. Jones and the art of ethnography: Inside the spinning, whirling world. *Austin Chronicle, 18*(51), 1–6.

Turner, V. (1986). Performing ethnography. In V. Turner, *The anthropology of performance* (pp. 139–155). New York: AJ Publishing.

Further Reading

Jones, J. (1996). The self as other: Broken circles. *Text and Performance Quarterly, 16*(1), 131–145.

Jones, J. (2002a). Performance ethnography: The role of embodiment in cultural authenticity. *Theatre Topics, 12*(1), 1–15.

Jones, J. (2002b). Conjuring as radical re/membering in the plays of Shay Youngblood. In P. C. Harrison, V. L. Walker II, & G. Edwards (Eds.), *Black theatre: Ritual performance in the African Diaspora* (pp. 206–228). Philadelphia: Temple University Press.

Jones, J. (2002c). Teaching in the borderlands: The performance of African-American literature in the multi-ethnic classroom. In C. Wimmer & N. Stucky (Eds.), *Teaching performance studies* (pp. 175–190). Carbondale: Southern Illinois University Press.

Jones, J. (2003). sista-docta. In L. C. Miller & J. Taylor (Eds.), *Voices made flesh: Performing women's autobiography* (pp. 128–142). Madison: University of Wisconsin Press.

Joni L. Jones /
Iya Omi Osun Olomo

Photo courtesy of Joni L. Jones/Iya Omi Osun Olomo

1956	Born in Chicago, Illinois.
1973	Graduated from high school and attended MacMurray College in Jacksonville, Illinois.
1977	Graduated summa cum laude from MacMurray College with a bachelor's degree in speech and theatre.
1978	Graduated from Northwestern University with a master's degree in performance studies.
	Became an instructor at the University of Maryland (1978–1982).
1982	Accepted position as instructor at the College of William & Mary.
1984	Accepted position as instructor at Howard University.
1990	Accepted position as associate professor at the University of Texas at Austin.
1992	Conceived and directed *Wild Women and Rolling Stones*.
1993	Received doctorate in educational theatre from New York University.
1994	Conceived, performed, and directed *sista-docta*, which offers a challenging critique of the academy's commitment to diversity, equal opportunity, and inclusion (performed numerous times between 1994 and 2002).
	Conceived, performed, and directed *Broken Circles: A Journey Through Africa and the Self*.
2001	Conceived, performed, and directed *Searching for Osun* (performed in 2001 and 2002).

2002   Received Leslie Irene Coger Award for Distinguished
        Performance.

        Published "Performance Ethnography: The Role of
        Embodiment in Cultural Authenticity," in Theatre Topics.

        Published "Teaching in the Borderlands: The Performance of
        African-American Literature in the Multi-ethnic Classroom,"
        in Teaching Performance Studies.

2004   Published "Improvisation as a Performance Strategy for
        African-based Theatre."

10

Dorthy L. Pennington

Too often intercultural study is confined to a description and awareness of the differences between and or among cultures. Although necessary, this treatment alone is inadequate. Beyond recognizing differences, which is analogous to noticing the tip of the iceberg while the bottom  *goes unseen, there is the need to understand the reasons for and the nature of the differences. Probing cosmological issues allows one to penetrate deeper, to really begin to understand the nature of culture.*

(Pennington, 1985, p. 31)

❖ INTRODUCTION

Dorthy L. Pennington, associate professor of African and African-American Studies and Communication Studies at the University of Kansas, is a scholar whose research has helped to illuminate the concept of power in studies of intercultural and interracial communication. Although her early research interests centered on Black rhetoric, she became increasingly interested in the development of intercultural communication theory as a young scholar. Pennington insists that research investigations of power dynamics and perceived privilege are crucial in the development of intercultural/interracial communication theory as well as an appreciation of cultural diversity and improved race relations in the United States. Her interest in improving the quality of intercultural exchanges between people has made her an important figure in both local and national circles. In 2004, Pennington was awarded a Lawrence, Kansas Sesquicentennial observance public programming grant for a project titled: *African American Churches in Early Lawrence: Citadels of Faith, Hope, and Community.* As project director, Pennington coordinated a panel discussion and ecumenical choir float presentation for the Lawrence Sesquicentennial celebration, designed to promote awareness of the role of African American churches in the history of the Lawrence community.

Pennington has been recognized locally and nationally as an outstanding mentor, teacher, scholar, and community leader. During her illustrious career, she has received numerous awards, honors, and nominations: a teaching award by the Teachers on Teaching series of the National Communication Association, recognition in several biographical listings of distinguished intellectuals, and an award for being a Distinguished Alumnus of a Historically Black Institution (Rust College), given by the National Association of Equal Opportunity in Higher Education. Moreover, on April 20, 2004, Pennington was inducted into the prestigious Kansas University Women's Hall of Fame. She was selected by The Commission on the Status of Women at the University of Kansas for her unique contributions to women of the University of Kansas and Lawrence communities.

Pennington's contributions to the field of communication have also been outstanding. She is a cofounder of the National Communication Association's (NCA) Black Caucus, for which she served as chair from 1974 until 1976, and played a key role in establishing the NCA African American Communication and Culture Division in 2000. She has served on many editorial and advisory boards and on national association governance committees. Pennington is an active participant in the NCA

Feminist and Women's Studies Division, which honored her with a spotlight convention program on her life and work in 1995. She is widely recognized as a communication theorist, educator, and mentor.

Pennington's book chapters appear in groundbreaking works concerning intercultural/interracial communication. In particular, her contributions to the development of interracial communication theory are included in Asante, Newmark, and Blake's *Handbook of Intercultural Communication* (Pennington, 1979); Asante and Vandi's *Contemporary Black Thought: Alternative Analyses in Social and Behavioral Science* (Pennington, 1980); and Samovar and Porter's *Intercultural Communication: A Reader* (Pennington, 1985). Pennington also appears in other volumes concerning the nature and processes of communicating across cultural spaces.

Pennington is a highly noted writer, mentor, and community advocate. Although each of these roles could easily be discussed in distinct chapters, the remaining sections of this chapter will highlight her early life, academic experiences, and contributions to communication research.

❖ BIOGRAPHICAL INFORMATION

Dorthy Pennington was born on May 24, 1946, in rural Mississippi. She was born into an extended family of aunts and uncles, including her mother's eight siblings. This sibling support network was unusually tight-knit because Pennington's maternal grandparents died early in their own children's lives. Pennington spent much of her early life on her family's farm with her aunts and uncles, who were cotton and soybean farmers. One of her aunts cared for her during the day while both her parents worked. Her mother worked as a schoolteacher and later became a principal in the Mississippi public school system. Pennington was the only child of her parents for many years, and because neighboring farms were miles apart, she could see her friends only on weekends. Thus, she spent all of her formative years on the family farm, in which she learned some "very important values" (D. L. Pennington, personal communication, July 12, 2004) such as self-determination, self-sufficiency, hard work, community collaboration, and the importance of family cohesion. Year after year, Pennington observed her uncles and other neighboring farmers help each other harvest their crops and noted that "this allowed everyone the opportunity to share in each other's success." These family values taught her to be kind and generous to all people. Those who know her well consider her a wonderfully compassionate and giving individual.

Pennington spent many childhood afternoons reading books, and her memories of the solitude of reading under a tree on sunny afternoons remain clear to this day. Despite her personable nature, Pennington remembers being very shy as a young child. While some kids were out playing and horsing around, she expended many hours fueling her love of learning and "curiosity about how things worked." Even during these early years, she was gaining an early appreciation for systematic investigation. Her passion for knowledge, thirst for understanding, and curiosity about how things functioned served her well in both her scholarly and community endeavors (D. L. Pennington, personal communication, July 12, 2004).

Pennington was quite fond of music as a child. She learned piano as an adolescent, and eventually became proficient enough to play the piano and/or sing for small church programs and school functions. She has always enjoyed singing, particularly gospel music, and has worked to develop her talents as both a singer and musician. Her love of music has remained a stable part of her life. She continues to perform as a musician and is currently a church organist for special occasions. Her personal affinity for music and its innocent emotional effect on all human beings, despite one's race, perhaps drove her closer to that mode of entertainment.

Racial tensions between Black and White people of the segregated south were very influential on Pennington. She was vividly aware of the oppressive Jim Crow laws that restricted the lives of many African Americans and ultimately left them with no devices to defend themselves against discrimination. She also became aware of the community resistance efforts of the late 1950s throughout the south, which marked the beginning of the civil rights movement. The various marches, protest speeches, and groundbreaking litigation (i.e., Brown v. Topeka Board of Education) awakened the nation to the power of organized resistance and gave people hope for the prospect of change. As a product of this magnificent moment in American history, Pennington has asked (and answered) some very important questions about how we might continue to strive for improved human relations for all people.

❖ ACADEMIC BACKGROUND AND EXPERIENCE

Dorthy Pennington began elementary school as one of the youngest students in her class. She excelled in her studies from the very beginning and recalled completing coursework in a single year that took some of her classroom colleagues twice as long to finish. Pennington described the first school she ever attended as "a three room building where the teacher taught the curricula for three or four different grade levels in the same room." She describes herself during these years as one who was always in search of new understandings and discoveries (D. L. Pennington, personal communication, July 12, 2004).

Pennington's early education emphasized the value of oral delivery skills. She recalled how effective her teachers were at encouraging her to speak out and to share her views with others. She felt significantly supported by teachers during these early years. Her abilities as a leader, scholar, and musician were all cultivated in a small rural school, in which she could express her ideas and explore her potential. From these early beginnings, Pennington developed a profound sense of self worth and value in achievement. In this way, her early educational experiences served to build her confidence and encourage her to reach her full potential into adulthood.

Pennington was an athlete in middle school. She played basketball and softball and ran track throughout her junior high school years. She believes that her participation in athletics and leadership opportunities helped her to develop a more outgoing personality. Although she left athletics later in high school, she remembers vividly how much her involvement as a student athlete helped her grow socially. Nonetheless, Pennington maintained her focus on academics in high school. She was an honors student, member of the school choir, and was elected to a variety of leadership roles.

Her early educational and religious experiences also shaped her desire to attend Rust College in Holly Springs, Mississippi—a private Methodist institution established in 1866 by the Freedman's Aid Society of the Methodist Episcopal Church. Rust College is the oldest of the 11 historically Black colleges and universities related to the United Methodist Church, the oldest historically Black college in the state of Mississippi, and one of the remaining five historically Black colleges in the United States founded before 1867 (Rust College, 2005). Pennington decided to attend Rust because many of her teachers were alumni of Rust and encouraged her to go there.

At Rust College, Pennington found a place where her religious and educational priorities were valued and nurtured. Although she initially believed that she would major in music, she won a first-place honor at a statewide high school oratory contest and was subsequently offered a scholarship. Thus, her undergraduate major was English, with a minor degree emphasis in French. The opportunity to earn a cost-free college education was far too valuable for Pennington to decline. This decision proved to serve her well, as she appeared on the dean's academic honor list for most of her undergraduate career.

While at Rust College, Pennington continued to perform as a musician and accept leadership opportunities. Her exuberance for learning was fed by the supportive environment there and resulted in her early graduation—after only three and a half years. During her senior year, Pennington served as a tutor for her peers in English and French. She viewed her work with fellow students as an opportunity to return Rust's generosity. Rather than leaving her cherished educational community, Pennington decided to remain in residence at Rust during what would have been the final semester of her senior year to prepare for the Graduate Record Exam. Pennington had high hopes of continuing her education. While her peers were preparing to become teachers in the Mississippi school system, Pennington applied to graduate programs and taught English and French courses for Rust College as an instructor.

After applying for entrance into several graduate programs, Pennington chose to attend the University of Kansas. She recalls coming to this decision in part because "they wrote the most cordial and warm letters, welcoming me to most certainly become a part of the University of Kansas." With her hopes to further her education confirmed, Pennington relocated to Kansas with the intention of leaving the field of English behind and studying in a field focused more on fundamentals of oral communication. She was immediately attracted to the speech communication and human relations program at the University of Kansas (D. L. Pennington, personal communication, July 12, 2004).

In hindsight, Pennington believes that her decision to attend the University of Kansas was valuable for several reasons. She found herself in an academic environment in which she was free to explore issues that interested her. She specifically recalled the rare opportunity to take a course called "The Rhetoric of Black Americans." In the course, Pennington was able to study the strategies of Black speakers, an important focal shift for Pennington because her previous coursework gave her little exposure to Black public address. She recalled being so intrigued by the course and how it "spoke" to her everyday realities that she was motivated to remain in the program and pursue a doctorate in speech communication and human relations, with an emphasis in rhetoric, at the University of Kansas (D. L. Pennington, personal communication, July 12, 2004).

After becoming more familiar with the field of classical rhetoric in the doctoral program, Pennington's ideas about communication took her scholarship in a different direction. The social milieu during her time as a graduate student in the late 1960s and early 1970s was both exciting and tumultuous. With the intensity of the civil rights movement came a surging academic interest in the study of culture and race relations. Pennington became interested in a newly emerging field of study: intercultural communication. She enrolled in every course that was available in that area of inquiry on her campus. She utilized her training in classical rhetoric to explore the then-unorthodox fields of Black rhetoric and intercultural communication. Pennington noted the connection she made between her academic study of these fields and her lived experiences: "When I began to study intercultural communication theory I began to see, that in my mind at least, there needed to be a marriage between what I lived and saw and how I could understand theory to help me explain what I'd seen, so I merged intercultural theory in a classic sense with interracial realities." Her desire to use newly emerging intercultural communication theories to describe her life experiences as a woman of color growing up in the segregated south led to new approaches to the study of the relationship between African American cosmologies and communication patterns between Black and White Americans. She became part of a group of innovators in communication who emphasized the importance of recognizing African American cosmological and epistemological perspectives in contemporary communication scholarship (D. L. Pennington, personal communication, July 12, 2004).

Pennington found a great deal of support for her interests at Kansas. She recalled feeling very welcomed and included by both faculty and fellow graduate students. With her strong sense of independence and inclusion into the informal networks of her academic department (which she suggested were very important to her success there), she was able to overcome some of the obstacles of being one of the first African American graduate students to study communication on the campus and receive a graduate degree.

The newly emerging field of interracial communication would have a profound effect on Pennington's future scholarship. Studies in the field helped to provide a theoretical basis for her to understand many of her own life experiences. As a student and developing scholar in the field, she felt very fortunate to have had the opportunity to share her work with other scholars who were equally as interested in exploring issues of race and human relations in the United States.

Despite the many advantages of the supportive environment at Kansas, she distinctly remembered navigating through the experience of usually being the only graduate student of color in her classes. She reported that the biggest transitional turning point for her was "going from a strongly, staunchly segregated society to a strongly Caucasian society" (Pennington, 2003). Over time, she saw more and more diversity at the University of Kansas, primarily because of newly initiated efforts to diversify predominantly White institutions of higher learning in the United States. However, she still recalled the feeling of being different from others in her cohort on the campus and within the classroom (D. L. Pennington, personal communication, July 12, 2004).

In 1974, Pennington completed her doctoral dissertation, titled *Temporality among Black Americans: Implications for Intercultural Communication* (Pennington, 1974). She was offered a faculty position at the University of Kansas that same year and became the first African American faculty member of the communication studies department. Pennington continues to teach there, with a split appointment in both communication studies and African American studies. The past 30 years of her academic career have brought Dorthy Pennington significant opportunities to tie the everyday realities she observed as a young girl in Mississippi to the training she received at the University of Kansas. These opportunities have allowed her to make significant scholarly contributions to the field of communication.

❖ CONTRIBUTIONS TO COMMUNICATION RESEARCH

Dorthy Pennington's scholarship has contributed to the growing body of knowledge in three areas. Focus on theory development in these areas has motivated her to challenge the ways in which key concepts in the field of communication are articulated by other scholars. She identifies both her scholarly and teaching interests as Black rhetoric, Black women's studies, and intercultural/interracial communication. Pennington's efforts to expand the scope of inquiry in these areas have resulted in several collaborative works with other notable communication scholars such as Larry Samovar and Richard Porter (Pennington, 1985), Arthur Smith (aka Molefi Asante; Pennington 1979; 1980; 1989), and William Gudykunst (Pennington, 1989).

Black Rhetoric

Although Pennington's doctoral degree emphasis was in classical rhetoric, little of her disciplinary training provided a unique space to write about the strategies of contemporary Black speakers. In her chapter entitled: "Guilt Provocation: A Strategy in Black Rhetoric," which appears in *Contemporary Black Thought: Alternative Analyses in Social and Behavioral Science*, Pennington argued that "representative black speakers, while using the same concept [guilt], employ a basis of application structurally different from traditional notions provided by theorists on guilt" (Pennington, 1980, p.112). Her objective was to argue for the incongruity of traditional conceptualizations of guilt with the rhetorical practices of notable African American orators. Although the writings of Jaspers (1947) and others advanced theoretical discussions of guilt provocation by identifying different types, these conceptualizations also argued that guilt could only be provoked internally. Pennington asserted the argument that the act of being "guilty" is an individual act that cannot be applied to appeals toward groups or collectives. Pennington found this paradigm for understanding guilt provocation as a rhetorical strategy to be limited and inefficient to describe the ways in which speakers such as Martin Luther King, Jr., Frederick Douglass, and Malcolm X used guilt provocation to indict White America for its transgressions against Blacks. Pennington concluded her analysis of critical discourse by arguing:

> The point of significance is that black speakers are making a judgment about America based upon some criteria. And in the cases where the term "guilty" is used by black speakers, their meaning is clear. This tendency violates the postulates of Jaspers and suggests that from the point of view of some black speakers, at least, judgments of guilt can be externally imposed upon others. (Pennington, 1980, p. 123)

In this way, Pennington challenged the validity of traditional conceptualizations of guilt provocation in explaining how Black speakers use guilt to "awaken the consciousness" of White America about the burdens of racism and discrimination in *their* lives (D. L. Pennington, personal communication, July 12, 2004). She identified the uniqueness of Blacks' experiences in the United States (as expressed by Black speakers) as an argumentative base for how social groups can be externally charged with moral and metaphysical guilt. This work implied that the concept of guilt is more expansive and has larger applications and implications for rhetorical studies than previously postulated. Pennington also noted that the act of guilt provocation on the part of Black speakers is best understood contextually because it is linked to the sociopolitical relationships of the time. These ideas paved the way for the development of new theories.

Black Women's Studies

Pennington's interest in theory development and her perceived need for communication scholarship to reflect the experiences of non-White and female communicators led her to write about Black Women's experiences. In the book *Seeing Female: Social Roles and Personal Lives* (Pennington, 1988), edited by Sharon Brehm, Pennington argued that African American women have successfully reconciled the contradictions between traditional conceptions of Caucasian American women as docile, fragile, and sexually innocent in concert with the negative images of them constructed by Caucasian Americans as a result of chattel slavery. She posited that such reconciliation was achieved mainly by Black women's pure resilience to stereotypical messages and images of them as "breeders, concubines, mammies, [and] mules (Pennington, 1988, p. 33). Pennington also suggested that traditional African worldviews (which place women at the center of most religious, family, political and social affairs) "served as the motivation and principles guiding Afro-American women toward specific strategies of achievement, in spite of their ascribed status of being Afro-American, female, and often, poor" (Pennington, 1980, p. 34).

In the chapter titled "Afro-American Women: Achievement Through the Reconciliation of Messages and Images" (Pennington, 1980), Pennington identified the important link between articulating religious values in African American communities and teaching Black women compassion and tolerance (in spite of their ascribed social status). She argued that this ongoing struggle has inspired them to fight for the improvement of the lives of African Americans:

> Just as religion served as a basis of hope for Afro-Americans, it also served as a basis for the motivation needed to actively resist oppression. The religious values of Afro-American women caused them to employ strategies that combined compassion with forcefulness in order to reconcile conflicting messages and images, and to advance their cause. (Pennington, 1980, p. 35)

In this way, Black women were encouraged through religion to see themselves as "warriors" waged in a battle to uplift themselves and their communities, regardless of the ascribed inferiority imposed upon them. Thus, according to Pennington, religion serves as a reconciling agent that offers Black women a sense of purpose and positive self-worth (Pennington, 1980).

Pennington described the strategy of becoming trained and educated as important in the lives of Black women. She contended that their sense of purpose and strength, as articulated through religious values, motivated them to become leaders in their communities by becoming knowledgeable about social and political activities, seeking professional proficiency, and organizing themselves to assist other disadvantaged African American women. Hence, the Black Women's Club movement emerged. Pennington posited:

"Love thy neighbor as thyself" was a motivating theme that Cynthia Hope [an African American leader in Atlanta in 1908] and other educated Afro-American women adopted to show their concern for the masses deprived of educational and training opportunities. This legacy inspired much of the effort of Afro-American women in the Club movement. Their motto was "Lifting as We Climb." The most prominent organization of the Club Movement was the National Association of Colored Women, formed in 1896. (pp. 37)

This agent of reconciliation was undoubtedly the most profound in forging a positive identity for African American women and giving them a voice in society.

The need to balance social, family, and work responsibilities was also a point of reconciliation for Black women. Pennington explained the complex roles of African American women who managed large families (sometimes single-handedly), participated in community activities, and worked as heavy laborers alongside African American men on farms. To resolve the contradictory view of Caucasian American women, who had very few social and work responsibilities, with the view of themselves as "beasts of burden," African American women "combined this image with their view of themselves as industrious and reconciled the two" (Pennington, 1980, p. 39). She eloquently concluded the chapter with the following statement:

They [African American women] have walked between the highly negative images held of Black women and the highly passive images held of White women to find a vision of women, strong *and* tender. Under the most difficult of circumstances, Afro-American women have struck a balance for all women. (Pennington, 1980, p. 40)

Pennington's in-depth analysis of Black women's experiences and social adaptation strategies brings to light the need to contextualize Black women's rhetoric as centered in their connection to spirituality, family, and unwavering strength.

Pennington's work in this area includes the book *African American Women Quitting the Workplace* (Pennington, 1999), which provides an analysis of interviews she conducted over two years with African American women who decided to end their careers and leave their places of employment. Pennington identified the significance and consequences of this decision in the lives of the women as she made theoretical links to the idea that the conception of African American women as laborers is alive and well in the American workplace. According to Pennington, many Black women are deciding to "free" themselves from the power of this conception by leaving the workplace and moving elsewhere to find a more conducive atmosphere for growth, to gain respect, and to assert their own agency to define who they are (Pennington, 1999).

Intercultural/Interracial Communication

One of Pennington's' first published works was a coauthored project with Jon A. Blubaugh. The book, *Crossing Difference: Interracial Communication* (Blubaugh & Pennington, 1976), had a tremendous impact on the way race, a social construct, was discussed in communication literature during the late 1970s. Additionally, in her chapter "Intercultural Communication" in the Samovar and Porter book, *Intercultural Communication: A Reader*, Pennington postulated:

> Real intercultural communication is not so much the idea of cultural entities coming together and merely alternating in their influence upon one another; it is, rather, the transactions that occur at the point of intersect. Each culture is in some way different as a result of the interaction. (Pennington, 1985, p. 31)

Pennington described her approach to rhetorical and intercultural communication as "phenomenological" (D. L. Pennington, personal communication, July 12, 2004). She contended that all communication practice is informed by cosmological, axiological, and epistemological factors that shape how communicators view the world. Thus, the notion of "difference," as it relates to the practice of communication with others is rooted in differences along these dimensions. This approach to understanding intercultural exchanges was distinct from other scholarly discussions of race, culture, and communication of the time in significant ways. Pennington took issue with earlier discussions because, in her view, they ignored the multiplicity of ways in which cultural standpoints are informed, understood, and negotiated in interpersonal contexts:

> Too often intercultural study is confined to a description and awareness of the differences between or among cultures. Although necessary, this treatment alone is inadequate. Beyond recognizing

differences, which is analogous to noticing the tip of the iceberg while the bottom goes unseen, there is the need to understand the reasons for and the nature of the differences. Probing cosmological issues allows one to penetrate deeper, to really begin to understand the nature of culture. (Pennington, 1985, p. 31)

In the chapter (Pennington, 1985), Pennington identified several "significant cultural components" that she used to develop a model of culture. At the center of this model lies the "essence of cosmology and worldview," which she argued informs all existential behavior. Pennington argued that existential worldview, ontology, and cosmology "permeate" all other ways of informing and being informed by the social world. According to Pennington, this component influences the language, schemas, beliefs/attitudes/values, temporality, proxemics, expressive forms, social relationships, and interpolation patterns of all people. Thus, differences in these components are the rudimentary differences that require acknowledgment and extensive study in intercultural transactions. In this way, Pennington called for the extension of traditional intercultural theories to communication contexts that are marked by fundamental differences in cosmological approaches to life, rather than differences in nationality alone. Her work encourages a "prescriptive" approach to intercultural communication, based on the assumption that the *quality* of intercultural transactions between people could be improved with acknowledgment and acceptance of cultural differences.

In addition to her interest in intercultural communication, Pennington saw the potential applications of her model of culture to interracial communication contexts marked by a shared social history and heavily influenced by racism and volatile sociopolitical relationships. However, she made clear in much of her writing that the two forms of communication are not synonymous. Pennington distinguished intercultural and interracial forms of human communication in her article, "Mainstreaming Interracial Communication," in *Speech Communication Teacher* with the following statement:

Some of the research on interracial communication in recent years has been subsumed under the general rubric of intercultural communication. In so doing, scholars have highlighted issues as identity, assimilation, diversity, and multiculturalism. Yet, none of these concepts seems to have had a serious impact on what is a growing reality in US America: the racial bigotry that leads to ethnoviolence and intimidation. (Pennington, 1997, p. 13)

Pennington's work and that of others (for example, Orbe & Harris, 2001), argued that the most significant difference between intercultural and interracial communication is "the difference of power" (Blubaugh & Pennington, 1976; Pennington, 2003). Pennington contended that her biggest objection to using intercultural theory to explain interracial communication realities is that intercultural theory "presumes that we enter such communication contexts as equals, that there is a reciprocal and egalitarian relationship between participants," which does not characterize many interracial communication contexts in the United States (Pennington, 2003). Another important distinction is a greater sensitivity to the historic legacy of race relations in America than to that of intercultural relations. This sensitivity, Pennington suggested, is because of a heightened awareness of the importance of race in shaping most aspects of American life. For Pennington, interracial communication is a "microset" of the intercultural communication experience (D. L. Pennington, personal communication, July 12, 2004).

Of the numerous books and journals containing her work, several of Pennington's key contributions have received attention within the field of communication, including her essay, "Intercultural Communication," in the fourth edition of *Intercultural Communication: A Reader* (Pennington, 1985). After its first printing, the essay was adapted as part of an instructional manual for the U.S. Department of Defense Race Relations Institute.

Until recently, scholarship on interracial communication was limited to the few books published almost 30 years ago. Pennington's work shifted toward larger pedagogical concerns in the 1990s. Not only is her scholarship instrumental to understanding the process of interracial communication but it is also significant in its encouragement of a multicultural curriculum in all learning institutions. In fact, Pennington believes that the invisibility of interracial communication scholarship hurts teachers of interracial communication and students of communication and culture who are forced to rely on dated materials to discuss contemporary social struggles. She recommends that all students of communication receive some formal training in intercultural and/or interracial communication. Pennington described the ability to communicate in diverse environments as a "life skill" similar to learning reading and writing skills (D. L. Pennington, personal communication, July 12, 2004).

Because Pennington views culture as central to communication, she advanced the notion of its centrality to her research interest in public address. Her article, "A Culture Based Approach to Teaching African American Public Address" (Pennington, 1998), emphasized the necessity of studying the "I Have a Dream" speech by Martin Luther

King, Jr., within the context of the assumptions of an oral culture to understand the speech's influence during the time of its delivery. The article showed how King appealed to particular assumptions held by members of his audience and how they, in turn, connected with him through spontaneous interplay and rhythm.

Dorthy Pennington has contributed to communication research through her conceptual and analytic research concerning Black women and interracial/intercultural communication. She has been a forerunner in the study of interracial communication, which is perhaps her most significant and heuristic contribution to the field.

❖ CONCLUSION

Over her career, Dorthy Pennington has served the academy, her discipline, and her community in significant ways. She has been honored on several occasions for her efforts to offer insights into the process of intercultural/interracial communication as well as to provide prescriptions for effectiveness in interracial relationships. Pennington has also received numerous national and international awards for her pedagogical contributions. By challenging the applicability of several contemporary communication theories to African American and interracial communication contexts, Pennington's' work has not only helped to advance communication theory but has also encouraged scholars to seek explanations for communication phenomena that are consistent with their everyday realities. Dorthy Pennington continues to be a significant contributor to the advancement of the communication discipline.

❖ REFERENCES

Blubaugh, J. A., & Pennington, D. L. (1976). *Crossing difference: Interracial communication.* Columbus, OH: Charles Merrill.

Jaspers, K. (1947). *The question of German guilt.* New York: Dial Press.

Orbe, M., & Harris, T. M. (2001). *Interracial communication: Theory to practice.* Belmont, CA: Wadsworth.

Pennington, D. L. (1974). *Temporality among Black Americans: Implications for intercultural communication.* Unpublished doctoral dissertation, University of Kansas, Lawrence.

Pennington, D. L. (1979). Black-White communication: An assessment of the research. In M. K. Asante, E. Newmark, & C. Blake (Eds.), *Handbook of intercultural communication* (pp. 383–401). Beverly Hills, CA: Sage.

Pennington, D. L. (1980). Guilt provocation: A strategy in Black rhetoric. In
    M. K. Asante & A. Vandi (Eds.), *Contemporary Black thought: Alternative
    analyses in social and behavioral science* (pp. 111–125). Beverly Hills, CA: Sage.
Pennington, D. L. (1985). Intercultural communication. In L. Samovar &
    R. Porter (Eds.), *Intercultural communication: A reader* (pp. 30–39). Belmont,
    CA: Wadsworth.
Pennington, D. L. (1988). Afro-American women: Achievement through the
    reconciliation of messages and images. In S. Brehm (Ed.), *Seeing female:
    Social roles and personal lives* (pp. 33–41). New York: Greenwood Press.
Pennington, D. L. (1997). Mainstreaming interracial communication. *Speech
    Communication Teacher, 11*(2), p. 13.
Pennington, D. L. (1998). A culture-based approach to teaching African
    American public address. *Speech Communication Teacher, 12*(4), pp. 7–8.
Pennington, D. L. (1999). *African American women quitting the workplace.*
    Lewiston, New York: E. Mellen Press.
Rust College. (2005). *History of Rust College.* Retrieved January 11, 2005, from
    www.rustcollege.edu.

Further Reading

Pennington, D. L. (1989a). Felix Boateng: Time in African culture. In
    M. K. Asante & K. Welsh-Asante (Eds.), *African culture: The rhythms of unity*
    (pp. 158–173). Trenton, NJ: Africa World Press.
Pennington, D. L. (1989b). Interpersonal power and influence in intercultural
    communication. In M. K. Asante & W. Gudykunst (Eds.), *Handbook of inter-
    national and intercultural communication* (pp. 261–274). Thousand Oaks, CA:
    Sage.
Pennington, D. L. (1993). Culture as symbolic: The challenge of intercultural
    communication. In J. Ward (Ed.), *African American communications: An
    anthology* (pp. 137–165). Dubuque, IA: Kendall-Hunt.
Pennington, D. L. (2003). The discourse of African American women: A case for
    extended paradigms. In R. L. Jackson III & E. B. Richardson (Eds.),
    *Understanding African American rhetoric: Classical origins to contemporary
    innovations* (pp. 303–317). NY: Routledge.
Pennington, D. L. (Forthcoming). *Interracial communication: Cases and critical
    incidents.* Thousand Oaks, CA: Sage.

Dorthy L. Pennington

**Photo Courtesy of the University of
Kansas Departments of Communication Studies
and African and African-American Studies**

1946	Born in rural Mississippi on May 24.
1968	Graduated from Rust College with a bachelor's degree in English.
1970	Graduated from the University of Kansas with a master's degree in speech communication and human relations.
1974	Earned a doctorate from the University of Kansas in speech communication and human relations. Her dissertation topic, "Temporality Among Black Americans: Implications for Intercultural Communication" was probably the first in-depth scholarly study completed on Black chronemics.
	Appointed assistant professor at the University of Kansas in African and African-American Studies and Communication Studies (still on the faculty as a tenured associate professor).
1976	Became educational consultant to the Department of Defense Race Relations Institute (1976–1984).
	Published *Crossing Difference: Interracial Communication* with Jon A. Blubaugh.
1977	Became educational Consultant to the Department of Defense Equal Opportunity Management Institute.
1978	Nominated for the Outstanding Young Teacher award of the Central States Speech Association.
	Listed in *Outstanding Young Women of America* (1978 and 1981).
	Listed in the *World's Who's Who of Women*.

Listed in *The International Who's Who of Intellectuals.*

Listed in *Who's Who of American Women.*

1980 — Authored a groundbreaking conceptual essay, "Guilt Provocation: A Strategy in Black Rhetoric," for the book *Contemporary Black Thought: Alternative Analyses in Social and Behavioral Science* (by Asante and Vandi).

1981 — Honored as a Distinguished Alumnus of a historically black institution (Rust College) by the National Association for Equal Opportunity in Higher Education, Washington, D.C. (1981–1986).

1985 — Published "Intercultural Communication" essay in *Intercultural Communication: A Reader.*

1988 — Served as visiting faculty member, Texas Tech University.

1993 — Nominated for the University of Kansas Women's Hall of Fame.

1995 — Honored as teacher, mentor, and intercultural scholar by the Speech Communication Association's Feminist and Women's Studies Division.

1997 — Received award from the Teachers on Teaching Series of the National Communication Association. A convention program was held in her honor.

1999 — Published *African American Women Quitting the Workplace.*

2001 — Invited to present at the Loccum Academy, Loccum, Germany.

Received Highest Service award from the Consortium of Women Doctors.

2002 — Received a teaching excellence award from the University of Kansas Center for Teaching Excellence.

2003 — Contracted with Sage to publish *Interracial Communication: Cases and Critical Incidents.*

11

Orlando L. Taylor

❖ ❖ ❖

Few standardized tests take culturally based communication or language issues into account at any level of the assessment process. Indeed, most standardized tests, and the communicative environments in which they are administered are culturally discriminatory  *against many cultural groups in the United States, since specific norms have not been established for them, and since insufficient numbers of persons from the groups are typically included in norming samples. African Americans, the nation's largest "minority group" are among the groups most vulnerable to test bias, particularly those persons who come from low-income, poorly educated or socially isolated communities.*

(Taylor & Lee, 1987, p. 68)

❖ INTRODUCTION

Orlando Taylor, a visionary researcher and transformative leader, became the first African American president of the National Communication Association (NCA) in 1998. In its almost 100-year history, there has not been another African American who has been elected to lead this major communication association. During his leadership of NCA, Taylor not only provided the leadership to move communication to a more prominent location geographically but also with respect to the national academic community and to the funding agencies and foundations that have cyclically given money to other disciplines to do the work in which communication researchers specialize. Because of his efforts and those of his successors, communication has reached unprecedented levels of respect and recognition from such entities as the National Research Council, American Association of Higher Education, and the Carnegie Foundation for the Advancement of Teaching. Additionally, the National Research Council has now decided to include the field of communication in its periodic rankings of doctoral programs, a useful tool for assessing placement and recruitment strategies. Taylor did not stop lobbying for communication after his presidency. He also served as chair and member of the board of directors for the Council for Graduate Schools and the Advisory Council of the Jacob Javits National Fellowship Program in the Humanities, which is supported by the U.S. Department of Education. Subsequently, he became president of the Council of Social Science Associations, which represents most social science disciplinary associations in the United States.

Mentored by J. Jeffrey Auer and Robert Milisen at Indiana University to have a prodigious career, Taylor never took rare opportunities for granted. In 1967, when Milisen was funded for an important project, he named Taylor, a young junior professor, to be one of the investigators. This appointment set Taylor up nicely to eventually become a principal investigator on a subsequent grant with Milisen. From these grants, Taylor could begin writing publications and his own grant proposals. The first grant became a catalyst for many others to come. At this point in his career, Taylor, vice provost of Graduate Research and graduate school dean at Howard University, has received more than $30 million in federally and privately sponsored research, graduate training, and program development grants.

Many institutions have recognized Taylor's achievements in research, teaching, and service. In 2003, he was awarded Yale University's Bouchet Leadership Award in Minority Graduate Education, named in honor of Edward Bouchet, the first African American to earn a doctorate in the United States. Moreover, he has received honorary doctorate degrees from Purdue, Hope, and DePauw Universities, and distinguished alumni awards from Hampton University and University of Michigan. Beyond these accolades, two of the greatest moments of his career were when he was designated as an "Old Master" at Purdue and given the highest honors within the American Speech, Language, and Hearing Association ("Honors of the Association").

Taylor is a pioneer of research in the fields of communication sciences and disorders, educational linguistics, sociolinguistics, and communication. He has always had a passion for education and has been an advocate for educational progress of minority students, as is clearly implied in the opening epigraph. He is author of nearly a dozen scholarly books and more than 50 refereed scholarly articles and chapters. Taylor's research employs multiple methods, although his work is primarily quantitative, often experimental, and conceptually theoretic. Although Taylor is known within academia for his ubiquitous leadership, prolific record of publications, and countless grants, he was also one of the members of the well-known and controversial "Bloomington Nine" (a group of eight student activists and their advisor, Taylor, at Indiana University [IU] in Bloomington, Indiana, in 1969). As Taylor worked to outline and develop a description for a new executive university leadership position titled vice president of Minority Affairs, the IU president decided to appoint Taylor to the position. Just before Taylor was to take office, eight Black students interrupted a faculty senate meeting, in which the senate was conferring with the senior university leaders, including the president The eight students presented a set of demands and refused to allow anyone to leave, except Taylor because they knew him. The students kept the rest of the university leaders there for three days. Their demands were directly related to the university's climate of racial hostility. Taylor recalled, "Indiana was the home of the Ku Klux Klan, and there were some threats of violence by the Klan and others against me and other African Americans—very bad threats, threats of life. It was hard to be liberal, active, and Black in Indiana circa 1969." Although the negotiations ended right before the National Guard arrived, a grand jury panel was assembled and wanted detailed answers to questions about who was involved and what happened. One person remembered the chancellor asking Taylor to make the students leave, to which Taylor replied, "I know these students. They are good students and they would not be here if there was not a big problem, and I think we better sit here and listen to them." Taylor remembered that he decided then "that if I was supposed to be the Black person designated to 'keep the natives quiet,' I would have no credibility with the constituents, and I refused to do it." The grand jury indicted the eight students and Taylor, their advisor, for conspiracy to take over the flagship state university of Indiana. After many faculty members put up their houses and bailed everyone out of jail, Taylor discovered the university's unwillingness to honor the offer to become vice president of Minority Affairs, and he had already resigned from his faculty appointment to take the position. Taylor was then without a job, but "wisdom is going through life and paying attention." Taylor was wise enough to have a backup option: he went to Washington D.C. to conduct a $500,000 Ford Foundation project at the Center for Applied Linguistics to address issues of language diversity in the nation's schools, particularly those with large numbers of African American students.

Taylor has consistently exercised wisdom and has been a persistent go-getter—someone who has refused to allow his God-given talents to subside and dreams to be deferred (O. L. Taylor, personal communication, February 3, 2004).

❖   BIOGRAPHICAL INFORMATION

Orlando LeRoy Taylor was born to the late Carrie and LeRoy Taylor in Chattanooga, Tennessee. Carrie, an elementary and secondary schoolteacher, finished two years of college at Selma University and received an associate degree in 1930, which was a sufficient credential for teaching in the Alabama public schools. However, LeRoy, who had only a sixth-grade education, wanted to move his family to Chattanooga—where better industrial job opportunities were available for Black people. Taylor suggested, "They were part of a migration of Blacks from the rural south to the north and the urban south." A few years after Carrie's graduation, she and LeRoy were married and decided to make the move. LeRoy worked in a steel mill, and Carrie planned to teach. When they arrived, however, she discovered that all teachers were required to have a four-year degree. For 16 years, while raising her two children, Carrie did not teach. In 1948, at the age of 40, she completed her bachelor's degree at Alabama State University and resumed her teaching career in 1950. Taylor was in high school at that time, and his younger brother Robert was in elementary school. Before his mother's shift to teaching, Taylor viewed his parents in blue-collar jobs, and knew nothing except what he called a "traditional working class background." Despite their class and racial background, Taylor's parents decided to move to an all-White neighborhood in the Chattanooga metropolitan area when Taylor was 5 years old. Because of school segregation, Taylor could not attend the neighborhood all-White elementary school, but had to attend an all-Black school several blocks away (O. L. Taylor, personal communication, February 3, 2004).

Taylor's parents were inspirations for Taylor. His mother is still alive, and his father passed away only three years ago. They instilled self-discipline, independence, perseverance, self-respect, and respect for others—values that became constitutive aspects of Taylor's personality, even into adulthood. Because he lived in an all-White neighborhood during segregation, Taylor grew up with no friends in his neighborhood. Consequently, he learned to be creative as he sought to entertain himself. He remembered:

> I was caught up with strategies for being self-sufficient, and I learned to entertain myself. Even to this day I'm not really a group person; I'm sort of a loner. Of course, I'm a friendly person, I interact with people, but I don't need a crowd to be entertained. (O. L. Taylor, personal communication, February 3, 2004)

Taylor also developed a love for music. In the 1940s and 1950s, there were not very many options for those interested in listening to Black music. In fact, there was only one radio station whose signal was audible: WLAC-Radio broadcast out of Nashville, Tennessee. "The dee-jay was a guy who was known throughout the south as his pseudonym Randy, borrowing the name of a famous record store in Gallatin, Tennessee," recalled Taylor. Both Randy and Randy's record store were well-known. In the early 1950s, Black music was a neglected part of the market. After realizing that there was a niche, a White radio station in Chattanooga, WDXB, entered the market with an R & B platform. The radio station managers hired someone named Ted Bryant as the disc jockey, who Taylor claimed was "a real pioneer in Black radio." Ted was scheduled to go on a vacation, and the station held a contest in which the winner's prize was to substitute for Ted for two weeks. Taylor participated and won, although he was only 14 years old and a high school sophomore. He noted, "My voice was recognized every time I was on the radio because I was the only kid. After two weeks when Ted returned, by audience demand, they gave me my own weekend show." Shortly thereafter, a Black radio station, WFMS, came to Chattanooga, and Taylor was offered his own daily R & B radio show called "Teen Time." He served as dee-jay and accepted song requests every day after school, 5–6 p.m. In the summer, he worked full-time at the station. Although these radio experiences became stimuli for Taylor's interest in the field of communication, his motivation for attending college was cemented by his parents and teachers since elementary school (O. L. Taylor, personal communication, February 3, 2004).

❖ ACADEMIC BACKGROUND AND EXPERIENCE

Taylor attended Orchard Knob elementary and junior high school and was a good student. He knew that poor grades would not be tolerated by his parents, but he loved school so grades were not a problem. Taylor attended Howard High School at the age of 14 and graduated right before his 17th birthday. Howard High School was one of several educational and medical institutions throughout the south that was named after, initiated by, and supported by the Freedman's Bureau (Howard University is another such institution). Taylor explained, "Pretty much everyone was expected to go to college. That was common in those days." Of course, the fact that his mother was an educator facilitated Taylor's love for books and general discovery. He had a cultivated thirst for knowledge that could easily be satiated in college. In his senior year of high school, Taylor won a four-year scholarship to attend college at Hampton Institute, a well-known historically Black college in Hampton, Virginia. Although Taylor never lived anywhere except Tennessee, he wanted to try something different, so he confronted any anxieties he had and enrolled in college in 1953. Several of his classmates went to Morehouse, Spelman, or Fisk. Taylor reminisced, "From where I was, in Tennessee, going to Virginia was going up north," so the prospects seemed exciting (O. L. Taylor, personal communication, February 3, 2004).

With his developed interests and skills in communication, Taylor found himself working on the student newspaper and periodically working as a dee-jay at the campus radio station. Over the next few years, he would have a lot to discuss via these media outlets. In 1954, the Brown v. Board of Education Supreme Court case would be won by Thurgood Marshall, and 14-year-old Emmett Till would be beaten and shot to death one year later for allegedly whistling at a White female. The year of 1955 is also historically important: Rosa Parks's refusal to give up her seat for a White person at the front of a bus instigated the bus boycotts in Montgomery, Alabama, led by young Reverend Martin Luther King, Jr. Virginia had many boycotts, sit-ins, and other civil rights activity, and the city of Hampton was no exception.

During his undergraduate matriculation at Hampton, Taylor was an active student. He even pledged Kappa Alpha Psi Fraternity, a predominately Black fraternity whose mission as a social organization emphasizes service and educational achievement. Taylor's major was communication, and the field included speech communication, speech pathology, and theater. He took courses in each of these areas and added psychology and sociology classes to round out his broad liberal arts curriculum. Taylor explored other opportunities and found that Hampton had a student exchange program in which Black and White universities sent students to the other college for a year. One of the conditions of this arrangement was that any student activities the student was involved in had to be replicated at the new host institution. Because Taylor was a member of a Black fraternity, he met the brothers of the predominately White fraternity, Delta Upsilon, at Denison University, his almost all-White host university, which was located in the all-White town of Granville, Ohio. The Delta Upsilon members allowed him to stay at their fraternity house, and Taylor's interest in interracial and intercultural communication was piqued. He began to notice everything—nonverbal communication, language and communication styles, politeness and request strategies—that distinguished him from others in the house. For example, "I learned that White people would always look me in the eye when they would listen to me talk, which signified to me they were staring at me and didn't like me. That was a perceived insult that I later learned was a misunderstanding. They really were just showing they were paying attention to me, so when I averted my gaze, they thought I was ignoring them." Taylor also noticed that they enacted indirect requests such as "Do you want to open that door?" or "Do you want to open that window?" He viewed this as a "sneaky way to get me to do something for them." He wondered why they did not simply say, "Would you open the door for me please?" He said this was starkly contrasted to what he experienced when he left Denison to visit Columbus, Ohio, for a weekend and had a chance to resume interaction with Black people. Those observations became paramount to his later research interests concerning interracial language differences and his subsequent grant-funded work with the U.S. Army concerning cross-cultural communication (O. L. Taylor, personal communication, February 3, 2004).

While Taylor was at Denison, Lionel Crocker, one of the early intellectual giants in communication, mentored him and taught him phonetics. Taylor thrived in his classes and came to understand that he could easily compete intellectually with White students in the classroom. When he left Denison, returned to Hampton, and graduated in

1957 with a bachelor's degree in education, Taylor knew he would go to a predominately White university for graduate school—and he did. He applied for and received financial support from Indiana University and a scholarship from the Indiana state government, which paid for his entire graduate program. As a master's degree student, Taylor worked as a speech clinician, identifying speech disorders in patients. In the same year as his graduation from Hampton, Taylor was married and had two children immediately who were only 11 months apart in age: Orlando Taylor II and Ingrid Gelete Taylor.

In 1960, Taylor earned his master's degree from Indiana University. Through nurturing mentors and a solid interdisciplinary communication curriculum, Taylor learned the essential skills necessary to succeed in academia. Between the mentorship of Robert Milisen and J. Jeffrey Auer, Taylor was well-equipped. Milisen was a highly respected teacher and researcher. Auer, who was certainly a well-respected scholar in his own right, was executive vice president and then president of the National Communication Association (then Speech Association of America) and editor of *Speech Monographs*. So Taylor witnessed up close the inner workings of highly successful academic careers in communication. Taylor took an eclectic mix of courses, including speech, psychology, reading, and sociology, and became acquainted with the methodologies and vocabularies associated with those areas of study. At the urging of a professor at Purdue University, Taylor left IU to pursue his doctorate degree. He was very aware of what it meant to be an academician. Between 1960 and 1962, he directed the speech and hearing clinic at the Fort Wayne State School in Indiana. In 1962, Taylor enrolled in the doctoral program in education at University of Michigan in 1962. It was a decade of social upheaval, and students and community citizens were protesting all over the nation. In 1966, the year he graduated with his doctorate in education, people were still mourning the 1965 death of Malcolm X, and the Black Power movement was born with the advent of the Black Panther Party, founded by Huey P. Newton and Bobby Seale.

Taylor had just completed his dissertation on linking brain function with language and communication behaviors when he was invited back to Indiana University to be a tenure-track assistant professor—an appointment that would position him as one of only a handful of Black scholars at major research institutions. Although the University of Michigan had five Black tenured or tenure-track scholars across all the disciplines, Indiana University had no Black tenured scholars and only two that were untenured. Taylor became the third Black tenure-line faculty member at the university, and the first in communication. He turned down an offer from Southern University to come to IU to remain consistent with his dream of teaching at a major research university. Taylor stayed at IU for five years before moving on to the Center for Applied Linguistics in Washington, D.C., where he produced research concerning sociolinguistics, educational linguistics, and intercultural communication. This proximity to many area universities gave Taylor the opportunity to teach at Federal City College (now called the University of the District of Columbia) between 1970 and 1973 while intermittently teaching at Howard University, the nation's only urban land grant institution. Taylor joined the Howard University faculty as a full-time professor 1973 and has been there ever since.

When Taylor arrived at Howard, Lyndrey Niles was leading the speech department, which had just initiated a doctoral program in 1971. From 1975 to 1980, Taylor was chair of the department, which graduated its first doctoral students in 1976. During his tenure, Taylor hired several new faculty members, including Melbourne Cummings. He later became dean of the School of Communication and served from 1985 through 1993. Taylor supported the development of the *Howard Journal of Communications* with its founding editor, William J. Starosta. He also played a leading role in enhancing the School of Communication's national reputation, which later resulted in a ranking as third in the nation in the field of intercultural communication, being the annual producer of one of the nation's largest number of communication doctoral students, and the absolute largest number of African American doctoral recipients in communication.

❖ CONTRIBUTIONS TO COMMUNICATION RESEARCH

In a profession in which researchers are expected to develop and specialize in only one or two lines of research throughout their careers, Orlando Taylor chose a much more multifaceted career. His pioneering program of communication research can be characterized as having five major strands (which are described in the following sections): (1) aphasia and language acquisition; (2) culture, language, and communication disorders; (3) Black English; (4) children's educational performance and test bias; and (5) graduate education.

Aphasia and Language Acquisition, 1969–1974

Not every scholar can claim to have written a magnum opus by midcareer, or even later in life, but Orlando Taylor's quintessential work in the field of communication sciences and disorders was published when he was 35 years old. It was among the first in a set of experimental research studies that emerged from both his dissertation and the funded research grants with Robert Milisen. After spending a couple of years researching the rehabilitation of aphasia, Taylor uncovered some interesting facets of aphasia. This work with aphasics by him and his associates would come to be frequently cited as major monographs connecting neurology to speech capacity. Aphasia is defined as "The loss or impairment of the power to use words, usually resulting from a brain lesion" (Woolf, 1977, p. 52). Taylor's principal concern in this line of research was discovering what happens when normal linguistic storage processes and functional neuroanatomy of language are interrupted by the occurrence of brain damage. His argument was that aphasia, when linked to short-term memory loss, could be discovered to severely limit human beings' capacity to produce speech. Taylor and Swinney (1971) explained:

It is obvious that some type of memory system is necessary for sentences to be held long enough (in memory) for comprehension. . . . It seems logical to assert that research on the processes underlying the storage of linguistic segments in STM (short-term memory) is mandatory for a complete theory of language decoding for normal subjects. . . . Further, as language comprehension difficulties and reduced auditory memory span are often characteristics of the aphasic disorder, it could be argued that aphasics' comprehension problems may be directly related to memory deficits. (Taylor & Swinney, 1971, pp. 578–579)

In this 1971 study, which compared short-term memory recognition in eight adult aphasics and eight adult nonaphasics, Taylor's results indicated that verbal responses to stimuli were more latent for adult aphasics because their limited memory storage capacity caused them to self-terminate their memory search much more quickly than the adult nonaphasics, who could perform an exhaustive memory search of recently occurred events. This study of neuroanatomical functioning was heuristic because it helped explicate how aphasia operates as a consequence of language decoding, memory recognition, and brain trauma. Whether it was about the effects of language loss of language reacquisition, each of Taylor's early speech pathology studies of aphasics advanced the field beyond its known parameters. Taylor's interest in intercultural communication never subsided, so he decided to pursue that theme within the context of language and communication disorders research.

Culture, Language, and
Communication Disorders, 1969–1994

In 1969, several things were happening in Orlando Taylor's life. Not only were his two children turning teenagers soon but he also left Indiana University to become associate director and senior research fellow at the Center for Applied Linguistics in Washington, D.C. The Bloomington Nine controversy was over, but the experience introduced him to social justice activism. As a fairly new scholar in the field of speech and hearing, Taylor noticed the absence of Black people and their experiences within the communication disorders conferences and literature and knew he had to become an academic change agent. Taylor and Charles Hurst, Ronald Williams, Gloria Walker, Earnest Moore, and others developed an agenda to forcefully petition change in the American Speech and Hearing Association (ASHA), the nation's largest and most respected organization of speech and hearing professionals. The result was the founding of a unit of the association called the Black Caucus, which promoted another thriving organization known as the National Black Speech, Language, and Hearing Association. Grounding their ideas in the scientific literature of the field, Taylor, Stroud, Hurst, Moore, and Williams (1969) wrote:

> Unfortunately, far too many speech pathologists view legitimate language differences among Afro-Americans from a pathology model. The result is that a number of Black children are receiving speech and language therapy, particularly in urban areas, when they in fact, have no pathology. Negative psychological effects on the Black child are obvious. . . . All too often clinicians fail to understand the Black child's language, as well as the child himself. (Taylor, Stroud, Hurst, Moore, and Williams, 1969, p. 221)

Shortly after this unit was created, Taylor learned of Black scholars trying to initiate the same type of intellectual activism in the Speech Association of America (now the National Communication Association). Taylor and his cohort met and organized with Jack Daniel, Molefi Asante, Lyndrey Niles, and others to lay the foundation for the beginning of the Speech Association of America Black Caucus. Because Taylor's educational training occurred in departments that taught both speech pathology and speech communication, he shared common interests with both segments of the field of communication and wrote one of the earliest pieces that called for the broad inclusion of Black perspectives in the communication curricula.

This project led Taylor to begin researching Black language concerns, which became a significant line of inquiry. After a few years away from communication disorders research, Taylor and Bruce Williams published a well-received book, *International Issues in Black Communication* (Taylor & Williams, 1980). As he worked back and forth between his research on Ebonics and communication disorders, Taylor began to link language acquisition and use with racial identity politics among speech pathology practitioners. He and his research associates began to study service delivery and diagnoses of speech pathology among urban Blacks—an extension of his early call for this in his 1969 article explaining the philosophy of the newly formed Black Caucus (Taylor, 1969). In their study of rehabilitation, Taylor and his colleagues found that speech pathologists and audiologists were not always accurately diagnosing Blacks for communication disorders because they did not understand the significance of speech differences among linguistically diverse populations. This research prompted Taylor to begin developing a tome that resulted in a two-volume anthology: *Nature of Communication Disorders in Culturally and Linguistically Diverse Populations* (Taylor, 1986a) and *Treatment of Communication Disorders in Culturally and Linguistically Diverse Populations* (Taylor, 1986b). These books covered the historical, conceptual and scientific speech and hearing issues among multiple populations—Whites, Blacks, Jews, Mexicans, Native Americans, and Pacific Islanders. This first-of-its-kind monumental effort also offered suggestions for the diagnosis and treatment of disorders among these multiple constituencies. Taylor wrote consistently and expanded this line of research until the late 1990s, working with scholars such as Kay Payne and many of his graduate students and doctoral recipients, and writing chapters for many books, including one for a book edited by Geneva Smitherman-Donaldson and Teun van Djik.

Black English, 1969–1999

One area of research productivity among Orlando Taylor's multiple and overlapping lines of research is Black English. There have been multiple names given to the study of Black language differences, but Black English (Harrison & Trabasso, 1976; Rodriguez, 2000; Smitherman, 1994), Black English Vernacular (Labov, 1972), and Ebonics (Perry & Delpit, 1988) were the most popular terms and Taylor uses these three variations most often in his research. *Ebonics* is a term coined in 1971 by psychologist Robert Williams. Derived from the combination of *ebony* and *phonics*, it was defined as "Black sounds." With Taylor's background in the production, acquisition, and auditing of verbal communication, as well as his investigative interests in the mistreatment and misdiagnoses of Black children, this area was a logical next step for him. The emerging field of sociolinguistics was dominated by scholars such Geneva Smitherman, William Labov, Dell Hymes, Lorenzo Turner, and J. L. Dillard. In the most sophisticated of these studies, the term *Black English* facilitated explanation of African American linguistic carryovers of Africanized phonetics and grammar while speaking English. In his research, Taylor maintained that school-aged children are often objects of racial and linguistic prejudice inflicted upon them by their teachers and peers because of the way they talk and because of ignorance about the rich cultural history and origins of Black English. Taylor felt the need to join the cadre of scholars fighting for the linguistic integrity and legitimacy of Black English, realizing that the life chances of Black children hung in the balance. He produced several studies concerning the nature of bidialecticalism (Taylor, Payne, & Cole, 1983), educational equity and language attitudes (Taylor & Payne, 1983), language variations and communication disorders (Taylor & Payne, 1983; Taylor & Stewart, 1986), and educational policy (Taylor, 1975; Taylor & Leonard, 1999).

Children's Educational Performance and Test Bias, 1972–1999

For Orlando Taylor, the entire conversation about Ebonics and the open protest against it in 1997 by the Oakland, California school board was always about Black children's self-esteem and educational success. The best way to ensure this was to become a cultural worker who enforced a radical progressive pedagogy that promoted respect of all cultural experiences, despite their differences. Consequently, Taylor decided to move the conversation forward by studying how Black language differences were entwined with Black children's educational performance. One of the most immediate areas to explore with respect to performance was standardized testing and latent cultural biases in test construction. He launched a series of investigations of valid testing procedures (Taylor, 1978; Taylor, Hoover, & Politzer, 1987; Taylor & Lee, 1987; Taylor & Payne, 1983). In one study (Cole & Taylor, 1990), Taylor found that in three articulation tests among Black children from working-class families, the children scored significantly higher when the test was constructed with a Black English Vernacular dialect and none was clinically diagnosed with a communication disorder. When administered in standard English form, the performance results were lower, and six Black students were diagnosed with a disorder. So, Cole and Taylor's argument

(1990) was that if standardized tests are to accurately measure knowledge content or academic competence, they ought to consider the biases inherent in the standard. In his most recent book, *Making the Connection: Academic Achievement and Language Diversity in African American Children* (Taylor, Adger, & Christian, 1999), Taylor and his coauthors synthesize his life's work on language variation, identity politics, and academic achievement.

Graduate Education, 1993-present

Orlando Taylor's fervor for studying academic success led him to his current line of research about graduate education. This broad area of research includes studies of student mentoring, recruitment, and retention as well as faculty diversity. The primary impetus for Taylor's preoccupation with this area of inquiry is evident in his work described so far. He has received more than $30 million in various types of research, training, and program development grants. In his roles as board member of the Council for Graduate Schools, advisory council member of the Jacob Javits National Fellowship Program in the Humanities, vice provost for Research at Howard University, and dean of the Howard University Graduate School, Taylor is engaged in the everyday research and practice of successful graduate education. It is natural for him to have delved into graduate education research.

Taylor's earliest work in this area, written in 1993, dealt with diversifying faculty and mentoring people of color. Quality graduate programs benefit from productive and nurturing faculty, as well as undying support of students via student mentoring and effective teaching. Certainly, there are things faculty must do and students must do, but peer group networks, positive reinforcement from significant others, and proper mentoring are key. This latter point, Taylor and Carter argue, cannot be underestimated because mentors are not all the same—some mentoring can lead to counterproductive decisions and outcomes. Taylor has devoted 10 years of his career to the development and promotion of the "Preparing Future Faculty" program. Through his research and several million dollars of grants from the U.S. government and such foundations as the Pew Charitable Trust, Taylor has become an ambassador for graduate education.

❖ CONCLUSION

Orlando L. Taylor is a pioneer of communication research and a pioneering academic leader. His accolades throughout his distinguished career are numerous and speak volumes about his service and research contributions. He is a genuinely wonderful human being. In all the discussions about disciplinary accomplishments and lifetime achievements, it is sometimes easy to overlook the simplest of attributes. Taylor is a father, brother, vice provost, dean, nationally recognized interdisciplinary academic leader, professor, and founding organizer of the ASHA and NCA Black Caucuses and the Black College Communication Association. He is a prodigious intellectual with a remarkable career and he continues to contribute tirelessly to the field of communication.

❖ REFERENCES

Cole, P., & Taylor, O. L. (1990). Performance of working class African American children on three tests of articulation. *Language, Speech and Hearing Services in Schools, 21*(3), 171–176.

Harrison, D. S., & Trabasso, T. (Eds.). (1976). *Black English: A seminar.* Hillsdale, NJ: Erlbaum.

Hoover, M., Politzer, R. L. & Taylor, O. L., (1987). Bias in reading tests for Black language speakers: A sociolinguistic perspective. *Negro Educational Review, 38*(2/3), 81–98.

Labov, W. (1972). *Language in the inner city: Studies in the Black English Vernacular.* Philadelphia: University of Pennsylvania Press.

Perry, T., & Delpit, L. (1998). (Eds.). *The real Ebonics debate: Power, language and the education of African American children.* New York: Beacon.

Rodriguez, A. (2000). *Diversity as liberation (vol. II): Introducing a new understanding of diversity.* Cresskill, NJ: Hampton Press.

Smitherman, G. (1994). *Black talk: Words and phrases from the hood to the amen corner.* New York: Houghton-Mifflin Co.

Taylor, O. L. (1969). Social and political responsibilities of the American Speech and Hearing Association. *ASHA, II,* 216–218.

Taylor, O. L. (1971). African origins of Black English. In R. Jeffrey & O. Peterson (Eds.), *Speech: A text with adapted readings.* New York: Harper and Row.

Taylor, O. L. (1972). An introduction to the historical development of Black English: Some implications for American education. *Language, Speech and Hearing Services in the School, 3*(1), 5–15.

Taylor, O. L. (1975). Black English and what to do about it: Some Black community perspectives. In R. Williams (Ed.), *Ebonics: The true language of Black folks.* St. Louis: Institute of Black Studies.

Taylor, O. L. (1978). Language issues in testing. *Journal of American Personnel and Guidance Association,* 125–133.

Taylor, O. L. (1986a). *Nature of communication disorders in culturally and linguistically diverse populations.* San Diego: College Hill Press.

Taylor, O. L. (1986b). *Treatment of communication disorders in culturally and linguistically diverse populations.* San Diego: College Hill Press.

Taylor, O. L. (1988). *Cross-cultural communication: An essential dimension of effective education.* Washington, DC: American University.

Taylor, O. L., Adger, C. T., & Christian, D. (1999) *Making the connection: Academic achievement and language diversity in African American children.* Washington, DC: Center for Applied Linguistics.

Taylor, O. L., & Anderson, C. (1969). Neuropsycholinguistics and language reacquisition. In J. Black & B. Jancosek (Eds.), *Language retraining in adults.* Columbus: Ohio State Foundation.

Taylor, O. L., & Lee, D. L. (1987). Standardized tests and African American children: Communication and language issues. *Negro Educational Review, 38(2/3),* 67–80.

Taylor, O. L., & Leonard, L. B. (1999). *Language acquisition in North America: A cross-cultural perspective.* San Diego: Singular Publishing Group.

Taylor, O. L., & Payne, K. (1983). Culturally valid testing: A proactive approach. *Topics in Language Disorders, 3,* 8–20.

Taylor, O. L., Payne, K., & Cole, P. (1983). A survey of bidialectal language arts in the United States. *Journal of Negro Education, 52(2),* 35–45.

Taylor, O. L., & Stewart, J. (1986). Prevalence of language, speech and hearing disorders in an urban preschool Black population. *Journal of Childhood Communication Disorders, 10(4),* 107–124.

Taylor, O. L., Stroud, V., Moore, E., Hurst, C., & Williams, R. (1969). Philosophies and goals of ASHA Black Caucus. *ASHA,* II, 221–225.

Taylor, O. L., & Swinney, D. (1971). Recognition search through short-term memory in adult aphasics. *Journal of Speech and Hearing Research, 14,* 578–588.

Taylor, O. L., & Williams, B. (1980). *International issues in black communication.* New York: Rockefeller Foundation.

Woolf, H. (1977). *Webster's new collegiate dictionary* (5th ed.). Springfield, MA: G. & C. Merriam Co.

Further Reading

Cummings, M. S., Niles, L., & Taylor, O. L. (1992). (Eds.) *Handbook of communication and development in Africa and the African Diaspora.* Boston: Ginn Press.

Dillard, J. L. (1972). *Black English: Its history and usage in the United States.* New York: Random House.

Taylor, O. L., & Campbell, L. (1992). ASHA-certified speech-language pathologists: Perceived competency levels with selected skills. *Howard Journal of Communications, 3(4),* 163–177.

Taylor, O. L., & Clarke, M. G. (1994). Culture and communication disorders. *Seminars in Speech and Language,* 103–114.

Taylor, O. L., & Ferguson, D. (1975). A study of cross-cultural communication between Blacks and Whites in the U.S. Army. *The Linguistic Reporter, 17,* 8–11.

Orlando L. Taylor

Photo courtesy of Orlando Taylor

Late 1930s ◆ Born in Chattanooga, Tennessee.

1957 ◆ Received a bachelor's degree from Hampton University.

1960 ◆ Received a master's degree from Indiana University.

1965 ◆ Became assistant professor at Indiana University, Bloomington (1965–1969).

1966 ◆ Received doctorate from the University of Michigan.

1969 ◆ Served as associate director and senior research fellow for the Language and Education Program Center for Applied Linguistics, Washington D.C. (1969–1975).

Published "Neuropsychololinguistics and Language Reacquisition" with Carol Anderson.

1970 ◆ Served as professor of Communication Sciences at the University of the District of Columbia (1970–1973).

1971 ◆ Served as Fellow, American Speech, Language, and Hearing Association.

Published "African Origins of Black English."

1973 ◆ Became graduate professor for Communication Arts and Sciences/Communication Sciences and Disorders at Howard University (1973–Present).

1975 ◆ Published "Black English and What To Do About It: Some Black Community Perspectives."

Served as department chair, Communication Arts and Sciences/Communication Sciences and Disorders at Howard University (1975–1980).

1980 ◆ Published *International Issues in Black Communication*.

1984 ◆ Received the Distinguished Scholar Teacher Award from Howard University.

1985 ◆ Served as dean of the School of Communications at Howard University (1985–1993).

1986 ◆ Published *Nature of Communication Disorders in Culturally and Linguistically Diverse Populations*.

Published *Treatment of Communication Disorders in Culturally and Linguistically Diverse Populations*.

1988 ◆ Published *Cross Cultural Communication: An Essential Dimension of Effective Education*.

1991 ◆ Received the Honors of the Association (the highest award given by the American Speech, Language, and Hearing Association).

Appointed Old Master of Purdue University.

1992 ◆ Became member, Board of Directors, American Speech and Hearing Foundation (1992–1994).

Published *Handbook on Communication and Development in Africa and the African Diaspora* (with Melbourne S. Cummings and Lyndrey A. Niles).

1993 ◆ Received the Presidential Award for education in journalism and mass communication from Howard University.

Served as dean of the Graduate School, Howard University (1993–2003).

1994 ◆ Became interim vice president for Academic Affairs, Howard University.

Received honorary doctorate of letters from Purdue University.

1995 ◆ Edited the series *Culture, Rehabilitation, and Education*.

1996 ◆ Served as dean-in-residence for Council of Graduate Schools.

Served as member of the board of the directors for the Council of Graduate Schools (1998–2002).

1998 ◆ Elected president of the National Communication Association.

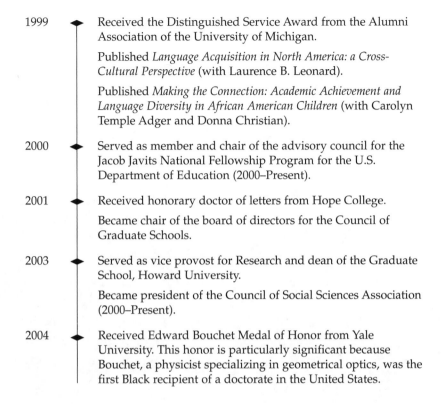

1999   Received the Distinguished Service Award from the Alumni Association of the University of Michigan.

Published *Language Acquisition in North America: a Cross-Cultural Perspective* (with Laurence B. Leonard).

Published *Making the Connection: Academic Achievement and Language Diversity in African American Children* (with Carolyn Temple Adger and Donna Christian).

2000   Served as member and chair of the advisory council for the Jacob Javits National Fellowship Program for the U.S. Department of Education (2000–Present).

2001   Received honorary doctor of letters from Hope College.

Became chair of the board of directors for the Council of Graduate Schools.

2003   Served as vice provost for Research and dean of the Graduate School, Howard University.

Became president of the Council of Social Sciences Association (2000–Present).

2004   Received Edward Bouchet Medal of Honor from Yale University. This honor is particularly significant because Bouchet, a physicist specializing in geometrical optics, was the first Black recipient of a doctorate in the United States.

Index

Abarry, A., 31
ABC (American Broadcasting
     Company), 122
Academic background/experience
     of Donald E. Bogle, 45–48
     of Dorothy L. Pennington,
          208–212
     of Hallie Quinn Brown, 66–73
     of Jack L. Daniel, 108–114
     of Joni L. Jones, 192–196
     of Marsha Houston, 176–178
     of Melbourne S. Cummings, 91–94
     of Molefi Kete Asante, 15–23
     of Orlando L. Taylor, 228–231
     of Oscar H. Gandy, Jr., 131–138
     of Stuart Hall, 158–163
Academy of Arts and Sciences
     Library, 55
Activism, 110–111, 133
     See also Civil rights movement
Adams, Bill, 135
Adams, Samuel, 17
Adger, C. T., 236
Africa
     Joni Jones in Nigeria, 190, 196
     Melbourne S. Cummings in, 86
     Molefi Kete Asante's travels
          in, 18
     proverbs from, 119, 120
African American Atlas (Asante and
     Mattson), 31
African American Churches in Early
     Lawrence: Citadels of Faith,
     Hope, and Community
     (Pennington), 206

African American Communication
     and Culture Division, 4
African American Communication
     and Identities: Essential
     Readings (Jackson, II.), 4
African American Criminological
     Thought (Gabbidon and
     Greene), 3
African American discourse,
     116–120
African American History: A
     Journey of Liberation (Asante
     and Abarry), 31
African American Images, 31
"African American Linkages to
     Africa through Oral Discourse"
     (Cummings and Daniel), 96
African American studies
     Afrocentricity and, 22
     doctoral program in, 12
     Jack L. Daniel's work in,
          105–106, 110
African American women
     Brown Sugar: Eighty Years of
          America's Black Female
          Superstars (Bogle), 51–54
     communication experiences
          of, 172
     Dorothy Dandridge: A Biography
          (Bogle), 55–57
     Dorothy Pennington's studies on,
          213–216
     Marsha Houston on
          communication
          experiences of, 172

Marsha Houston's early life and, 175–176

Marsha Houston's work on Black women's communication, 173–174, 177–178, 179, 181–183

performance of Joni Jones and, 199–200

African American Women Quitting the Workplace (Pennington), 215–216

African Americans
Hallie Quinn Brown and, 76–80
institutionalized racial bias, 121–123
performances of Joni Jones and, 198–199
test bias and, 223
See also Blacks

African Americans and Privacy (Gandy), 143

African Americans: Voices of Triumph (Cave and Britten), 59

African communication. See Black communication

African Diaspora, 13–14, 32

African Methodist Episcopal (AME) church
Bishop Henry McNeal Turner of, 98–99
Brown family and, 66
Hallie Quinn Brown's love of, 73

African Methodist Episcopal Church Review, 70

African Religions and Philosophies (Mbiti), 118

African scholarship, 1

Africana studies, 6, 28–30

"Afro-American Women: Achievement Through the Reconciliation of Messages and Images" (Pennington), 214

The Afrocentric Idea (Asante), 25

Afrocentricity
Joni Jones at Howard University and, 195
Molefi Kete Asante and, 11, 12, 13–14

Molefi Kete Asante's Africana studies, 28–30

Molefi Kete Asante's development of, 20–23

Molefi Kete Asante's early formulations about, 16–17

Molefi Kete Asante's rhetoric work and, 25

rap music and, 99–100

Afrocentricity: The Theory of Social Change (Asante), 25, 31

Agitator in American Society (Lomas), 16

Ali, Olu Hassan, 135

Allen, A., 27

Allen University, 68

Althusser, Louis, 153, 166

AMC (American Movie Classic), 41

AME. See African Methodist Episcopal (AME) church

American Broadcasting Company (ABC), 122

American Chautauqua Lecture School, 68

American Movie Classic (AMC), 41

American Museum of the Moving Image, 59

American Speech and Hearing Association (ASHA), 233

Amistad Press, 55

Anderson, L. M., 41

Ani, M., 14

Annenburg School for Communication at University of Pennsylvania, 129, 134–135, 138

Anthony, Susan B., 71

The Anthropology of Performance (Turner), 197–198

Antigua, 119

Aphasia, 9, 231–232

Aristotle, 22

Articulation theory
of Stuart Hall, 2, 8
Stuart Hall's development of, 166–167

Asante, Ana Yenenga, 19
Asante, Kariamu Welsh, 19
Asante, Kasina Eka, 19
Asante, Molefi, Jr., 19
Asante, Molefi Kete
    academic background, experience
        of, 15–23
    at UCLA, 111
    biographical information on, 14–15
    call-and-response and, 2
    communications research
        contributions of, 6, 23–31
    conclusion about, 31–32
    Dorothy Pennington and, 9,
        207, 212
    founding of National
        Communication Association's
        Black Caucus, 113
    Melbourne S. Cummings and,
        93, 94, 97
    on Afrocentricity, 11
    overview of, 12–14
    timeline, 36–38
Asante, Ngena, 19
ASHA (American Speech and
    Hearing Association), 233
Audience reception theory, 166
Auer, J. Jeffrey, 224, 230
Austin, Mrs., 91

Baker, David, 113
Baker, H., 66
Baltimore Afro American
    (newspaper), 43
Barber, J. T., 142
Barlow, W., 41
Baron, J., 142, 144
Barrett, Catherine, 157, 162
Bates, B., 41
BBC (British Broadcasting
    Corporation), 153
Beale, F., 181
The Beautiful: A True Story of
    Slavery (Brown), 73
Bennett College, 175, 176
Bertelsen, Phil, 55
Bethun, Mary McLeod, 97
Beyond Agenda Setting: Information

Subsidies and Public Policy
    (Gandy), 129, 139
Biographical information
    on Donald E. Bogle, 43–45
    on Dorothy L. Pennington,
        207–208
    on Hallie Quinn Brown, 65–66
    on Jack L. Daniel, 106–108
    on Joni L. Jones, 190–192
    on Marsha Houston, 174–176
    on Melbourne S. Cummings,
        87–90
    on Molefi Kete Asante, 14–15
    on Orlando L. Taylor, 226–228
    on Oscar H. Gandy, Jr., 130–131
    on Stuart Hall, 154–158
Bits and Odds: A Choice Selection
    Of Recitations for School,
    Lyceum, and Parlor
    Entertainments (Brown)
    Brown's contributions, 73, 80
    excerpt from, 78–79
    on elocution, 74
Black, Edwin, 108
"Black and White communication:
    Analyzing Work Place
    Encounters" (Asante and
    Davis), 26
Black Arts Annual: 1989–1990
    (Bogle), 42
Black Caucus of the National
    Communication Association.
    See National Communication
    Association (NCA) Black
    Caucus
Black church
    Asante on Black rhetoric, 24–25
    communal-oral discourse, 117–118
    Cummings and Daniel on Black
        rhetoric, 96
Black cinema
    Blacks in American Films and
        Television: An Illustrated
        Encyclopedia (Bogle), 54
    Bogle on, 39–40
    Bogle's contributions to
        communication research,
        49–60

Bogle's life and, 44–45
See also Film
Black communication
    Black Pioneers in Communication
        Research (Jackson and
        Givens), 1–10
    Jack L. Daniel on, 104
    Jack L. Daniel's academic
        background/experience,
        108–114
    Jack L. Daniel's contributions to,
        105–106, 114–123
    Marsha Houston on, 172
    Marsha Houston's academic
        background and, 177–178
    Marsha Houston's contributions
        to, 179–183
    Melbourne S. Cummings'
        academic background, 92–94
    Melbourne S. Cummings'
        contributions to, 94–100
    Melbourne S. Cummings on, 84
    National Communication
        Association's Black Caucus,
        founding of, 112–113
    Orlando Taylor's contributions to,
        233–236
    Stuart Hall's contributions to,
        163–168
Black Communication: Dimensions
    of Research and Instruction
    (Daniel), 113–114
Black community
    consciousness, 29–30
Black discourse, 116–120
Black English
    Orlando Taylor's research on,
        234–235
    test bias and, 235–236
Black English Vernacular (BEV)
    focus on Black men, 172
    Orlando Taylor's research on,
        234–235
    test bias and, 235–236
Black feminist theory, 181–183
Black Feminist Thought (Collins),
    179, 183

Black images
    Donald Bogle's work on, 6–7, 49–51
    Melbourne S. Cummings on, 7, 99
Black Lines (journal), 116
Black Panther Party
    expansion of, 115
    founding of, 230
    Oscar Gandy and, 134
Black Pioneers in Communication
        Research (Jackson and Givens)
    challenges in writing of, 9–10
    functions of, 1–5
    layout of, 6
    purpose/rationale of, 5
    scholars included in,
        contributions of, 6–9
Black popular culture, 99–100,
    164–165
Black Power movement, 115, 230
Black public address, 97–99
Black rhetoric
    Dorothy Pennington
        and, 212–213
    Dorothy Pennington's academic
        background in, 211–212
    Melbourne S. Cummings and,
        94–97, 99
Black scholars, 1–10
Black Studies, 105–106, 110
Black women. See African American
    women
Black Women's Club, 215
Blacks
    culture, language, communication
        disorders and, 233–234
    early life of Melbourne S.
        Cummings, 89–90
    interracial communication and,
        179–181
    media's representation of,
        165–168
    privacy/use of media and,
        143–144
    race, discrimination, media
        consumption and, 141–142
    Stuart Hall's early life in Jamaica,
        155–158

Blacks in American Films and
    Television: An Illustrated
    Encyclopedia (Bogle), 54
Blacks in film. *See* Film
Blake, C., 28, 207
Blankenship, Jane, 178
"Bloomington Nine", 225, 233
Blubaugh, Jon A., 216, 218
Board of Education of Topeka,
    Kansas, Brown v., 228
Bofah, Kete, 18
Bogle, Donald E.
    academic background, experience
        of, 45–48
    biographical information
        on, 43–45
    communication research
        contributions of, 6–7, 49–58
    conclusion about, 58–60
    on Blacks in films, 39–40
    overview of, 41–43
    timeline, 62–63
Bogle, John D., 41–42, 43, 44
Bogle, Robert, 43
Bogle, Robert Woods, 44
Bogle, Roslyn Woods, 43–44
Boker, George H., 78–79
Bolden, T., 41
"Bosom biscuits", 120
Bouchet, Edward, 225
Brain damage, 231–232
Brehm, S., 214
Bright Boulevards, Bold Dreams:
    The Story of Black Hollywood
    (Bogle), 43, 58–59
British Broadcasting Corporation
    (BBC), 153
British Chautauqua School, 69
British cultural studies
    Stuart Hall's academic
        background/experience and,
        158–163
    Stuart Hall's contributions to
        communication research, 8,
        163–168
    Stuart Hall's impact on, 154
Britten, L., 59

Broken Circles: A Journey through
    Africa and the Self (Jones), 196
BrothersJudd.com, 57, 59
Brown, Frances Jane (Scoggins),
    65–66, 67
Brown, Hallie Quinn
    academic background, experience
        of, 66–73
    biographical information on, 65–66
    communication research
        contributions of, 2, 7, 73–80
    conclusion about, 80
    overview of, 65
    photograph of, 64
    quote of, 64
    timeline, 82–83
Brown, Lloyd, 113
Brown, Sterling, 44, 48
Brown, Thomas Arthur, 65–66, 67
Brown Sugar: Eighty Years of
    America's Black Female
    Superstars (Bogle), 51–54
Brown Sugar: Eighty Years of
    America's Black Female
    Superstars (PBS television
    series), 42, 54
Brown v. Board of Education of
    Topeka, Kansas, 228
Bryant, Ted, 227
BSA (Emory Black Student
    Alliance), 176

Call-and-response
    Afrocentricity and, 21
    description of, 117–118
    feature of speech, 2
    in Black church, 24–25
Calloway Thomas, C., 173
Canada, 66–67
Capitalism, 137–138, 144
Carmen Jones (film)
    Donald Bogle and, 42
    Dorothy Dandridge: A Biography
        (Bogle) and, 55, 56
Carnoy, Martin, 137, 141
Casmir, Fred, 16
Cassata, M., 26

Cave, J., 59
CCCS (Centre for Contemporary
    Cultural Studies), 161–162
Center, 1, 10
Center for African American Studies
    at University of Texas at Austin,
    190, 195–196
Center for Applied Linguistics,
    231, 233
Center of African American Studies,
    18, 19
Centering Ourselves: African
    American Feminist and
    Womanist Studies of Discourse
    (Houston and Davis), 183
Central Michigan University, 109
Central State University, 68
Centre for Contemporary Cultural
    Studies (CCCS), 161–162
Challengers to Capitalism:
    Marx, Lenin, Stalin and Mao
    (Gurley), 136
Chaminade High School, 131–132
"The Changing Image of the Black
    Family on Television"
    (Cummings), 99
Changing the Players and the Game:
    A Personal Account of the
    Speech Communication
    Association Black Caucus
    Origins (Daniel), 112, 114
Chatham, Ontario, Canada, 66–67
Chattanooga, Tennessee, 226–228
"Check It Out" program, 135
Chelsea College, 161
Chen, K. H.
    on Stuart Hall at CCCS, 162
    on Stuart Hall's academic
        background, 159–160
    on Stuart Hall's life, 155, 158
Chen, V., 181, 183
Children
    Black English and, 235
    educational performance/test bias
        and, 235–236
    institutionalized racial bias and,
        121–123
    proverbs and, 119, 120
Christian, D., 236

Chronicle of Higher Education, 6
Church. See Black church
Cinema. See Black cinema; Film
Civil rights, 71–73
Civil rights movement
    Black Studies programs
        and, 110–111
    class-based communication
        studies and, 114–116
    Dorothy Pennington and, 208, 211
    Joni Jones and, 190–191
    Orlando Taylor and, 228–229
Civil Rights Voting Act of 1965, 115
Clark, John Henrick, 29
Clark, Kenneth and Mamie, 121–122
Clark College, 177
Class-based communication
    studies, 114–116
Classical Africa (Asante), 31
Classical African Activity Book
    (Asante and Mitchell), 31
Clevenger, Theodore (Ted), 109
Clinkscales, Marcia, 93
Code-Switching in Black Women's
    Speech (Houston), 178
Cole, P., 235
College of William & Mary, 195
Colleges, 110–111
Colley, Jerlean Evelyn, 108, 109
Collins, Patricia Hill, 179, 183
Color caste system, 155–158
Colored Women's League of
    Washington, D.C., 71–72
Columbia University, 47
Commoditization, 128, 147
Communal-oral discourse, 116–118
Communication
    Black Pioneers in Communication
        Research on (Jackson and
        Givens), 1–10
    Jack Daniel's academic
        background/experience in,
        108–114
    Orlando Taylor's academic
        background/experience in,
        228–231
    See also Black communication;
        Intercultural communication;
        Interracial communication

Communication and Race: A
    Structural Perspective
    (Gandy), 140
Communication disorders
    aphasia and language acquisition,
        231–232
    culture, language and, 233–234
Communication Education, 105
Communication Quarterly, 105
Communication research
    Donald E. Bogle's contributions
        to, 49–58
    Dorothy L. Pennington's
        contributions to, 212–219
    Hallie Quinn Brown's
        contributions to, 73–80
    Jack L. Daniel's contributions to,
        114–123
    Joni L. Jones's contributions to,
        196–200
    Marsha Houston's contributions
        to, 179–183
    Melbourne S. Cummings'
        contributions to, 94–100
    Molefi Kete Asante's
        contributions to, 23–31
    Orlando Taylor's contributions to,
        225–226, 231–236
    Oscar Gandy's contributions to,
        129–130, 138–147
    Stuart Hall's contributions to,
        163–168
The Communist Manifesto (Marx),
    158–159
Conquergood, Dwight
    Joni Jones and, 194, 198
    on performance, 201
Conrad, Jeff, 54
Contemporary Black Thought:
    Alternative Analyses in
    Social and Behavioral Science
    (Asante and Vandi), 24, 207, 212
Contemporary Public
    Communication (Asante
    and Frye), 25–26
Copper, Anna Julia, 71
Coppin, Fannie Jackson, 71
The Cosby Show (television show), 99
Couch, William, 91, 92

Council for Graduate Schools,
    224, 236
Council of Social Science
    Associations, 224
Coward, Janice, 174
Coward, Jather, 174
Coward, Josephine, 174, 175
Cripps, T., 41
Crispus Attucks High School, 92
"Critical Analysis of Selected
    Dramatic Plays of Eugene
    O'Neill" (Cummings), 92
Critical paradigm, 161
Critical Studies in Mass
    Communication (journal), 166
Crocker, Lionel, 229–230
Cronen, Vernon, 177
Crossing Difference: Interracial
    Communication (Blubaugh
    and Pennington), 216
Crouch, S., 29
Cultural studies
    Stuart Hall's academic
        background/experience,
        158–163
    Stuart Hall's contributions to, 8,
        153–154, 163–168
Culture. See Black popular culture
"A Culture Based Approach To
    Teaching African American
    Public Address" (Pennington),
    218–219
Cummings, Melbourne S.
    academic background, experience
        of, 91–94
    biographical information on,
        87–90
    call-and-response and, 2
    communication research
        contributions of,
        7, 94–100
    conclusion about, 100
    on Black communication, 84
    Orlando Taylor and, 231
    overview of, 85–87
    timeline, 102–103
Cummings, Robert, 92, 93
Cummings, Samir, 94, 100
Cummings, Samori, 93, 100

Customs and Culture of
    Contemporary Egypt
    (Asante), 31

Daly, Ms., 46
Dandridge, Dorothy
    Dorothy Dandridge: A Biography
        (Bogle), 55–57
    in Carmen Jones, 42
    Otto Preminger and, 47
Dandridge, Vivian, 47, 55
Daniel, Gracie, 106–107
Daniel, J. E., 121–122
Daniel, Jack L.
    academic background, experience
        of, 108–114
    African American rhetoric and,
        84, 96
    biographical information on,
        106–108
    call-and-response and, 2
    communication research
        contributions of, 7, 114–123
    conclusion about, 123
    founding of National
        Communication Association's
        Black Caucus, 17
    on Black communication, 104
    on conference, 86
    overview of, 105–106
    timeline, 126–127
Daniel, Jerlean Evelyn Colley,
    108, 109
Daniel, Marijata, 107, 122
Daniel, Omari
    birth of, 111
    name of, 122
    values of, 107
    We Fish: The Journey to
        Fatherhood (Daniel and
        Daniel), 114, 123
Daniel, Russell, Sr., 106–107
Daniel, S. I., 65
Daniel, Sadie, 79
Dates, J., 41
Dates, J. L., 140
Daughters of the American
    Revolution, 72

Davis, Alice, 26
Davis, E. L., 66, 72
Davis, J., 140, 141
Davis, Olga, 183
Dayton, Ohio, 68, 69
de Certeau, M., 197
Decker, Phillip, 194
Deep structures, 117
Delpit, L., 234
Denison University, 229
DePauw University, 225
Desert Island Discs (Radio 4), 153
Detroit, Michigan, 119–120
Diop, Chiekh Anta, 29
Discourse, 116–120
Discrimination, 140–142
    See also Racism
Distinguished Book Awards, 173
Divas, 52–53
Dominant code, 166
Donawerth, J., 73, 75
Dorothy Dandridge: A Biography
    (Bogle), 47, 55–57
Douglas Ehninger Award for
    Distinguished Rhetorical
    Scholarship, 28
Douglass, Frederick
    Hallie Quinn Brown and, 70
    preservation of home of, 72
    speech by, 95
Dow, B., 183
Du Bois Club, 133
DuBois, W. E. B., 96

Early, G., 27
Early, Sarah J., 71
Ebonics
    Orlando Taylor's research on,
        234–235
    test bias and, 235–236
Ebony magazine, 47
Economics
    class-based communication
        studies, 114–116
    Leicester Centre research on, 161
    of education, 137–138
    Oscar Gandy's education in, 136
    TrEE model and, 145–146

Education
    after emancipation, 76
    assimilation through, 122–123
    children's educational
        performance/test bias,
        235–236
    economics of, 137–138
    Hallie Quinn Brown as educator,
        68–69
    Marsha Houston's early interest
        in, 175
    Orlando Taylor's contributions to,
        225–226
    Orlando Taylor's work on
        graduate education, 236
    See also Academic
        background/experience
Education subsidy, 139–140
Educational Policies Board of the
    Speech Communication
    Association, 173
Edwards, Michael, 113
"Effective and Ineffective
    Communication on the Parts
    of Professionals and
    Non-Professionals When
    Communicating with Poor
    People" (Daniel), 105, 109
Effective Expression: A New
    Approach to Better Speaking
    (Hurst), 20
Effinger, M., 119, 120
Egypt vs. Greece in the American
    Academy (Asante and
    Mazama), 31
The Egyptian Philosophers
    (Asante), 31
Eighth National Conference on
    Research in Gender and
    Communication, 173–174
Elocution
    Hallie Quinn Brown as lecturer,
        70–71
    Hallie Quinn Brown's
        academic background/
        experience, 66–73
    Hallie Quinn Brown's
        contributions to, 65, 73–80

Elocution and Physical Culture:
    Training for Students, Teachers,
    Readers, and Public Speakers
    (Brown), 73, 74–75, 80
Emery, Julia, 71
Emory Black Student Alliance
    (BSA), 176
Emory College, 173
Emory University, 176
"Encoding/Decoding" (Hall), 166
England, 159–163
Entertainment Weekly, 59
Espinosa, P., 145
Essentialism, 29
Ethnicity, 163–165
Eurocentricity, 21–23, 122–123
Events, 152, 166

Faculty, 236
FAMU (Florida Agricultural &
    Mechanical University), 92
Fanon, Frantz, 114
Farrell, H. Alfred, 46
Fathers, 114, 123
Federal City College, 231
The Federal Theatre's Black Units: A
    Study of their Social Relevance
    (Houston), 177
Feminist theory, 181–183
Film
    Blacks in American Films and
        Television: An Illustrated
        Encyclopedia (Bogle), 54
    Bogle on Blacks in films, 39–40
    Bogle's academic experience
        in, 45–48
    Bogle's life and, 44–45
    Bogle's work on Blacks in film,
        41–43, 58–60
    Brown Sugar: Eighty Years of
        America's Black Female
        Superstars (Bogle), 51–54
    Donald Bogle's contributions
        to, 6–7
    Dorothy Dandridge: A Biography
        (Bogle), 55–57
    Toms, Coons, Mulattoes, Mammies
        & Bucks: An Interpretive

History of Blacks in American
   Films (Bogle), 49–51
Film Forum, 59
First Lessons in Public Speaking
   (Brown), 73, 75, 80
Fisher, V., 66
Fitz, Clifford, 130–131
Florida, 14
Florida Agricultural & Mechanical
   University (FAMU), 92
Florida International
   University, 93
Florida State University, 18
Foucault, M., 143
Francine Merritt Award for
   Distinguished Service to
   Women in the Communication
   Discipline, 174
Frazer, K., 140, 141
Frazier, E. Franklin, 96
Freire, Paul, 165
Frye, J., 25–26

Gabbidon, Shaun, 3–4
Gandesha, S., 159, 161
Gandy, Imani, 138
Gandy, Judith, 134, 138
Gandy, Oscar H., Jr.
   academic background, experience,
      131–138
   biographical information, 130–131
   communication research
      contributions, 7–8, 138–146
   conclusion about, 146–147
   on commodification, 128
   overview of, 129–130
   timeline, 150–151
   TrEE model of, 7
Gandy, Oscar, Sr., 130
Gandy, Rita, 130
Gandy, Sheila, 130, 131
Garner, T., 41
Gates, Henry Louis
   Afrocentricity and, 29
   citation of book by Hallie Quinn
      Brown, 73
   "Wonders of the African World"
      series of, 22

Gender, 179, 181–183
   See also African American women
Georgia, 14–15
Gerbner, George
   data from, 139
   Oscar Gandy and, 134, 135
Ghana, 13
Gilroy, P., 153, 165
Gilyard, K., 76
Giovanni, Nikki, 133
Giroux, H. A., 154, 165
Gonzalez, A., 181, 183
Goshorn, K., 140
Gottlieb, Inez, 134–135
Government
   media and, 129
   privacy/surveillance and, 142–144
Government and Media: An
   Annotated Bibliography
   (Gandy), 129
Graduate education, 236
Gramsci, Antonio, 164
"Gramsci's Relevance for the
   Study Of Race and Ethnicity"
   (Hall), 164
Greene, Helen Taylor, 3
Greensboro, North Carolina,
   174–176
Groff, Edward, 46
Grossberg, L.
   articulation theory and, 166
   Stuart Hall's approach and, 165
   trained by Stuart Hall, 163
   Without guarantees: In honour
      of Stuart Hall (Gilroy,
      Grossberg and
      McRobbie), 153
Gudykunst, W. B., 28, 212
Guilt provocation, 212–213
"Guilt Provocation: A Strategy
   in Black Rhetoric"
   (Pennington), 212–213
Gurley, John, 136

Hall, Catherine Barrett, 157, 162
Hall, George, 155
Hall, Jess, 157
Hall, Rebecca, 157

Hall, Stuart
  academic background, experience
    of, 158–163
  articulation theory of, 2
  as Caribbean, 5
  biographical information on,
    154–158
  communication research
    contributions of, 8, 163–168
  conclusion about, 168
  historical events, 152
  life/work covered in book, 3
  overview of, 153–154
  timeline, 170–171
"Hallie Quinn Brown: Black Woman
  Elocutionist" (McFarlin), 65
Hamlet J., 12, 29
Hampton Institute, 228–229
Hampton Press, 183
Handbook of Communications and
  Development in Africa and the
  African Diaspora (Cummings,
  Niles, and Taylor), 87
Handbook of Gender &
  Communication (Wood and
  Dow), 183
Handbook of International and
  Intercultural Communication
  (Asante and Gudykunst), 28
Handbook of International and
  Intercultural Communication
  (Asante, Newmark, and Blake),
  28, 207
Hands, T., 140, 141
Harding, Warren, 72
Hardy, Martha Nell, 177
Hare, Nathan, 111
Harper, Frances Watkins, 71
HarperCollins, 50
Harris, T., 41
Harrison, D. S., 234
Harris-Stewart, C., 31
Hawthorne, Lucia
  founding of National
    Communication Association's
    Black Caucus, 17
  Melbourne S. Cummings and, 85
  paper by, 113

HBO (Home Box Office), 41
Health information, 139–140
Hernandez, D., 27
Herskovitz, Melville, 96
Hine, D. C, 66, 72
Hines, Imogine, 113
Historical and Cultural Atlas of
  African Americans (Asante
  and Mattson), 30
Historical event, 152
Hitler Jugend (HJ), 16
Hitler Youth, 16
Hoggart, Richard, 153, 161
Holism, 118
Hollywood, 58–59
Home Box Office (HBO), 41
Homespun Heroines and Other
  Women of Distinction (Brown),
  73–74, 75
Homosexuality, 23
Hoover, M., 235
Hope, Cynthia, 215
Hope University, 225
Houston, Lillian Tyson, 174–175
Houston, Marsha (aka Marsha
  Houston Stanback)
  academic background, experience
    of, 176–178
  as mentor to Joni Jones, 194
  biographical information on,
    174–176
  communication research
    contributions of, 8, 179–183
  conclusion about, 183–184
  on Black women's
    communication, 172
  overview of, 173–174
  timeline, 186–188
Houston, Roosevelt, 174
Houston Stanback, Marsha.
    See Houston, Marsha (aka
    Marsha Houston Stanback)
"How I Got Over: Communication
  Dynamics in the
  Black Community"
  (Daniel and Smitherman-
  Donaldson), 7, 106,
  117–118

How to Talk to People of Other
    Races (Asante, Allen, and
    Hernandez), 27
Howard High School, 228
Howard Journal of
    Communications, 231
Howard University
    Black Studies program at, 111
    Joni Jones at, 195
    Melbourne S. Cummings and,
        85–86, 93–94
    Molefi Kete Asante as professor
        at, 19
    Orlando Taylor and, 224,
        231, 236
    Oscar Gandy and, 138, 145
Hughes, Frances, 72–73
Hughes, Langston, 176
Hurst, Charles
    American Speech and Hearing
        Association and, 233
    founding of National
        Communication Association's
        Black Caucus, 17, 112–113
    Molefi Kete Asante and, 20

"I Have a Dream" speech (Martin
    Luther King, Jr.), 218–219
Ideologies
    media communication and,
        166, 167
    Stuart Hall's theories about, 154,
        164–165
Illinois, 190–192
Imports, 136–137
Improvisation, 198, 199
"Improvisation as a Performance
    Strategy for African-based
    Theatre" (Jones), 198
Indiana University
    "Bloomington Nine" of,
        225–226, 233
    Donald Bogle as student at, 47
    Orlando Taylor as professor at,
        230–231
    Orlando Taylor at, 224
Indianapolis Times
    (newspaper), 71

Information technology
    Gandy's work related to,
        129, 139–140
    privacy/surveillance and, 142–144
Institute of Race Relations, Fisk
    University, 110
Institutionalized racial bias, 121–123
Interacial caste system, 155–158
Intercultural communication
    Dorothy Pennington on, 205
    Dorothy Pennington's academic
        background in, 211–212
    Dorothy Pennington's
        contributions to, 206–207,
        208, 216–217
    interracial communication vs., 218
    Marsha Houston's contributions
        to, 179–181
    Molefi Kete Asante's
        contributions to, 26–28
    Orlando Taylor's interest in, 229
    Stuart Hall's contributions to,
        163–165
Intercultural Communication: A
    Reader (Samovar and Porter),
    207, 216, 218
"Intercultural Communication"
    (Pennington), 216–217, 218
Internal Revenue Service, 142
International Council of Women's
    Conference, 72
International Institute of Visual Arts,
    London, 153
International Issues in Black
    Communication (Taylor and
    Williams), 234
Interpersonal communication, 8
Interracial communication
    Dorothy Pennington and, 211–212,
        217–219
    Marsha Houston's contributions
        to, 179–181
    Melbourne Cummings and, 93
    Molefi Kete Asante's
        contributions to, 26–28
    Orlando Taylor and, 229
    Stuart Hall's contributions to,
        163–165

Intrapsychic community, 21
"It Ain't Half Racist, Mum" (BBC 2
    Open Door program), 153
Iya Omi Osun Olomo, 200
    See also Jones, Joni L.

Jackson, Blydon, 91
Jackson, R. L., II., 4, 29
Jacob Javits National Fellowship
    Program in the Humanities,
    224, 236
Jamaica
    Stuart Hall's academic
        background/experience
        and, 159
    Stuart Hall's life in, 154–158
    Stuart Hall's relationship to, 160
Jamaican Rastafarian groups, 157–158
James B. Dudley High School, 176
Jaspers, K., 213
The Jeffersons (television show), 99
Jeremiah, M., 119–120, 121
Johannesburg City Press, 20
John H. Johnson School of
    Communications, 86
Johnson, Charles S., 110
Johnson, Fern, 177
Johnstown, Pennsylvania, 106–108
Joint Math Meetings, 193
Jones, A. LaVerne Love, 191, 192
Jones, C., 183
Jones, Dorothy Mae Brown, 191–192
Jones, Joni L.
    academic background, experience
        of, 192–196
    biographical information on,
        190–192
    communication research
        contributions of, 8, 196–200
    conclusion about, 200–201
    on performance work, 189
    overview of, 190
    timeline, 203–204
Jones, Regina Elaine Patrick,
    191, 192
Jones, Willetta Doreen Wordlaw,
    191, 192
Jones, William Edward, 191, 192

Journal of Black Studies
    article by Melbourne Cummings
        in, 95
    founding of, 12, 18
Journal of Communication
    Inquiry, 164
Journal of Popular Culture, 99

Kael, Pauline, 48
Karenga, Maulana
    Molefi Kete Asante and,
        16–17, 18
    Us organization, 115
Kates, S.
    o Hallie Quinn Brown as
        lecturer, 70
    on Brown's approach to
        elocution, 77
    on Brown's contributions to
        elocution, 78
    on Hallie Quinn Brown as
        activist, 71
    on work of Hallie Quinn
        Brown, 65
    poem by Hallie Quinn Brown,
        78–79
Kemet, Afrocentricity, and
    Knowledge (Asante), 25
Kennedy, John Fitzgerald, 132
Kibler, Robert, 17
King, Martin Luther, Jr.
    assassination of, 115
    bus boycotts led by, 228
    communication conference
        about, 173
    Cummings's study of speeches of,
        97, 98
    Dorothy Pennington and, 218–219
    Jack L. Daniel and, 109–110
    Marsha Houston and, 176
Kisch, John, 57
Klebe, Joerg, 42, 54
Kopp, K., 140, 141
Kramarae, Cheris, 178
Ku Klux Klan, 225

Labov, W., 234
L'Afrocentricité (Asante), 31

Language, Communication, and Rhetoric in Black America (Asante), 27
Language acquisition, 231–232
"Language and Black Women's Place: Evidence from the Black Middle Class" (Houston Stanback), 182
Lawrence, Kansas, 206
Lee, D. L., 223, 235
Lee, Spike, 41, 59
Leeman, R., 71
Lefkowitz, M., 14, 29
Leicester Centre, 161
Leonard, L. B., 235
Leslie Irene Coger Award for Distinguished Performance, 190, 200
Levin, Hank, 137, 141
Lewin, Olivia, 113
Library Journal, 59
Lincoln Center's Library of the Performing Arts, 48, 55
Lincoln University, 44, 45–46
Locke, Alain, 44
Logan, R. W., 69, 70
Lomas, Charles, 16
Louisiana, 87–91
Lucaites, J., 173
Lumumba, Patrice, 135
Lumumba-Zapata College, 135–136
Lyceum, 69, 70

MacMurray College, 193–194
Madison, D. Soyinyi, 194, 198
"Mainstreaming Interracial Communication" (Pennington), 217
Making the Connection: Academic Achievement and Language Diversity in African American Children (Taylor, Adger, and Christian), 236
Malcolm X, 115, 230
Manley, Michael, 157–158
Mann, A., 31
Mansfield, Mrs., 91
Mapp, Edward, 57

Marable, M., 110–111
"Markings of an African Concept of Rhetoric" (Asante), 25
Marshall, Thurgood, 228
Marshall College, 135
Martin Luther King Jr. and the Sermonic Power of Discourse (Lucaites and Calloway Thomas), 173
Martin Luther King, Jr. Center for Nonviolent Social Change, 173
Marx, Karl, 158–159
Marxism
  beliefs of, 129
  intercultural/interracial communication and, 164
  Oscar Gandy's education at Stanford and, 136
  Oscar Gandy's work related to, 139
  Stuart Hall's academic background/experience and, 158–159, 161
  Stuart Hall's theoretical framework and, 153–154
Mass Communication: Principles and Practices (Asante and Cassata), 26
Mass media
  Donald Bogle and, 6–7
  Molefi Kete Asante and, 25–26
  Oscar Gandy and, 138–146
  Stuart Hall and, 165–168
Matabane, P., 142
Mattson, M., 30, 31
Maxwell, R., 135
Mazama, Ama, 31
Mbiti, John, 118
McAnany, Emile, 136
McFarlin, Annjennette
  on Brown as educator, 68
  on Brown as elocutionist, 71
  on Brown as lecturer, 70
  on Brown family, 66
  on Brown's approach to elocution, 77
  on Brown's early life, 66, 67
  on Brown's loves, 73

on lack of recognition of
    Brown, 65
quote of Brown, 64, 67–68
speech by Brown, 76
McRobbie, A., 153
Means-Coleman, R., 41
Media
    Centre for Contemporary
        Cultural Studies' research
        on, 161–162
    Oscar Gandy's academic
        experience in, 134–138
    Oscar Gandy's contributions to
        communication research,
        138–147
    Oscar Gandy's work related to,
        129–130
    privacy/surveillance, 142–144
    Stuart Hall's scholarship on
        media communication,
        165–168
Media consumption, 140–142
Media development, 144–146
Media framing, 139–140
Media Training Needs in Zimbabwe
    (Asante), 26
Meier, Howard, 130, 133
Mentoring
    by Jack L. Daniel, 105
    by Marsha Houston, 183
    by Melbourne S. Cummings,
        85, 100
    of Orlando Taylor, 229, 230
    Orlando Taylor's work on
        graduate education, 236
Micheaux, Oscar, 48
Michile—The African (Brown), 73
Microinequities, 193
Milhouse, V., 28
Milisen, Robert
    mentor of Orlando Taylor,
        224, 230
    Orlando Taylor's work and, 232
Mind, 21
The Mind Managers (Schiller), 135
Minority groups
    class-based communication
        studies, 114–116

founding of NCA's Black Caucus
    and, 112
media and, 146–147
privacy/surveillance and, 143–144
representation in media, 140–142
Mississippi, 207–210
Mitchell, J., 31
Mo' Better Blues (film), 41
Mo' Funny: Black Comedy in
    America (HBO special), 41
Montage of a Dream Deferred
    (Hughes), 176
Moore, Earnest, 233
Moreland, Mantan, 48
Morrison, Carlos, 4
Morton College, 160
Movies. See Black cinema; Film
Multiple Perspectives: African
    American Women Conceive
    Their Talk" (Houston), 183
Muse, Clarence, 48

NACW. See National Association of
    Colored Women
Names, 121–122
Nashville Christian Institute, 15
Nassau Community College,
    131, 132
National Afrocentric Institute, 13
National Association of Colored
    Women (NACW)
    establishment of, 72, 215
    Hallie Quinn Brown's
        love of, 73
National Black Feminist
    Organization, 191
National Black Speech, Language,
    and Hearing Association, 233
National Communication
    Association (NCA)
    award given to Joni L. Jones,
        190, 200
    award given to Molefi Kete
        Asante, 28
    Marsha Houston's contributions
        to, 173
    Melbourne S. Cummings and
        Jack L. Daniel and, 7

members from Howard
  University, 86
Mentor Award given to
  Melbourne S. Cummings, 85
Orlando Taylor as president
  of, 224
Robert J. Kibler Memorial Award
  given to Melbourne S.
  Cummings, 86
National Communication Association
  (NCA) Black Caucus
cofounded by Dorothy
  Pennington, 206–207
cofounded by Jack L. Daniel,
  105, 111–114
cofounded by Molefi Kete
  Asante, 12–13
Distinguished Service Award
  given to Melbourne S.
  Cummings, 86
Dorothy Pennington and, 8–9
Jack Daniel and, 7
Molefi Kete Asante and, 17
Orlando Taylor and, 233
surveys of members of, 4
National Endowment for the
  Humanities, 113
Nature of Communication Disorders
  in Culturally and Linguistically
  Diverse Populations
  (Taylor), 234
NCA. See National Communication
  Association
NCUU (North Carolina Central
  University), 91–92
Negotiable code, 166
Negotiating Boundaries: The
  Language of Black Women's
  Intercultural Encounters
  (Houston and Scott), 183
Negritude, 20
The Negro and His Orations
  (Woodson), 94
Negro Orators and Their Orations
  (Woodson), 24
New Left, 160–163
New Left Review (journal)
  edited by Stuart Hall, 154,
    160–161, 163

Stuart Hall as founding editor
  of, 168
The New Reasoner (journal), 160–161
New York Times (newspaper), 72
New York University
  Donald Bogle as professor at, 43, 49
  Joni Jones at, 195
Newmark, E., 28, 207
News, 140
Newspapers, 141
Newton, Huey P., 230
Nhiwatiwa, Naomi, 19
Nigeria, 190, 196
Niles, Lyndrey
  at Howard University, 93
  Handbook of Communications
    and Development in Africa
    and the African Diaspora
    (Cummings, Niles, and
    Taylor), 87
  Melbourne S. Cummings and, 7
  oratory of Martin Luther
    King, Jr., 98
  Orlando Taylor and, 231
  World Congress on
    Communications and
    Development in Africa and
    the African Diaspora and, 86
North Carolina, 174–177
North Carolina Agricultural &
  Technical (A&T) State
  University, 175, 176
North Carolina Central University
  (NCUU), 91–92
Northern Caribbean
  University, 158
Northwestern University, 194
Not Gifts but Opportunity
  (Brown), 76
Notable Black American Women
  (Smith), 65
Nwosu, P., 28

Obafemi Awolowo University,
  Nigeria, 190, 196
Ogbonnaya, Okechukwu, 21
Ogelsby, Gloria, 175
Ohio, 68, 69
Oklahoma Christian College, 16

Omachonu, J., 142
100 Greatest African Americans
    (Asante), 31
O'Neal, Ms., 46
O'Neill, Eugene, 91–92
Open University, 162–163
Oppositional code, 166
Oral discourse, 116–120
Oratory. *See* Elocution
Orature, 87
Orbe, M., 41
Orchard Knob elementary and
    junior high school, 228
Ordover, J., 145
Our Voices: Essays in Culture,
    Ethnicity, and Communication
    (Gonzalez, Houston and Chen),
    181, 183
Our Women: Past, Present and
    Future (Brown), 73
Oxford University, 159–160

The Padlock (film), 44
The Panoptic Sort: A Political
    Economy of Personal
    Information (Gandy), 143
Panopticon, 143
Parents
    naming of children, 121–122
    use of proverbs, 119, 120
    We Fish: The Journey to
        Fatherhood (Daniel and
        Daniel), 123
Parks, Rosa, 228
Payne, Daniel Alexander, 67–68
Payne, K., 234, 235
PBS (Public Broadcasting Service),
    42, 54
Pearce, W. Barnnett, 177, 179–180
Pen Pictures of Pioneers of
    Wilberforce (Brown), 73
Pennington, Dorothy L.
    academic background, experience,
        208–212
    as president of Black Caucus, 113
    biographical information,
        207–208
    communication research
        contributions, 8–9, 212–219

conclusion about, 219
    Marsha Houston and, 178
    Melbourne S. Cummings
        and, 85
    on intercultural study, 205
    overview of, 206–207
    timeline, 221–222
Pennsylvania, 106–108
Peoples Publishing Group, 31
Pepperdine University, 16
Performance ethnography,
    196–198
Performance studies
    academic background/experience
        of Joni Jones, 192–196
    contributions of Joni Jones, 8, 190,
        196–201
Perry, T., 234
Pew Charitable Trust, 236
The Philadelphia Tribune (newspaper),
    41, 42, 43
Phillips, D., 140, 141
Pittsburgh, Pennsylvania, 119–120
Poitier, Sidney, 45, 59
Political economy
    approach of Leicester Centre, 161
    Gandy's work on information
        technology and education
        subsidy, 139–140
Political symbols, 53
Politics
    class-based communication
        studies, 114–116
    Stuart Hall's academic
        background/experience
        and, 159
Politzer, R. L., 235
Polyrhythm, 25, 118
Poor people, 114–116
The Popular Arts (Whannel and
    Hall), 161
Popular culture, 99–100, 164–165
Porgy and Bess (film), 56
Porter, R.
    collaboration with Dorothy
        Pennington, 212
    Intercultural Communication: A
        Reader (Samovar and Porter),
        207, 216, 218

Poststructuralism, 129
Power of the Spoken Word: The
    Oratory of Dr. Martin Luther
    King, Jr. Conference, 173
Preminger, Otto
    Donald Bogle's work with, 43, 47
    Dorothy Dandridge: A Biography
        (Bogle) and, 55
"Preparing Future Faculty"
    program, 236
"Preschool Children's Selection Of
    Race-Related Personal Names"
    (Daniel and Daniel), 121
Prime Time Blues: African
    Americans on Network
    Television (Bogle), 57–58, 59
Primetime Blues (Bogle), 42
Privacy, 142–144
"The Problem of Ideology: Marxism
    without Guarantees" (Hall), 164
"Problems of Researching Black
    Rhetoric" (Cummings), 95
Protests, 110–111
Proverb tradition, 119–120
Public address, 97–99
Public Broadcasting Service (PBS),
    42, 54
Public communication, 25–26
Public speaking, 70–71
    See also Elocution
Purdue University, 17, 225
Putnam, Lou, 46

Quarterly Journal of Speech,
    117, 179

Race
    Black public address and, 97–99
    institutionalized racial
        bias, 121–123
    interracial communication,
        163–165, 179–181, 217–219
    media communication and,
        140–142, 165–168
    Stuart Hall's early life and,
        155–158
Racial stereotypes, 122
Racism

class-based communication
    studies and, 114
Hallie Quinn Brown's experiences
    of, 67
institutionalized racial
    bias, 121–123
interracial communication and,
    164–165, 217–219
Joni Jones and, 193
Melbourne S. Cummings
    and, 89–90
Molefi Kete Asante's experience
    with, 27
Radio, 227–228
Rap music, 99–100
Rayville, Louisiana, 87–91
Rayville Rosenwald School, 91
Real, Mike, 136
Reddick, L. D., 48
Redemption Song (BBC series), 153
References, 94–100
Religion, 214
    See also Black church
Repetition, 24
Research in Mass Communication:
    A Guide to Practice (Asante), 26
Rhetoric
    "classical", 29
    Dorothy Pennington and, 210–211
    Hallie Quinn Brown as lecturer,
        70–71
    Hallie Quinn Brown's
        contributions to, 65, 73–80
    Hallie Quinn Brown's education
        in, 67
    Hallie Quinn Brown's work on, 7
    Jack L. Daniel's work on,
        116–120
    Melbourne S. Cummings and,
        84, 85, 93
    Molefi Kete Asante and, 17, 24–25
"The Rhetoric of Bishop Henry
    McNeal Turner, Leading
    Advocate of the African
    Emigration Movement,
    1868–1907" (Cummings), 93
Rhetoric of Black Revolution
    (Asante), 17, 24

Rhetoric of Revolution (Asante and Rich), 17
Rich, Andrea, 17, 93
Right On! program, 134–135
Robb, S., 17, 24
Robertson, Professor, 68
Rodriguez, A., 234
Rosenthal, Paul, 16
Ross, Gerlene, 113
Roy, A., 99–100
Rust College, 209–210

SAA. *See* National Communication Association
Sage Publications, 18
Samovar, L.
  collaboration with Dorothy Pennington, 212
  Intercultural Communication: A Reader (Samovar and Porter), 207, 216, 218
San Francisco State University, 111
Sarris, Andrew, 48
Scattered to the Wind (Asante), 31
Schechner, Richard, 197, 198
Schiller, Herbet I., 135–136, 137
"Scholarship of the oppressed", 109
Schomburg Center for Research in Black Culture, 48, 55
School of Communication, Howard University, 231
Scoggins, Frances, 65–66
Scott, Karla, 183
SDS (Students for a Democratic Society), 133
Seale, Bobby, 230
Searching for Osun (Jones), 196
Seeing Female: Social Roles and Personal Lives (Brehm), 214
Segmentation, 140–142
Senghor, Leopold, 20
Senora Plantation School, 68–69
A Separate Cinema: Fifty Years of Black Cast Posters (Kisch and Mapp), 57
Seymour, Charlena, 178

Shakin' the Mess Outta Misery (Jones), 190
Shea, C., 12
Shearer, Ned, 16
Shifting: The Double Lives of Black Women in America (Jones and Shorter-Gooden), 183
Shoemaker, J. W., 75
Shorter-Gooden, K., 183
Short-term memory, 232
Sierra Leone, 119
SIETAR (Society for International Education, Training and Research), 13, 27
"Signification, Representation, Ideology: Althusser and the post-Structuralist Debates" (Hall), 166, 167
Signorielli, N., 141
Sinclair, T., 59
Singleton, Robert, 12, 18
Sista-docta (Jones)
  contributions of Joni Jones, 196
  description of, 199–200
  Joni Jones most noted for, 190
Slater, A., 154
Slavery
  Hallie Quinn Brown and, 76
  media communication and, 167
  names and, 121
  Stuart Hall and, 157
Small Steps, Big Strides (AMC documentary), 41
Smith, Arthur Lee, Jr.. *See* Asante, Molefi Kete
Smith, Arthur Lee, Sr., 14–15
Smith, Donald, 17
Smith, J. C., 65, 68–69, 72
Smith, Mrs., 91
Smith, Plenty, 14
Smitherman, G., 234
Smitherman-Donaldson, Geneva
  de-Africanization, 121
  "How I Got Over: Communication Dynamics in the Black Community (Daniel and Smitherman-Donaldson), 106, 117–118

Jack Daniel's work with, 7
mentoring of Jack L. Daniel, 114
on proverbs, 119–120
Social symbols, 53
Social transformation, 198,
199, 200
The Social Uses of Mass
Communication (Asante and
Cassata), 26
Socialist Society, 160–161
Society for International Education,
Training and Research
(SIETAR), 13, 27
Southern Journal of
Communication, 180
Southern States Communication
Association Outreach
Award., 173
Southern University, 91
Southwestern Christian
College, 15
Sowande, Fela, 113, 114
Speech
aphasia and language acquisition,
231–232
culture, language and
communication disorders,
233–234
Speech Association of America
(SAA). See National
Communication Association
Speech Communication Teacher
(Pennington), 217
The Speech Teacher (journal), 105
Sperry Gyroscope Corporation,
131, 132
Spiritual diunitality, 118
Spivak, Gayatri, 165
Stanback, Howard, 177
Stanback, Zuri Akili, 177, 178
Standardized tests, 223, 235–236
Stanford University
Jack L. Daniel at, 109, 111
Oscar Gandy at, 136–138
Starosta, William J., 231
State University of New York
(SUNY) at Buffalo, 19
Stenson, Emma Virginia Elizabeth
Brown, 87–89

Stenson, Melbourne Jean, 87–92
See also Cummings, Melbourne S.
Stenson, Theolis, 87–88
Stereotypes
created by surveillance, 142
minority representation in media,
140, 141, 142
names and, 122
of Black women, 214
surveillance and, 143
Stetson, E., 69
Stevens, Mrs., 91
Stewart, J., 235
Strom, C., 66
Strother, K., 41
Stroud, V., 233
Structuralism, 154
Students for a Democratic Society
(SDS), 133
Sungai Books, 31
SUNY (State University of New
York) at Buffalo, 19
Superstate: Readings in the
Military-Industrial Complex
(Schiller), 135
Surface structures, 117
Surveillance
media privacy/surveillance,
142–144
Oscar Gandy's work related to,
129, 130
Surveys, 143
Swanson, C. D., 197
Swinney, D., 232

Tales My Father Told, and Other
Stories (Brown), 67, 73
"Talking to 'The Man': Some
Communication Strategies Used
By Members Of 'Subordinate'
Social Groups" (Houston
Stanback and Peace), 179–180
Taylor, Carrie, 226–227, 228
Taylor, Ingrid Gelete, 230
Taylor, LeRoy, 226–227, 228
Taylor, Orlando, II., 230
Taylor, Orlando L.
academic background, experience
of, 228–231

at Howard University, 93
biographical information on,
226–228
communication research
contributions of,
9, 231–236
conclusion about, 236–237
founding of National
Communication Association's
Black Caucus, 113
Handbook of Communications
and Development in Africa
and the African Diaspora
(Cummings, Niles, and
Taylor), 87
Melbourne S. Cummings and,
7, 94
on test bias, 223
overview of, 224–226
timeline, 239–241
World Congress on
Communications and
Development in Africa
and the African Diaspora
and, 86
Taylor, Robert, 226
Teacher's Guide for African
American History (Asante,
Harris-Stewart, and Mann), 31
Television
Blacks in American Films and
Television: An Illustrated
Encyclopedia (Bogle), 54
Donald Bogle and, 42, 48,
49–50, 54
Donald Bogle's contributions
to communication,
6–7, 59–60
effects on Black consciousness,
25–26
Melbourne S. Cummings
and, 7, 99
Oscar Gandy and, 134–135
Prime Time Blues: African
Americans on Network
Television (Bogle), 57–58
Temple University, 19
Temporality among Black
Americans: Implications for

Intercultural Communication
(Pennington), 212
Tennessee, 226–228
Tests, 223, 235–236
Theatre. See Performance studies
Third College, 135
Third world nations, 144–146
Thomas, O., 77
Thompson, E. P., 160
Till, Emmett, 228
Timeline
of Donald E. Bogle, 62–63
of Dorothy L. Pennington,
221–222
of Hallie Quinn Brown, 82–83
of Jack L. Daniel, 126–127
of Joni L. Jones, 203–204
of Marsha Houston, 186–188
of Melbourne S. Cummings,
102–103
of Molefi Kete Asante, 36–38
of Orlando L. Taylor, 239–241
of Oscar H. Gandy, Jr., 150–151
of Stuart Hall, 170–171
Today's Speech (journal), 105, 115
Toll, R. C., 41
Toms, Coons, Mulattoes, Mammies
& Bucks: An Interpretive
History of Blacks in American
Films (Bogle)
Bogle on, 39–40
discussion of, 49–51
Edward Groff and, 46
recognition of, 42
Toward Transracial Communication
(Asante), 27
Trabasso, T., 234
Transcultural Realities (Milhouse,
Asante, and Nwosu), 28
Transracial Communication
(Asante), 27
Treatment of Communication
Disorders in Culturally and
Linguistically Diverse
Populations (Taylor), 234
TrEE (Transformation, Effectiveness,
and Efficiency) model
description of, 145–146
Oscar Gandy most known for, 8

Oscar Gandy's development
of, 136–137
Tulane University, 173
Turner, Bishop Henry McNeal,
97, 98–99
Turner, D.
interview with Molefi Kete
Asante, 14–15
on Molefi Kete Asante, 13, 31
on Molefi Kete Asante's
Afrocentricity, 17
on Molefi Kete Asante's move to
UCLA, 18
Turner, R., 12
Turner, Victor, 196, 197, 198
Tuskegee Institute
Clifford Fitz educated at, 131
Hallie Quinn Brown at, 68

UCLA. See University of California,
Los Angeles
UCSD (University of California at
San Diego), 135–136
Underground Railroad, 66, 105
Universities, 110–111
Universities and Left Review
(journal), 154, 163
University of Alabama at
Birmingham, 173
University of Birmingham, 161–162
University of California at San
Diego (UCSD), 135–136
University of California, Los Angeles
(UCLA)
Afrocentricity development at, 21
Melbourne S. Cummings at,
85, 92–93
Molefi Kete Asante at, 16, 18–19
University of Kansas, 206, 210–212
University of Maryland, 195
University of Massachusetts at
Amherst, 177–178
University of Miami, 93
University of Michigan, 230
University of New Mexico, 129–130,
132–133
University of North Carolina at
Chapel Hill, 176–177

University of Pennsylvania
Donald Bogle as professor
at, 43, 49
Oscar Gandy as professor
at, 129, 138
Oscar Gandy as student
at, 133–135
University of Pittsburgh
"Black Communication
Conference" at, 113
Jack L. Daniel as professor at,
109–110
Jack L. Daniel at, 106, 108–109
University of Texas at Austin, 190,
195–196
Us organization, 115
Utne Reader, 6, 32

Vandi, A. S., 24, 207
Victoria, Queen of England, 67, 68
Vidor, King, 48
Vietnam War, 108
Voice, 75
The Voice of Black Rhetoric:
Selections (Asante and Robb),
17, 24

Walker, Gloria
American Speech and Hearing
Association and, 233
founding of National
Communication Association's
Black Caucus, 113
Melbourne S. Cummings and, 94
Walter H. Annenburg School
for Communication at
University of Pennsylvania,
129, 134–135, 138
Ware, Opoku, II, 18
Washington, Booker T.
dialogues of, 96
Hallie Quinn Brown and, 68
Melbourne S. Cummings and, 97
speech by, 95
Tuskegee Institute founded
by, 131
Waters, Ethel, 53
WDXB radio station, 227

We Fish: The Journey to Fatherhood
    (Daniel and Daniel), 114, 123
Weber, Shirley, 93
Welsh, Kariamu, 19
Wertheimer, M., 71
West, C.
    Afrocentricity and, 29
    criticism of Molefi Kete Asante, 14
    Stuart Hall and, 164
WFMS radio station, 227–228
Whannel, Paddy, 161
What Makes Scholarship About
    Black Women and
    Communication Feminist
    Communication Scholarship?
    (Houston Stanback), 182
"When Black Women Talk with
    White Women: Why Dialogues
    Are Difficult" (Houston), 183
"White talk Black talk: Inter-racial
    friendship and communication
    amongst adolescents" (Houston
    Stanback), 180
Whites
    Black rhetoric and, 213
    founding of NCA's Black Caucus
        and, 112–113
    interracial communication and,
        179–181
    Melbourne S. Cummings and, 90
    Orlando Taylor's communication
        with, 229
    race, discrimination, media
        consumption and, 141–142
    white women, stereotypes of,
        214, 215
WHO (Women's Honor
    Organization), 176
Who's Who in Colored America, 75
Wilberforce College
    Hallie Quinn Brown at, 67–68
    Hallie Quinn Brown's love of, 73
    Hallie Quinn Brown's trip to
        Europe for, 70–71
    professorship offer to Hallie
        Quinn Brown, 68
Wild Women and Rolling Stones
    (Jones), 196

Wilkson, Lillie Mae, 14–15
Williams, Bruce, 234
Williams, Chancellor, 29
Williams, Fannie Barrier, 71
Williams, Lorraine, 94
Williams, Maggie, 131
Williams, Raymond, 153
Williams, Robert, 234
Williams, Ronald, 113, 233
Wilson, William, 47
Wimbish, Emery, 46
Winston, M. R., 69, 70
Winston-Salem State University, 92
The Wisdom of Sixth Mount Zion
    from the Members of Sixth
    Mount Zion and Those Who
    Begot Them (Daniel), 119–120
Wise, J. M., 154
Without guarantees: In honour of
    Stuart Hall (Gilroy, Grossberg
    and McRobbie), 153
WLAC-Radio, 227
Women
    Brown Sugar: Eighty Years of
        America's Black Female
        Superstars (Bogle), 51–54
    civil rights of, Hallie Quinn
        Brown and, 71–73, 80
    Dorothy Dandridge: A Biography
        (Bogle), 55–57
    Hallie Quinn Brown's realization
        about, 67
    See also African American women
Women Builders (Daniel), 79
Women's Honor Organization
    (WHO), 176
"Wonders of the African World"
    television series, 22
Wood, B., 154
Wood, J., 183
Woods, Nellie Hunter, 44
Woods, Robert Clisson, 43
Woodson, Carter G., 24, 94
Woolf, H., 232
World Congress on Communications
    and Development in Africa and
    the African Diaspora, 86–87
The World University, 13

World's Congress of Representative
    Women, 71
Wretched of the Earth (Fanon), 114
Wright, A. A., 70
Wright, Trina, 4
"Writing for My Life: Intercultural
    Methodology and the Study of
    African American Women"
    (Houston), 183

Yale University, 224–225
Yenenga, Ana, 19
Yoruba performance, 198
Young, Andrew, 97–98

Zapata, Emiliano, 135
Zeigler, D. H.
    admiration of Molefi
        Kete Asante, 14
    Afrocentricity paradigm
        and, 12
    book on mass media in Africa, 26
Zimbabwe
    mass communication in, 26
    Molefi Kete Asante in, 19
Zimbabwe Institute of Mass
    Communication (ZIMCO), 19
Zimbabwe National Dance
    Company, 19

About the Authors

Ronald L. Jackson II is associate professor of Culture and Communication Theory in the Department of Communication Arts & Sciences at the Pennsylvania State University. He is author of *The Negotiation of Cultural Identity* (Praeger Press), *Think About It!* (Iuniverse.com), *African American Communication: Identity and Culture* (with Michael Hecht and Sidney Ribeau; Erlbaum), *African American Rhetorics: Interdisciplinary Perspectives* (with Elaine Richardson; Southern Illinois University Press), *Essential Readings in African American Communication Studies* and *Understanding African American Rhetoric* (with Elaine Richardson). Forthcoming is another book, titled *Scripting the Black Masculine Body in Popular Media: Identity, Discourse, and Racial Politics in Popular Media* (SUNY Press). Dr. Jackson's theory work includes the development of two paradigms, coined "cultural contracts theory" and "black masculine identity theory."

Sonja M. Brown Givens is assistant professor of Interpersonal Communication in the Department of Communication Arts at the University of Alabama in Huntsville. Her research interests include the influence of mass-mediated portrayals of socially marginalized groups on social decision-making processes. Her collaborative work appears in the *Quarterly Journal of Speech* with Dr. Celeste Condit from the University of Georgia. Her latest manuscript, "Mammies, Jezebels, and Other Controlling Imagery: An Examination of the Influence of Televised Stereotypes of Perceptions of an African American Woman," is currently under review for *Media Psychology*. Works in progress include a manuscript titled "Coping from the Margins: The Intersection of Race, Gender, Spirituality and Professional Identity in African American Graduate Student Experiences" which is currently being prepared for submission to the *Western Journal of Communication*.